A ROM
RENAISSANCE

D0885157

"THE BEST OF PLIMPTON
shows how much fun there can be in life."
—*The Boston Globe**

The Best Of

PLIMPTON

GEORGE PLIMPTON

ATLANTIC MONTHLY PRESS

THE 1990/1991 PUSHCART PRIZE

BEST OF THE SMALL PRESSES

EDITED BY BILL HENDERSON
WITH THE
PUSHCART PRIZE EDITORS.
INTRODUCTION BY
RUSSELL BANKS

"... the single best measure of
the state of affairs in
American literature today."
NEW YORK TIMES
BOOK REVIEW

"Get it, read it, lug it around
with you; as always, this book
is essential."

LIBRARY JOURNAL

"A national literary treasure ..."
KIRKUS REVIEWS

XV

JUST PUBLISHED.
581 PAGES
CLOTHBOUND
$27.95

PUSHCART PRESS
P.O. BOX 380
WAINSCOTT, NEW YORK 11975

The Paris Review

Publisher	Deborah S. Pease
Editors	George A. Plimpton, Peter Matthiessen, Donald Hall, Robert B. Silvers, Blair Fuller, Maxine Groffsky
Managing Editor	James Linville
Editor-at-Large	Jeanne McCulloch
Senior Editor	Antonio Weiss
Associate Editors	Beth Drenning, Elizabeth Gaffney
Assistant Editor	Charles Rogers
Poetry Editor	Patricia Storace
Art Editor	Richard Marshall
Paris Editor	Harry Mathews
London Editor	Shusha Guppy
Business Manager	Lillian von Nickern
Print Directors	Joan Krawczyk, Christopher Lightfoot Walker
Special Consultant	Robert Phillips
Contributing Editors	William Plummer, Patsy Southgate, Lucas Matthiessen, Joanie McDonnell, Charles Russell, David Michaelis, Ron Bailey, Helen Bartlett, Robert Becker, Joanna Laufer, John Glusman, Gerald Howard, Tom Jenks, Mary Maguire, Michael Sagalyn, Ileene Smith, Dan Max, Elise Paschen, William Wadsworth, Barbara Jones, Allan Peacock
Editorial Assistants	Rose Styron, Jill Fox, Mary B. Lumet, Kevin Richardson, Matthew Rose, Jill Birdsall, Michele Somerville, Jennifer Egan, Cheryl Sucher, Margaret Broucek, Adam Begley, Ian Ganassi, Julia Myer, Kip Azzoni, Daniel Ellen, Dini von Mueffling, Laura Gerrity, Elizabeth Ziemska, Gerry Visco, Joanna Hernandez, Anne Gimm, Claudia Grazioso, Melissa Anderson, Barry Munger, Jonna Espey, Kendra Taylor, Paul Nastu, Susannah Hunnewell
Advisory Editors	Nelson Aldrich, Patrick Bowles, Joan Dillon, William Pène du Bois, Drue Heinz, John Train, Harold L. Humes, Ben Johnson, Jonathan Miller, John Phillips, Thomas H. Guinzburg, Lawrence M. Bensky, Frederick Seidel, Terry Southern, Max Steele, Philip Roth, William Styron, Eugene Walter, Christopher Cerf, Tom Clark, Ron Padgett, Maggie Paley, Fayette Hickox, Molly McKaughan, Francine du Plessix Gray, Lindy Guinness, Hallie Gay Walden, David Robbins, David Evanier, Mona Simpson, Jonathan Galassi, Jonathan Dee
Consultants	Squaw Valley Community of Writers, Timothy Dickinson
Founding Publisher	Sadruddin Aga Khan
Former Publishers	Bernard F. Conners, Ron Dante

The Paris Review is published quarterly by The Paris Review, Inc. Vol. 32, No. 117, Winter 1990. Office: 45–39 171 Place, Flushing, New York 11358 (ISSN #0031-2037). Paris Office: Harry Mathews, 67 rue de Grenelle, Paris 75007 France. London Office: Shusha Guppy, 8 Shawfield St., London, SW3. Distributors in the U.S.A.: Eastern News Company, Sandusky, OH. Typeset and printed in USA by Capital City Press, Montpelier, VT.

Price for single issue in USA: $6.00; in France: 50F; in the UK: £3. Post-paid subscription for four issues $20, for eight issues $40, for twelve issues $60, lifetime Associate $1000. Postal surcharge of $6.00 per four issues outside USA (excluding life subscriptions). Subscription card is bound within magazine. Please give six weeks notice of change of address using subscription card.

Fiction manuscripts should be submitted to George Plimpton, poetry to Patricia Storace c/o The Paris Review, 541 East 72nd Street, New York, N.Y. 10021. Manuscripts will not be returned unless accompanied by addressed envelope and stamps or international postage coupons.

Charter member of the Council of Literary Magazines and Presses.
This publication is made possible, in part, with public funds from the New York State Council on the Arts.
Second Class postage paid at Flushing, New York, and at additional mailing office.
Postmaster: Please send address changes to 45-39 171st Place, Flushing, N.Y. 11358.

The Paris Review

45-39 171 Place
Flushing, New York 11358

Eastern News Distributors, Inc.
1130 Cleveland Road
Sandusky, Ohio 44870

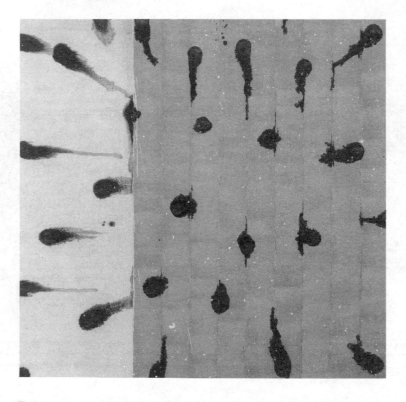

Frontispiece by William Pène du Bois.
Cover by Mike Kelley, *Empathy Displacement: Humanoid Morphology (2nd and 3rd Remove) #7*, detail, 1990, acrylic on panel.
Table of contents illustration by Jacqueline Humphries, *After*, 1989, oil on canvas.

Number 117

From Kings, an Account of Books 1 and 2 of Homer's Iliad *by Christopher Logue*

"Who's there?"
"Manto, sir."
"Manto?"
"Yes, sir. Your youngest son."

"Shine the light on your face.

"Come here.

"Now wipe my mouth.
No-no-no-no-no-no. Take it from there.
I like a clean one every time.

"Ah, Soos . . .

"Soos, this is my youngest son.
Soos is my herald, boy. He must be . . ."
"80, sire."
"And you are?"
"15, sir.
Queen Neday's child."
"Of course.
Your mother was my eighth, full, wife,
Resigned to . . . Soos?"
"Lord Rebek, sire.
Queen Hecuba's first nephew."

"Now, Manto—tell me truthfully,
Have you killed your first Greek?"

"I think so, sir. Today.
When the car stopped I shot one in the back."
  "Who had the reins?"
  "The Prince Aeneas, Sir."

  A pause. A look at Soos. And then,
Priam stands:
  Some six foot six; his brush thick hair
Vertical to his brow; blue white;
Correctly known as the Great King of Troy;
And says:

  "Aeneas is no more a prince than you a king.
He is Anchises' son, not mine.
Anchises cannot sire a prince.
Lords—yes; but princes—no.
  "You, Manto, might—note I say *might*, Soos—"
  "Sire—"
  "Be king of Phrygia, one day, and tax
My hilltop cousin, lord Anchises, of some beef.
But that is all.
  "So do not trust the gods too much, young man.
Gods fail their worshippers—but not themselves."

  "Your chair is here, sire."

Priam turns.

They go.

                    *

  "He took to drink."
  "He had a stroke."
  "She told his wife."
  "He ran off with a slave."

Like monumental wings
The doors that overlook the acropolis' main court
Open onto the evening air
And Priam's portico

And when his chair appears
(Four sons of his beside each quilted arm)
   Then
Neomab, Soos' next, declares:
   "All rise for Priam, Laomedon's son,
Great King of Troy, and Lord of Ilium."
Old Priam seats his Council of 100 with his hand,
Gathers his strength, and cries:

   "Where is my son? My only son?
I do not see my son! He has no twin!
Take all my sons, Achilles, saving him."
But only to himself.

   Aloud, he says:

   "I reign with understanding for you all.
Antenor, as the eldest, will speak first.
   "Our question is:
How can we win this war?"

   "And I reply," Antenor, standing, says,
"How can we lose it?
   "Troy has been challenged 50 times —
But never taken.
   "Your line goes back 900 years.
The Greeks have been here nine. Surely their chance
To take our city worsens in the tenth?
   (Anchises' face is stone.
His kinsman, Panda, spits.)
   "If we have difficulties, so do they;
If we are tired, so are they;

And we are tired at home; behind our wall.
    "These are their facts:
Full tents, thin blankets, gritty bread, no shes,
With agitators picking at their weariness.
    And one thing more: they have a case.
Their hospitality is absolute.
You are a guest, you are a king. The house is yours.
Helen left Sparta with her husband's guest, your eldest son.
They want her back. They want her treasure back.
Not an unreasonable demand.
Women are property for them.
And stolen property can be returned.

    "My king,
The winners of a war usually get
Something out of it. What will we get?
The camp. Their ditch. And who wants those?
Only, Kakanaphag, the god of shit—
    "Or do we have some honour happy oaf
Raring to heave a Trojan fleet to Greece
And Panachea back into its cave?
    "Dear my dear lord, some here would garrison the clouds
In case we are invaded from the moon.

    "Stand Helen on a transport piled with gold—
Supplied by Paris—covered with silk tarpaulins,
Frogged with pearl—likewise supplied.
And as they rumble through the Scean Gate
Let trumpets from its terracing
Bray charivari to her long white back's
Disgusting loveliness."

    Applause.

    And under it:
"Where can that Hector be?" the old king asks.
    "On his way here, sire. From the Temple,"
As Antenor ends:

"Achilles is no different from the rest.
Let him face stone. Sixty by thirty feet of it.
Height before width. Our dam. The wall. The death of fear.
Keep its gates down and send our allies home.
Since men have lived, they lived in Troy.
Why fight for what is won?"

Now more—(too much)—applause,
Into the last of which:

"This is the why," Anchises said,
As Panda helped him up—

For long ago
As he was swimming in a mountain lake
My Lady Aphrodité liked
The undulation of his glistening flesh
And rising through the water by his side
Brushed his torso with her breasts
Then led him by his penis to the bank.
    Them done,
She told him who she was, and said:
    "Our son, who you will name *Aeneas*, will be king.
Mention our bond to anyone but him,
You will be struck."

Gods always ask too much.
As sixteen lines ago Anchises said:
    "This is the why,"
One day he answered those who claimed
A new bought templemaid to be:
    "As good as Aphrodite."
    "She's not. I know, because I've had them both."
And withered instantly from hip to foot.

Withered or not:

"This is the why," Anchises said.
"Troy is not Ilium. And without Ilium
Troy will not last.
    "You say: 'Give Helen back, they will go home.'
O sorry orator, they have no home.
They are a swarm of lawless malcontents
Hatched in the chaff we cast five centuries ago,
Tied to the whim of their disgusting gods,
Knowing no quietude until they take
All quiet from the world; ambitious, driven, thieves;
Our speech, like footless crockery in their mouths;
Their way of life, perpetual war;
Inspired by violence, compelled by hate,
Peace is a crime, to them, and offers of diplomacy
Like giving strawberries to a dog.
    "Indeed, what sort of king excepting theirs
Would slit his daughter's throat to *start* a war?

    "They must be beaten. Preferably, destroyed.
Return their she, her boxes, they will think:
'Ilium is weak.' —and stay. Retain them, they will think:
'Ilium is fat.' —and stay. As either way
They want your city whole; your wives,
Your stuff and stock, floodlit by fire, while they
Pant in their stinking bronze and lick their lips.
    "Ask who you like from Troy Beyond.
They say: 'For us, the time to die is ripe.'
The Dardanelles, Negara Point,
Arisbe, Hellespont, then south,
Larissa, Paran, Tollomon and Hac,
Inland as far as Thebe-under-Ida,
Seaward to Chios and to Samothrace,
All raided, many burnt,
Nothing to spare except their injuries,
'And where is Troy?' they say, 'We paid her well,
Great Priam had our princess for a queen,
Now turns his back, now sends our allies home,
As if Pe'leus son was nothing but his name.

"Ask Hector's wife. Andromache has lost
A father and four brothers at Achilles' hands.
She will not underestimate that boy's ferocity.
  "He is what they call Best. That is to say:
Proud to increase the sum of human suffering;
To make a wife, a widow; widows, slaves;
Hear, before laughter, lamentation;
Rather burn, than build. Our only question is:
How best to kill him? Panda has planned for that.
  "The saying goes:
Not the dog in the fight but the fight in the dog.
And you, Antenor, have no fight.
You speak from cowardice. You plan from fear."

Then Panda's "True." was mixed with someone's "Shame."
"Shame." mixed with "Answer him," and "Fool," with "Stand,"
Their voices rising through the still, sweet air

  As once, from our hotel,
  Elly and Hugo Claus and I
  Smoked as we watched
  The people of the town of Skopje
  Stroll back and forth across their fountained square,
  Safe in their laughter on our balcony, one dusk,
  Just days before an earthquake tipped
  Themselves and their society aside.

  Now,
Almost as if by touch,
The Council's agitation fails, as
Gowned and trousered, down the flight that joins
Temple to court to royal portico,
Surrounded by his lords, Prince Hector comes.

Whether it is his graceful confidence,
His large and easy legs, his fearless, open look
That let him fortify your heart,
That make you wish him back when he has gone,
Trusting oneself to him seems right, who has belief,
And your belief respected, where he stands.

"My son!"

No sound aside from Priam's cry, as Hector led

Chylaborak,
Andromache's one brother left, king Etion's heir,
Across the courtyard; plus
Aeneas,
Brave, levelheaded, purposeful,
My Lady Aphrodité's son,
Treated by Ida's herdsmen as a god;
Troy's Lycian allies,
Glaucos, beside his prince, Sarpedon,
Anaxapart, Sarpedon's armourer;
And more, as valiant, as keen for fame,

The plumes of Ilium,
That you will meet before they die,
Followed their Hector up, onto the portico
Before the monumental wings, and stood
Around the king, who pulls his son's face down,
And kisses it, even as he whispers:
"Where have you *been*?"

And Hector lets the smile this brings
Fade from his lips, before he says:

"My friends,
Your faces bear your thoughts. Change them for these:

"My name means: He who holds.
Troy; Ilium; Troy Beyond; one thing.
 "The victory is God's.

 "Anchises harms the truth
By making it offensive;
Antenor hides the truth by making out
Greece has already lost.
 "Probably,
Leading my father's sons alone,
I could hold Troy until the sea runs dry.
 "And, yes: an inland king arrived today
Whose mercenaries promise Troy Beyond
Help when Achilles' sails say: Bad news.

 "God break the charm of facts! Excepting this:
That we are sick and tired of the wall.
Of waking up afraid. Of thinking: Greece.
Your life in danger all your life. Never to rise
Alone before the birds have left their nests
And ride through sunlit, silent, woods,
Deep snow to spring flowers in a single day,
And then, the sea . . .
 "To miss these things
When things like these are your inheritance
Is shameful.
 "Nine years of it, enough.

 "We are your heroes.
Audacious fameseekers who relish close combat.
Mad to be first among the blades;
Now wounded fifty times, stone sane.
And we will burn Greece out.
 "Achilles' name, that turns you whiter than a wall,
Tells me just this: although his mother is a god,

He is a man, and like all men, has just one life,
Can only be in one place at one time.
    "It is not hard to see whose part Heaven takes;
If God guides Hector's spearcast, or if not;
If God is pleased with Hector, or if not;
If not, it is a manly thing, an honourable thing
To die while fighting for one's country.
    "Be sure:
I know it is the plain that leads
Us to their ships, and them to the sea.
And when God shows the moment we should strike
I will reach out for it.
    "But I—
Not you, Anchises, and not you, Antenor,
Will recognize that moment when it comes.

    "All to their towers.
Sleep tight. But do not oversleep,
Or you may miss a crimson breakfast."

    Did our applause delay him?
Out of the corner of his eye, Chylaborak
Sees Soos make not-now signs to Neomab
Who—apologizing with a shrug—

Goes towards Priam.

    Our silence holds.

    Whispering on the portico.

    Then Soos declares:

    "Cryzez of Tolloman offers this news:
Achilles has walked out on Greece.
Tomorrow he sails home."

"So I am right!"
"So I am right!"
In unison, Antenor and Anchises called;
And so again, as in that fountained square,
"True," "Shame," "Right!" "Answer him . . ." and "Stand,"
Became the crosstalk of their dark, that grew
Slowly and slowly less, until
All were as quiet as children drawing.

Then Hector said:

"Listen to me, and take my words to heart.
This changes nothing.
    "I lift my hands to God
Whose voice knows neither alien head or land.
He is my word, my honour, and my force.
    "And I shall bury Greece."

Then he was gone.

But God,
Asleep by now beside his dimpled queen,
Heard nothing Hector said.

                    *

    Immediately below the parapet
Of Troy's orbital wall, wide, house-high terraces
Descend like steps until they mill
The flagstone circus ringing the acropolis
Whose acre top supports the palace, walk and wall,
Rooms by the flight where Priam's 50 sons
Slept safe beside their wives before Greece came.
    The Temple faces south.
In its geometry God's many names
(As from the sideshrines those of Lord Apollo,

Lady Aphrodite) are heard seriatim
Under breeze-touched lamps.
   And over there
(Beyond the columns, looking down)
Notice the winding steps that lead
Down to a balcony where Helen stands
And says:

   "They want to send me back."
And Paris answers her:
   "Heaven sent you here. Let Heaven send you back."

   And in his sleep king Priam shouts:
"You are too faithful to your gods!"

*

   Cut to the flat topped rock's west side, and see
Andromache touch Hector's shoulder, as she says:
   "My love,
I am a good and patient wife.
I speak the truth. My father was a king.
Yet when he slaughtered him,

Achilles did not shame his corpse,
But laced him in his plate and lifted him,
As tenderly I do our son, onto his pyre,
And let our 12-year-olds plant cypresses
Around his cairn, before he burnt our town
And led them to his ships.
   "Distrust cold words.
Friendship is yours, and openheartedness.
I hear your step—I smile behind my veil.
To measure you, and make your clothes,
Your armour, or to forge your blades,
Is privilege in Troy.

You fear disgrace above defeat. Shame before death.
And I have heard your bravery praised
As many times as I have washed my hands.
Be sure of it!—as you are sure of me.
As both of us are sure
Courage can kill as well as cowardice,
Glorious warrior."

Then as they walk along the pergola
Towards the tower of the Scean Gate:
"Half Troy is under twenty, love.
Half of the rest are wounded, widowed, old.
Hush . . ." raising her finger to his lips,
"Why else does Prince Aeneas take a boy
As young as Manto in his car?"

"Aeneas is my business— "

"My lord, you never yet
Treated me like a woman. Do not start now.
Your family quarrels are your own."
She said, and went before him through the horseshoe arch
Into the tower's belvedere; retied
The threads of her veil at the back of her head,
Then said:
"Dearest, nearest, soul, I know
It is not hard to needle Hector with the thought
It was the weakness of the Greeks, and not his strength
That kept them out, that kept them down.
But those who say so like to preach, not prove.
"Why sir, even if you sent
Sarpedon, Glaucos, and Anaxapart
Back home to Lycia, Aeneas to his hills,
Prior to shouldering Agamemnon's race
Into the Dardanelles, alone,
Those preachers would not change their tune.
"Day after day I wash Greek blood off you.

It teaches me that Greece is not so far
And not so strange to us, to be excused
Exhaustion.
    "Send Helen back.
Let her establish a world-record price.
Desire will always be her side-effect.
And Achilleus is out.
    "O love, there is a chance for peace.
Take it. We all die soon enough."

Hieee . . . Daughter of Etion,
From diadem to mirror slippered feet
You show another school of beauty.
    And as you look
Over the Trojan plain towards the Fleet
Your Hector says:
    "I know another way."
And moonlight floods the open sky.

The Virgin Suicides

Jeffrey Eugenides

On the morning the last Lisbon daughter took her turn at suicide — it was Mary this time, and sleeping pills, like Therese — the two paramedics arrived at the house knowing exactly where the knife drawer was, and the gas oven, and the beam in the basement from which it was possible to tie a rope. They got out of the EMS truck, as usual moving much too slowly in our opinion, and the fat one said under his breath, "This ain't TV, folks, this is how fast we go." He was carrying the heavy respirator and cardiac unit past the bushes that had grown monstrous and over the erupting lawn, tame and immaculate eleven months earlier when the trouble began.

Cecelia, the youngest, only thirteen, had gone first, slitting her wrists like Cato while taking a bath, and when they found her, afloat in her pink pool, with her yellow eyes of someone possessed and her small body giving off the odor of a mature woman, the paramedics had been so frightened by her tranquility that they had stood mesmerized. But then Mrs. Lisbon lunged in, screaming, and the reality of the room reasserted itself: blood on the bathmat; Mr. Lisbon's razor sunk in the toilet bowl, marbling the water. The paramedics fetched Cecelia out of the warm water because it quickens the bleeding and put a tourniquet on her arm. Her wet hair hung down her back and already her extremities were blue. She didn't say a word, but when they parted her hands they found the laminated picture of the Virgin Mary she held against her budding chest.

That was in June, fish fly season, when each year our town is covered by the flotsam of those ephemeral insects. Rising in clouds from the algae in the polluted lake, they blacken windows, coat cars and streetlamps, plaster the municipal docks and festoon the rigging of sailboats, always in the same brown ubiquity of flying scum. Mrs. Scheer, who lives down the street, told us she saw Cecelia the day before she attempted suicide. The girl was standing in the street, wearing the antique wedding dress with the shorn hem she always wore, looking at a Thunderbird encased in fish flies. "You better get a broom, honey," Mrs. Scheer advised. But Cecelia fixed her with her spiritualist's gaze. "They're dead," she said, "they only live twenty-four hours. They hatch, they reproduce, and then they croak. They don't even get to eat." And with that she stuck her hand into the foamy layer of bugs and cleared her initials—C.L.

We've tried to arrange the photographs chronologically. A few are fuzzy but nonetheless revealing. Plate #1 shows the Lisbon house shortly before Cecelia's suicide attempt. It was taken by a real estate agent, Ms. Carmina D'Angelo, whom Mr. Lisbon had hired to sell the house his large family was outgrowing. As the snapshot shows, the slate roof had not yet begun to shed its shingles, the porch was still visible above the grass, and the windows were not yet held together with strips of masking tape. A comfortable suburban home. The upper right second story window contains a blur that Mrs. Lisbon identified as Mary Lisbon. "She used to tease her hair because she thought it was limp," she said, recalling how her daughter had looked for her brief time on earth. In the photograph

Mary is caught in the act of blow-drying her hair. Her head appears to be on fire but that is only a trick of the light. It was June third, eighty-three degrees out, under sunny skies.

When the paramedics were satisfied they had reduced the bleeding to a trickle, they put Cecelia on a stretcher and carried her out of the house. She looked like a tiny Cleopatra on a palanquin. We saw the gangly paramedic with the Wyatt Earp mustache come out first—the one we'd call "Sheriff" when we got to know him better through these domestic tragedies—and then the fat one appeared, carrying the back end of the stretcher and stepping daintily across the lawn, peering at his police-issue shoes as though looking out for dog shit, though later, when we were better acquainted with the machinery, we knew he was checking the blood pressure gauge. Sweating and fumbling, burdened with reality, they moved toward the shuddering, blinking truck. The fat one tripped on a lone croquet wicket. In revenge he kicked it; the wicket sprang loose, plucking up a spray of dirt, and fell with a ping on the driveway. Meanwhile, Mrs. Lisbon burst onto the porch, trailing Cecelia's flannel nightgown. She let out a long wail which stopped time. Under the molting trees and above the blazing overexposed grass those four figures paused in tableau—the two slaves offering the victim to the altar (lifting the stretcher into the truck), the priestess brandishing the torch (waving the flannel nightgown) and the virgin, drugged, or dumb, rising up on her elbows, with an otherworldly smile on her pale lips.

Mrs. Lisbon rode in the back of the EMS truck, but Mr. Lisbon followed in the station wagon, observing the speed limit. Two of the Lisbon daughters were away from home. Therese was in Pittsburgh at a Science Convention, and Bonnie was at music camp, trying to learn the flute after giving up the piano (her fingers were too short), the violin (her chin hurt), the guitar (her fingers hurt) and the trumpet (she didn't want to get one of those big lips). Mary and Lux, hearing the siren, had run home from their voice lesson down the street with Mr. Jessup. Barging into that crowded bathroom, they registered the same shock as their parents at the sight of Cecelia with her spattered forearms and pagan nudity. Outside they hugged on a patch of uncut grass that Butch, the brawny boy who mowed it on Saturdays, had missed. Across the street, a truckful of men from the Parks Division attended to some of our dying elms. The EMS siren shrieked, going away. The botanist and his crew withdrew their insecticide pumps and watched the truck. When it was gone, they began spraying again. The stately elm tree, also visible in the foreground of Plate #1, has since succumbed to the Dutch elm beetles and has been cut down.

The paramedics took Cecelia to Bon Secours Hospital on Kercheval and Maumee. In the emergency room Cecelia watched the attempt to save her life with an eerie detachment. Her yellow eyes did not blink, nor did she flinch when they stuck a needle in her arm. Dr. Armonson stitched up her wrist wounds. Within five minutes of the transfusion he declared her out of danger. Chucking her under the chin, he said, "What are you doing here, honey? You're not even old enough to know how bad life gets."

And it was then Cecelia gave orally what was to be her only form of suicide note, and a useless one at that, because she was going to live: "Obviously, doctor," she said, "you've never been a thirteen-year-old girl."

The Lisbon girls were thirteen (Cecelia), and fourteen (Lux), and fifteen (Bonnie), and sixteen (Mary), and seventeen (Therese). They were short, round-buttocked in denim, with roundish cheeks that recalled the same dorsal softness. Whenever we got a glimpse, their faces looked indecently revealed, as though we were used to seeing women in veils. No one could understand how Mr. and Mrs. Lisbon had produced such beautiful children. Mr. Lisbon taught high school math. He was thin, boyish, stunned by his own gray hair. He had a high voice, and when Lux Lisbon told us how he had cried on the day he learned that Bonnie was pregnant with Joe the Retard's kid, we could easily imagine the sound of his girlish weeping.

Whenever we saw Mrs. Lisbon we looked in vain for some sign of the beauty that must have once been hers. But the

plump arms, the brutally cut steel-wool hair, the church choir
dresses and the librarian's glasses foiled us every time. We saw
her only rarely, in the morning, fully dressed though the sun
hadn't come up, stepping out to snatch up the dewy milk bottles, or on Sundays when the family drove in their panelled
station wagon to St. Paul's Catholic Church on the Lake. On
those mornings Mrs. Lisbon assumed a queenly iciness. Clutching her good purse, she checked each daughter for signs of
make-up before allowing her to get in the car, and it was not
unusual for her to send Lux back inside to put on a less revealing top. None of us went to church so we had a lot of time
to watch them, the two parents leeched of color, like photographic negatives, and then the five glittering daughters in
their homemade dresses, all lace and ruffle, bursting with their
fructifying flesh.

Only one boy had ever been allowed in the house. Peter Sissen had helped Mr. Lisbon install a working model of the solar
system in his classroom at school, and in return Mr. Lisbon had
invited him for dinner. He told us the girls had kicked him
continually under the table, from every direction so that he
couldn't tell who was doing it. They gazed at him with their
blue, febrile eyes and smiled, showing their crowded teeth, the
only feature of the Lisbon girls we could ever find fault with.
Bonnie was the only one who didn't give Peter Sissen a secret
look or kick. She only said grace and ate her food silently, lost
in the piety of a fifteen-year-old. After the meal Peter Sissen
asked to go to the bathroom, and because Cecelia and Mary
were both in the downstairs one, giggling and whispering, he
had to use the upstairs. He came back to us with stories of
bedrooms filled with crumpled panties, of stuffed animals
torn to shreds by the passion of the girls, of a crucifix draped
with a brassiere, of gauzy chambers of canopied beds, and of
the effluvia of so many young girls becoming women together
in the same cramped space. In the bathroom, running the faucet to cloak the sounds of his search, Peter Sissen found Mary
Lisbon's secret cache of cosmetics tied up in a sock under the
sink. Tubes of red lipstick and the second skin of blush and
base, and the depilatory wax that informed us she had a mus-

tache we had never seen. In fact, we didn't know whose make-up Peter Sissen had found until we saw Mary Lisbon two weeks later on the pier with a crimson mouth that matched the shade of his descriptions.

He inventoried the deodorants and the perfumes and the scouring pads for rubbing away dead skin, and we were surprised to learn that there were no douches anywhere because we had thought girls douched every night like brushing their teeth. But our disappointment was forgotten in the next second when Peter Sissen told us of a discovery that went beyond our wildest imaginings. In the trashcan was one Tampax, spotted, still fresh from the insides of one of the Lisbon girls. Peter Sissen had said that he wanted to bring it to us, that it wasn't gross but a beautiful thing, you had to see it, like a modern painting or something, and then he told us he had counted twelve boxes of Tampax in the cupboard. It was only then that Lux knocked on the door, asking if he had died in there, and he sprang to open it. Her hair, up in a barrette at dinner, was down, and fell over her shoulders. She didn't move into the bathroom but stared into his eyes. Then, laughing her hyena's laugh, she pushed past him, saying, "You done hogging the bathroom? I need something." She walked to the cupboard, then stopped and folded her hands behind her. "It's private. Do you mind?" she said, and Peter Sissen sped down the stairs, blushing, and after thanking Mr. and Mrs. Lisbon he hurried off to tell us that Lux Lisbon was bleeding between the legs that very instant, while the fish flies made the sky filthy and the streetlamps came on.

When Paul Borado heard Peter Sissen's story, he swore that he would get inside the Lisbons' house and see things even more unthinkable that Sissen had. "I'm going to watch those girls taking their showers," he vowed. Already at the age of fourteen Paul Borado had the gangster gut and hit-man face of his father, Black Bill Borado, and of all of the men who entered and exited the big Borado house with the two lions carved in stone on the front steps. He moved with the sluggish swagger of urban predators who smelled of cologne and had manicured nails. We were frightened of him, and of his imposing, doughy cousins, Rico Manollo and Vince Lametta, and not only because his house appeared in the paper every so often, nor because of the bulletproof black limousines that glided up the circular drive ringed with laurel trees imported from Italy, but because of the dark circles under his eyes and his mammoth hips and his brightly polished black shoes which he wore even when playing baseball. He had also snuck into other forbidden places in the past, and though the information he brought back was not always reliable, we were still impressed with the bravery of his reconnaissance. In sixth grade, when they took the girls into the auditorium to show them a special film, it was Paul Borado who had infiltrated the room, hiding in the old voting booth, to tell us what it was about. Out on the playground we kicked gravel and waited for him, and when he finally appeared, chewing a toothpick and playing with the gold ring on his finger, we were breathless with anticipation.

"I saw the movie," he said. "I know what it's about. Listen to this. When girls get to be about twelve or so," he leaned toward us, "their tits bleed."

Despite the fact that we now knew better, Paul Borado still commanded our fear and respect. His rhino's hips were even larger by then and the circles under his eyes had deepened to a cigar-ash-and-mud color that made him look acquainted with death. This was about the time the rumors began about the escape tunnel. A few years earlier, behind the spiked Borado fence patrolled by two identical white German shepherds, a group of workmen had appeared one morning. They hung tarpaulins over ladders to obscure what they did, and after three days, when they whisked the tarps away, there, in the middle of the lawn, stood an artificial tree trunk. It was made of cement, painted to look like bark, the size of a redwood, complete with fake knothole and two lopped limbs pointing at the sky with the fervor of amputee stubs. In the middle of the tree, a chain-sawed wedge contained a metal grill.

Paul Borado said it was a barbecue and we believed him. But, as time passed, we noticed that no one ever used it. The papers said the barbecue had cost $50,000 to install, but not one hamburger nor hot dog was grilled upon it. Soon the rumor began to circulate that the tree trunk was an escape tunnel, that it led to a hideaway along the river where Black Bill Borado kept a speedboat, and that the workers had hung tarps to conceal the digging. Then, a few months after the rumors began, Paul Borado began emerging in people's basements, through the sewer pipes. He came up in Miles Blunt's house, covered with a gray dust that smelled like friendly shit; and then he came up in Danny Zinn's house, this time with a flashlight, baseball bat, and a bag containing two dead rats; and finally he ended up on the other side of Tom Nihem's boiler which he clanged three times.

He always explained to us that he had been exploring the sewer system underneath his own house and had gotten lost, but we began to suspect that he was playing in his father's escape tunnel. When he boasted that he would see the Lisbon girls taking their showers, we all believed he was going to enter the Lisbon house in the same way he had entered the others. We never learned exactly what happened, though the police interrogated Paul Borado for over an hour. He told them only what he told us. He said he had crawled in the sewer duct underneath his own basement and had started walking, a few feet at a time. He described the cramped pipes, the coffee cups and cigarette butts left by workmen, and the charcoal drawings of naked women that resembled cave paintings. He told how he had chosen tunnels at random, and how as he passed under people's houses he could smell what they were cooking. Finally, he had come up through the sewer grate in the Lisbon's basement. After brushing himself off, he went looking for someone on the first floor, but no one was home. He called out again and again, moving through the rooms. He climbed the stairs to the second floor. Down the hall, he heard water running. He approached the bathroom door. He insisted that he knocked. And then Paul Borado told how he had stepped into the bathroom and found Cecelia, naked, her wrists oozing blood, and how after overcoming his shock he had run downstairs to call the police first thing, because that was what his father had always taught him to do.

* * *

The paramedics found the laminated picture first, of course, and in the crisis the fat one put it in his pocket. Only at the hospital did he think to give it to Mr. and Mrs. Lisbon. Cecelia was out of danger by that point, and her parents were sitting in the waiting room, relieved but confused. Mr. Lisbon thanked the paramedic for saving his daughter's life. Then he turned the picture over and saw the message printed on the back: *The Virgin Mary has been appearing in our city, bringing her message of peace to a crumbling world. As in Lourdes and Fatima, Our Lady has granted her presence to people just like you. For information call* 1–800–555–MARY.

Mr. Lisbon read the words three times. Then he said in a defeated voice: "We baptized her, we confirmed her, and now she believes this crap."

It was his only blasphemy during the entire ordeal. Mrs. Lisbon reacted by taking the picture and crumpling it in her fist. (It survived; we have a photocopy here.)

Our local newspaper neglected to run an article on the suicide attempt, because the editor, Mr. Baubee, felt such depressing information wouldn't fit between the front-page article on the Junior League Flower Show and the back-page photographs of the grinning brides. The only newsworthy article in that day's edition concerned the cemetery workers strike (bodies piling up, no agreement in sight), but that was on page four beneath the Little League scores.

After they returned home, Mr. and Mrs. Lisbon shut themselves and the girls in the house, and didn't mention a word about what had happened. Only when pressed by Mrs. Scheer did Mrs. Lisbon refer to "Cecelia's accident," acting as though she had cut herself in a fall. With precision and objectivity, however, already bored by blood, Paul Borado described to us what he had seen, and left no doubt that Cecelia had done violence to herself.

Mrs. Buck found it odd that the razor ended up in the toilet. "If you were cutting your wrists in the tub," she said, "wouldn't you just lay the razor on the side?" This led to the question as to whether Cecelia had cut her wrists while already in the bathwater, or while standing on the bath mat, which was bloodstained. Paul Borado had no doubts: "She did it on the john," he said. "Then she got into the tub. She sprayed the place, man."

Cecelia was kept under observation for a week. The hospital records show that the artery in her right wrist was completely severed, because she was lefthanded, but the gash in her left wrist didn't go as deep, leaving the underside of the artery intact. Both arteries were closed with dissolving sutures. She received twelve stitches in each wrist.

She came back still wearing the wedding dress. Mrs. Patz, whose sister was a nurse at Bon Secours, said that Cecelia had refused to put on a hospital gown, demanding that her wedding dress be brought to her, and Dr. Hornicker, the staff psychologist, thought it best to humor her. She returned home during a thunderstorm. We were in Joe Larson's house, right across the street, when the first clap of thunder hit. Downstairs Joe's mother shouted to close all the windows, and we ran to ours. Outside a deep vacuum stilled the air. A gust of wind stirred a paper bag which lifted, rolling, into the lower branches of the trees. Then the vacuum broke with the downpour, the sky grew black, and the Lisbon's station wagon tried to sneak by in the darkness.

We called Joe's mother to come see. In a few seconds we heard her quick feet on the carpeted stairs and she joined us by the window. It was Tuesday and she smelled of furniture polish. Together we watched Mrs. Lisbon push open her car door with one foot, and then roll out, holding her purse over her head to keep dry. Crouching and frowning, she opened the rear door. Rain fell. Mrs. Lisbon's hair fell into her face. At last, Cecelia's small head came into view, hazy in the rain, swimming up with odd thrusting movements because of the double slings that impeded her arms. It took her a while to get up enough steam to roll to her feet. When she finally tumbled out she lifted both slings like canvas wings and Mrs. Lisbon took hold of her left elbow and led her into the house. By that time the rain found total release and we couldn't see across the street.

In the following days we saw Cecelia a lot. She would sit on the front steps of her house, picking red berries off the bushes and eating them, or staining her palms with the juice. She was always wearing the wedding dress and her bare feet were dirty. In the afternoons, when sun lit the front yard, she would watch ants swarming in sidewalk cracks or lie on her back in fertilized grass staring up at clouds. One of her sisters always accompanied her. Therese brought science books onto the front steps, studying photographs of deep space and looking up whenever Cecelia strayed to the edge of the yard. Lux spread towels in the backyard and lay suntanning while Cecelia scratched Arabic designs on her leg with a stick. At other times Cecelia would accost her guard, hugging her neck and whispering in her ear.

Everyone had a theory as to why she had tried to kill herself. Mrs. Blunt said the parents were to blame. "That girl didn't want to die," she told us. "She just wanted out of that house." Mrs. Scheer added, "She wanted out of that decorating scheme." On the day Cecelia returned from the hospital, those two women brought over a Bundt cake in sympathy, but Mrs. Lisbon refused to acknowledge any calamity.

We found Mrs. Blunt much aged and hugely fat, still sleeping in a separate bedroom from her husband, the Christian Scientist. Propped up in bed she still wore pearled cat's-eye sunglasses during the daytime, and still rattled ice cubes in the tall glass she claimed contained only water, but there was a new odor of afternoon indolence to her, a soap-opera smell. "As soon as Lily and I took over that Bundt cake, that woman told the girls to go upstairs. We said, 'It's still warm, let's all have a piece,' but she took the cake and put it in the refrigerator. Right in front of us."

Mrs. Scheer remembered it differently. "I hate to say it, but Joan's been potted for years. The truth is, Mrs. Lisbon thanked us quite graciously. Nothing seemed wrong at all. I started to wonder if maybe it was true that the girl had only slipped and cut herself. Mrs. Lisbon invited us out to the sun-room and we each had a piece of cake. Joan disappeared at one point. Maybe she went back to her house to have another belt. It wouldn't surprise me."

We found Mr. Blunt down the hall from his wife, in a sepa-rate bedroom with a sporting theme. On the shelf stood a photograph of his first wife, whom he had loved ever since divorcing her, and when he rose from his desk to greet us, he was still stooped from the shoulder injury faith had never quite healed. "It was like anything else in this sad society," he told us. "They didn't have a relationship with God." When we reminded him about the laminated picture of the Virgin Mary, he said, "Jesus is the one she should have had a picture of." Mr. Blunt had been a pilot in the Second World War. Shot down over Burma, he led his men on a two-hundred mile hike through the jungle to safety. He never accepted any kind of medicine after that, not even aspirin. One winter he broke his shoulder skiing, and could only be convinced to get an X-ray, nothing more. From that time on he would wince when we tried to tackle him, and raked leaves one-handed, and no longer flipped daredevil pancakes on Sunday morning. Other-wise he persevered, and always gently corrected us when we took the Lord's name in vain. In his bedroom, so many years later, the shoulder had fused into a graceful humpback. "It's sad to think about those girls," he said. "What a waste of life."

The most popular theory at the time held Buzz Palazollo to blame. Buzz was the immigrant kid staying with relatives until his family got settled in New Mexico. He was the first boy in our neighborhood to wear sunglasses, and within a week of arriving, he had fallen in love. The object of his desire wasn't Cecelia but Diana Porter, a girl with chestnut hair and a horsey though pretty face who lived in an ivy-covered house on the lake. Unfortunately, she didn't notice Buzz peering through the fence as she played her fierce tennis on the clay court, nor as she lay, sweating nectar, on the poolside recliner. On our corner, in our group, Buzz Palazollo didn't join in conversa-tions about baseball or busing because he could only speak a few words of English, but every now and then, he would tilt his head back so that the lenses of his sunglasses reflected the sky, and would say: "I love her." Every time he said it he seemed delivered of a profundity that amazed him, as though he had coughed up a pearl. When, at the beginning of June, Diana Porter left on vacation to Switzerland, Buzz Palazollo was stricken. "Fuck the Holy Mother," he said, despondent, "Fuck God." And to show his desperation and the validity of his love, he climbed onto the roof of his relatives' house and jumped off.

We watched him. We watched Cecelia Lisbon watching from her front yard. Buzz Palazollo, with his tight pants, his dingo boots, his pompadour, went into the house; we saw him passing the plate glass picture windows downstairs; and then he appeared at an upstairs window, with a silk handkerchief around his neck. Climbing onto the ledge, he swung himself up to the flat roof. Aloft, he looked frail, diseased, and temperamental, as we expected a European to look. He toed the roof's edge like a high diver, and whispered, "I love her," to himself as he dropped past the windows and into the yard's calculated shrubbery.

He didn't hurt himself. He stood up after the fall, having proved his love, and down the block, some maintained, Cecelia Lisbon developed her own. Amy Schraff, who knew Cecelia in school, said that Buzz had been all she could talk about for the final weeks before commencement. Instead of studying for exams, she spent study halls looking up ITALY in the encyclopedia. She started saying "Ciao," and began slipping into St. Paul's to sprinkle her forehead with holy water. In the cafeteria, even on hot days when the place was thick with the fumes of institutional food, Cecelia always chose the spaghetti con carne, as though by eating the same food as Buzz Palazollo she could be closer to him. At the height of her crush she purchased the crucifix Peter Sissen had seen decorated with the brassiere.

The supporters of this theory always pointed to one central fact: the week before Cecelia's suicide attempt, Buzz Palazollo's family had called him to New Mexico. He went telling

God to fuck Himself all over again because New Mexico was even further from Switzerland where Diana Porter was strolling under summer trees, moving unstoppably away from the world he was going to inherit as the owner of a carpet cleaning service. Cecelia had unleashed her blood in the bath, Amy Schraff said, because the ancient Romans had done that when life became unbearable, and she thought when Buzz heard about it, on the highway amid the cactus, he would realize that it was she who loved him.

The psychologist's report takes up most of the hospital record. After talking with Cecelia, Dr. Hornicker made the diagnosis that her suicide was an act of aggression inspired by the repression of adolescent libidinal urges. For three wildly different ink blots, she had responded, "a banana." She also saw "prison bars," "a swamp," "an afro," and "the earth after an atomic bomb." When asked why she had tried to kill herself, she said only, "It was a mistake," and clammed up when Dr. Hornicker persisted. "Despite the severity of her wounds," he wrote, "I do not think the patient truly meant to end her life. Her act was a cry for help." He met with Mr. and Mrs. Lisbon and recommended that they relax their rules. He thought Cecelia would benefit by "having a social outlet, outside the codification of school, where she can interact with males of her own age. At thirteen, Cecelia should be allowed to wear the sort of make-up popular among girls her age, in order to bond with them. The apeing of shared customs is an indispensable step in the process of individuation."

From that time on, the Lisbon house began to change. Almost every day, and even when she wasn't keeping an eye on Cecelia, Lux would suntan on her towel, wearing the swimsuit that caused the knife-sharpener to give her a fifteen-minute demonstration for nothing. The front door was always left open, because one of the girls was always running through it. Once, outside Jeff Maldrum's house, while we were playing catch, we saw a group of girls dancing to rock and roll in his living room. They were very serious about learning the right ways to move, and we were amazed to learn that girls danced together for fun, while Jeff Maldrum rapped the glass and made kissing noises until they pulled down the shade. Before they disappeared we saw Mary Lisbon in the back near the bookcase. She was wearing bell-bottomed blue jeans with a heart embroidered on the seat.

There were other miraculous changes. Butch, who cut the Lisbon grass, was now allowed inside for a glass of water, no longer having to drink from the outside faucet. Sweaty, shirtless, and tatooed, he walked right into the kitchen where the Lisbon girls lived and breathed, but we never asked him what he saw because we were scared of his muscles and his poverty.

We assumed Mr. and Mrs. Lisbon were in agreement about the new leniency, but when we met with Mr. Lisbon years later, he told us his wife had never agreed with the psychologist. "She just gave in for a while," he said. Divorced from her by this time, he lived alone in an efficiency apartment, the floor of which was covered with shavings from his wood carvings. Whittled birds and frogs crowded the shelves. According to Mr. Lisbon, he had long harbored doubts about his wife's strictness, knowing in his heart that girls who were never allowed to dance would only attract husbands with bad complexions and sunken chests. Also, the odor of all those cooped-up girls had begun to annoy him. He felt at times as though he were living in the bird house at the zoo. Everywhere he looked he found hairpins and fuzzy combs, and because so many females roamed the house they forgot he was a male and discussed their menstruation openly in front of him. Cecelia had just gotten her period, on the same day of the month as the other girls who were all synchronized in their lunar rhythms. Those five days of each month were the worst for Mr. Lisbon, who had to dispense aspirin as though feeding the ducks and comfort crying jags that arose because a dog was killed on TV. He said the girls also displayed a dramatic womanliness during their menarche. They were more languorous, descended stairs in an actressy way, and kept saying with a wink, "Cousin Herbie's come for a visit." On some nights they would send him out to buy more Tampax, not just one box but four or five, and the young storeclerks with their thin mustaches would smirk. He loved his daughters, they were precious to him, but he longed for the presence of a few boys.

That was why, a week after Cecelia returned home, Mr. Lisbon persuaded his wife to allow the girls to throw the first of the innumerable parties they would have over the next year. We all received invitations, made by hand from construction paper, with balloons containing our names drawn in Magic Marker. Our amazement at being formally invited to a house where we had only gone in our bathroom fantasies was so great that we had to compare one another's invitations before we believed it. It was thrilling to know that the Lisbon girls knew our names, that their delicate vocal chords had pronounced their syllables, and that our names meant something in their lives. They had had to labor over the proper spellings and to check our addresses in the phone book or by the metal numbers nailed to the trees.

As the night of the party approached, we watched the house for signs of decorating or other preparations, but saw none. The yellow bricks retained their look of a church-run orphanage and the silence of the lawn was absolute. The curtains did not rustle and no delivery trucks arrived with six-foot submarine sandwiches or drums of potato chips.

Then the night arrived. In blue blazers, with khaki trousers and clip-on neckties, we walked along the sidewalk in front of the Lisbon house as we had so many times before, but this time we turned up the walk, and came up the front steps between the pots of red geraniums, and rang the doorbell. Peter Sissen acted as our leader, and even looked slightly bored, saying again and again, "Wait'll you see this." The door opened. Above us the face of Mrs. Lisbon took form in the dimness. She told us to come in, we bumped against each other getting through the doorway, and as soon as we set foot on the hooked rug in the foyer we knew that Peter Sissen's descriptions of the house had been all wrong. Instead of a heady atmosphere of feminine chaos, we found the house to be a tidy dry-looking place that smelled faintly of stale popcorn. A piece of needlepoint saying "Bless This Home" was framed over the arch, and to the right, on a shelf above the radiator, five pairs of bronzed baby shoes retained for all time the unstimulating stage of the Lisbon daughters' infancy. The dining room was full of stark colonial furniture. On one wall hung a painting of Pilgrims plucking a turkey. The living room revealed orange carpeting and a brown vinyl sofa. Mr. Lisbon's La-Z-Boy flanked a small table on which sat the partially completed model of a sailing ship, without rigging and with the busty mermaid on the prow painted over.

We were directed downstairs to the rec room. The steps were metal-tipped and steep, and as we descended, the light at the bottom grew brighter and brighter, as though we were approaching the molten core of the earth. By the time we reached the last step it was blinding. In addition to overhead strips of fluorescent lights, table lamps stood everywhere. Green and red squares of linoleum flamed beneath our buckled shoes. On a card table, the punch bowl erupted lava. The panelled walls gleamed, and for the first few seconds the Lisbon girls were only a patch of glare like a congregation of angels. Then, however, our eyes got used to the light and informed us of something we had never realized: the Lisbon girls were all different people. Instead of five replicas with the same blonde hair and puffy cheeks we saw that they were distinct beings, that their personalities were beginning to transform their faces and reroute their expressions. We saw at once that Bonnie, who introduced herself now as Bonaventure, had the bloodless cheeks and sharp nose of a nun. Her eyes watered and she was a foot taller than any of her sisters, mostly because of the length of her neck which would one day hang from the end of a rope. Therese Lisbon had a heavier face, the cheeks and eyes of a cow, and she came forward to greet us on two left feet. Mary Lisbon's hair was darker; she had a widow's peak and fuzz above her upper lip which suggested that her mother had found her depilatory wax. Lux Lisbon was the only one who accorded with our image of the Lisbon girls. She radiated health and mischief. Her dress fit tightly and when she came forward to shake our hands, she secretly moved one finger to tickle our palms, giving off at the same time a strange gruff laugh. Cecelia was wearing, as usual, the wedding dress with the shorn hem. The dress was vintage 1920s. It had sequins on the bust she didn't fill out, and someone, either Cecelia herself or the owner of the used clothing store, had cut off the bottom of the dress with a jagged stroke so that it ended above Cecelia's chafed knees. She sat on a bar stool, staring into her punch glass, and the shapeless bag of a dress fell over her. She had colored her lips with red crayon, which gave her face a deranged harlot look, but she acted as though no one was there.

We knew to stay away from her. The bandages had been removed, but she was wearing a collection of bracelets to hide the scars. None of the other girls had any bracelets on, and we assumed they'd given Cecelia all they had. Scotch Tape attached the undersides of the bracelets to Cecelia's skin, so they wouldn't slide. The wedding dress bore spots of hospital food, stewed carrots and beets. We got our punch and stood on one side of the room while the Lisbon girls stood on the other.

We had never been to a chaperoned party. We were used to parties when our parents went out of town, to dark rooms vibrating with heaps of bodies, musical vomiting, beer kegs beached on ice in the bathtub, riots in the hallways and the destruction of coffee table art. This was all different. Mrs. Lisbon ladled out more glasses of punch while we watched Therese and Mary play dominoes, and across the room Mr. Lisbon opened his tool kit. He showed us his ratchets, spinning them in his hand so that they whirred, and he showed us a long sharp tube he called his router, and another covered with putty he called his scraper, and one more with a pronged end he said was his gouger. His voice was hushed as he spoke about these implements, but he never looked at us, only at the tools themselves, running his fingers over their lengths or testing their sharpness with the tender whitened bulb of his thumb. A single vertical crease deepened in his forehead, and in the middle of his dry Nordic face his lips grew moist.

Through all this Cecelia remained on her stool.

We were happy when Joe the Retard showed up. He arrived on his mother's arm, wearing his baggy bermuda shorts and his blue baseball cap, and as usual he was grinning with the face he shared with every other mongoloid. He had his invita-

tion tied with a red ribbon around his wrist, which meant that
the Lisbon girls had spelled out his name along with our own,
and he came murmuring with his oversize jaw and loose lips,
his tiny Japanese eyes, his smooth cheeks shaved by his
brothers. Nobody knew exactly how old Joe the Retard was,
but as long as we could remember he had had whiskers. His
brothers used to take him onto the porch with a bucket to
shave him, yelling to keep still, saying if they slit his throat
it wouldn't be their fault, while Joe turned white and became
as still as a lizard. We also knew that retards didn't live long
and aged faster than other people, which explained the gray
hairs peeking out from under Joe's baseball cap. As children
we had expected that Joe the Retard would be dead by the
time we became adolescents, but now we were adolescents and
Joe the Retard was still a child.

Now that he had arrived we were able to show the Lisbon
girls all the things we knew about him, how his ears wiggled
if you scratched his chin, how he could only say, "Heads,"
when you flipped a coin, never "Tails," because that was too
complicated, even if we said, "Joe, try tails," he would say,
"Heads!" thinking he won every time because we let him. We
had him sing the song he always sang, the one Mr. Pappas
taught him. He sang "Oh, the monkeys have no tails in Sambo
Wango, oh, the monkeys have no tails in Sambo Wango, oh
the monkeys have no tails, they were bitten off by whales," and
we clapped, and the Lisbon girls clapped, Bonnie clapped,
and pressed against Joe the Retard who we thought was too
dense to appreciate it.

The party was just beginning to get fun when Cecelia
slipped off her stool and made her way to her mother. Playing
with the bracelets on her left wrist, she asked if she could be
excused. It was the only time we ever heard her speak, and we
were surprised by the maturity of her voice. More than anything she sounded old and tired. She kept pulling on the
bandage, until Mrs. Lisbon said, "If that's what you want,
Cecelia. But we've gone to all this trouble to have a party for
you."

Cecelia tugged the bracelets until the tape came unstuck.

Then she froze. Mrs. Lisbon said, "All right. Go up then. We'll
have fun without you." As soon as she had permission, Cecelia
made for the stairs. She kept her face to the floor, moving in
her personal oblivion, her sunflower eyes fixed on the predica-
ment of her life we would never understand. She climbed the
steps, closed the door behind her, and proceeded along the
upstairs hallway. We could hear her feet right above us. Halfway up the staircase to the second floor her steps made no
more noise, but it was only thirty seconds later that we heard
the wet sound of her body falling on the fence that ran along-
side the house. First came the sound of wind, a rushing we
decided later must have been caused by her wedding dress
filling with air. This was brief. A human body falls fast. The
main thing was just that: the fact of a person taking on completely physical properties, falling at the speed of a rock. It
didn't matter whether her brain continued to flash on the way
down, or if she regretted what she'd done, or if she had time
to focus on the fence spikes shooting toward her. Her mind
no longer existed in any way that mattered. The wind sound
huffed, once, and then the moist thud jolted us, the sound
of a watermelon breaking open, and for that moment everyone remained still and composed, as though listening to an
orchestra, heads tilted to allow the ears to work and no belief
coming in yet. Then Mrs. Lisbon, as though she were alone,
said, "Oh my God."

Mr. Lisbon ran upstairs. Mrs. Lisbon ran to the top and
stood holding the banister. In the stairwell we could see her
silhouette, the thick legs, the great sloping back, the big head
stilled with panic, the eyeglasses jutting into space and filled
with light. She took up most of the stairs and we were hesitant
to go around her until the Lisbon girls did. Then we squeezed
by. We reached the first floor. Through a window in the side
of the house we could see Mr. Lisbon's lower half bending into
the shrubbery. When we came out the front door we saw that
he was holding Cecelia, one hand under her neck and the
other under her knees. He was trying to lift her off the spike
which had punctured her left breast, travelled through her in-
explicable heart, separated two vertebrae without shattering

either, and come out her back, ripping the dress and finding
the air again. The spike had gone through so fast there was
no blood on it. It was perfectly clean. There was no blood at
all that we could see and Cecelia merely seemed balanced on
the pole like a gymnast. The fluttering wedding dress added
to this circusy effect. Mr. Lisbon kept trying to lift her off,
gently, but even in our ignorance we knew it was hopeless and
that despite Cecelia's open eyes and the way her mouth kept
contracting like that of a fish on a stringer it was just nerves
and she had succeeded, on the second try, in hurling herself
out of the world.

Blaise Cendrars

Panama, or the Adventures of My Seven Uncles

to Edmond Bertrand,
bartender at the Matachine

Books
There are books that talk about the Panama Canal
I don't know what the card catalogs say
And I don't pay any attention to the financial pages
Although the Stock Market quotations are our daily prayers

The Panama Canal is intimately linked to my childhood . . .
I used to play under the table
And dissect flies
My mother used to tell me about the adventures of her
    seven brothers
My seven uncles
And when she got letters
Dazzlement!
Those letters with beautiful exotic stamps inscribed with
    lines from Rimbaud
She didn't tell me any stories on those days
And I stayed sad under my table

It was also around that time that I read the story of the
    Lisbon earthquake
But I really believe
That the Panama crash had a much wider effect
Because it turned my childhood upsidedown.

I had a nice picture book
And for the first time I saw
The whale
The big cloud
The walrus
The sun
The great walrus
The bear the lion the chimpanzee the rattlesnake and the
    fly
The fly
The terrible fly
"Mommy, the flies! The flies! And the tree trunks!"
"Go to sleep now, child."
Ahasuerus is idiotic

I had a nice picture book
A big greyhound named Dourak
An English maid
As a banker
My father lost three-fourths of his fortune
Like a number of upright people who lost their money in
    that crash,
My father
Less stupid
Lost other people's money.
Bang bang.
My mother wept.
And that night I was sent to sleep with the English maid

Then after an enormous number of days . . .
We'd had to move
And the few rooms of our little apartment were crammed
    with furniture
We no longer had our villa on the coast
I was alone for entire days
Among the stacks of furniture
I could even break the dishes

Split open the armchairs
Demolish the piano . . .
Then after an enormous number of days
A letter came from one of my uncles

It was the Panama crash that made me a poet!
It's great
My whole generation is like that
Young people
Who experienced weird ricochets
You don't play with the furniture anymore
You don't play with old stuff anymore
You break every dish you can get your hands on
You sail away
You hunt whales
You kill walruses
You're always afraid of the tse-tse fly
Because we don't like to sleep

The bear the lion the chimpanzee the rattlesnake had taught
    me how to read . . .
Oh that first letter I deciphered alone, letter more teeming
    than all of creation
My uncle said:
I'm working as a butcher in Galveston
The slaughterhouses are 15 miles from town
I'm the one who takes the bleeding animals back along the
    sea, in the evening
And when I go by, the octopuses stand up
Sunset . . .
And there was still something else
Sadness
And homesickness.

Uncle, you disappeared in the cyclone of 1895
Since then I've seen the rebuilt town and strolled along the
    seashore where you took the bleeding animals

There was a Salvation Army band playing in a lattice band-
    stand
I was offered a cup of tea
They never found your body
And when I turned twenty I inherited the 400 dollars you'd
    saved
I also have the cookie box that served as your reliquary
It's made of tin
All your poor religion
A button from a uniform
A Kabyle pipe
Some cocoa beans
A dozen watercolors by you
And the photos of prize animals, the giant bulls you're hold-
    ing by the halter
You're in shirtsleeves with a white apron

I like animals too
Under the table
Alone
I'm already playing with the chairs
Wardrobes doors
Windows
Modern-style furniture
Preconceived animals
That sit enthroned in houses
Like reconstructed antediluvian beasts in museums
The first wooden stool is an aurochs!
I break the windowpanes
And I threw all that out
The city, a pasture for my dog
The pictures
The books
The maid
The visits
Ha ha!

How am I supposed to study for my tests?
You sent me to all the boarding schools in Europe
High schools
Prep schools
University
How am I supposed to study for my tests
When a letter slides under the door
I saw
This beautiful pedagogy!
In the movies, I saw the trip it took
It took sixty-eight days to get to me
Loaded with spelling errors
My second uncle:
I married the woman who makes the best bread in the district
I live three days away from my nearest neighbor
I'm prospecting for gold in Alaska now
I've never found more than 500 francs' worth in my shovel
Life doesn't get paid what it's worth, either
Three of my fingers have been frozen
It's cold here . . .
And there was still something else
Sadness
And homesickness.

O uncle, my mother told me everything
You stole some horses to run away with your brothers
You became a cabin-boy on a tramp steamer
You broke your leg jumping from a moving train
And after the hospital, you were in jail for sticking up a
  stagecoach
And you used to write poetry inspired by Musset
San Francisco
That's where you read the story of General Sutter who con-
  quered California
And who, a multimillionaire, lost all his money when gold was
  discovered on his land

For a long time you hunted in the Sacramento Valley where
 I worked clearing land
But what happened
I understand your pride
Eating the best bread in the district and the rivalry among
 neighbors 12 women in a thousand square kilometers
They found you
A rifle bullet through the head
Your wife wasn't there
Now she's married to a jam magnate

I'm thirsty
Good God
Jesus Christ
Christ!
I feel like reading the *Neuchâtel Tattler* or the *Pamplona
 Courier*
In the middle of the Atlantic you're no more comfortable than
 in an editorial office
I go round in the cage of meridians like a squirrel in his
Look there's a Russian with a friendly face
Where to go
He doesn't know where to put down his baggage either
In Leopoldville or in Sejera near Nazareth, at Mr. Junod's or
 my old friend Perl's
In the Congo in Bessarabia in Samoa
I know all the timetables
All the trains and the connections
Time of arrival time of departure
All the steamers all the fares all the taxes

It's all the same to me
I have some addresses
Sponging my way
I come back from America on board the *Volturno* for 35 francs
 from New York to Rotterdam

Now we're "crossing the equator"
The engines keep throwing endless left-rights
Boys
Splash
Buckets of water
An American his fingers stained with ink keeps time
Wireless telegraph
People are dancing with their knees among orange peels and
    empty cans
A delegation is seeing the captain
The Russian revolutionary erotic experiences
Gaoupa
The dirtiest Hungarian word
I'm escorting a Neapolitan marchioness 8 months pregnant
I'm the one taking the emigrants from Kishinev to Hamburg
It was in 1901 that I saw the first automobile,
Broken down,
At a street corner
That little train the Solothurnians call "the steam iron"
I'll call my consul
Send me over a 3rd-class ticket immediately
The Uranium Steamship Co.
I want my money's worth
The ship is dockside
A mess
The cargo doors wide open
I leave it the way you leave a filthy whore

En route
I didn't bring enough toilet paper
And I bring out
Like the god Tangaloa who fished the world up out of the water
The last letter of my third uncle:
Papeete, September 1, 1887
My dear, dear sister
I've become a Buddhist, a member of a political sect

I'm here to buy dynamite
You can buy it here at grocery stores the way you buy chicory
in France
In little packets
Then I'll go back to Bombay and blow up the English
Things are getting hot
I'll never see you again . . .
And there was still something else
Sadness
And homesickness.

Knocking around
I've done time in Marseille and they took me back to school
by force
All voices cry out together
The animals and the rocks
It's the mute who speaks most beautifully
I've been a libertine and have taken every liberty with the
world
You who used to have faith why didn't you arrive on time
At your age
Uncle
You used to be a cute kid and you really knew how to play the
cornet
That's what (as they say) did you in
You loved music so much that you preferred the whining of
bombs to evening dress symphonies
You worked with happy Italians building a railroad near
Baghavapur
A live wire
You were a natural leader
With your good humor and beautiful singing voice
You were the favorite of the women around the camp
Like Moses you flattened your crew boss
You fled
For 12 years there was no word of you
And like Luther a thunderbolt made you believe in God
In your solitude

You learned Bengali and Urlu to learn how to make bombs
You were in contact with secret committees in London
It was at Whitechapel that I picked up your trail again
You're a convict
Your life circumcised
So much so that
I feel like killing someone with a sap or a waffle iron just to
    get the chance to see you
Because I never have seen you
You must have a long scar across your forehead

As for my fourth uncle, he was the valet of General Robertson
    who fought in the Boer War
His letters came rarely and said things such as
His Excellency has deigned to increase my salary by £50
Or
His Excellency brings 48 pairs of shoes to war
Or
I do His Excellency's nails each morning . . .
But I know
There was still something else
Sadness
And homesickness.

Uncle Jean, you're the only one of my seven uncles I ever saw
You had come back because you were ill
You had a big trunk made of hippopotamus hide that was
    always buckled up
You shut yourself up in your room to recuperate
When I saw you for the first time, you were asleep
Your face showed terrible suffering
A long beard
You slept for two weeks
And as I was leaning over you
You woke up
You were crazy
You wanted to kill grandmother
They locked you up in the asylum

And that's where I saw you for the second time
Strapped
In the strait-jacket
They wouldn't let you off the ship
You made pathetic motions with your hands
As if you were going to row
Transvaal
You were in quarantine and the Horse Guards had trained a
    cannon on your ship
Pretoria
A Chinaman almost strangled you
Tugela
Lord Robertson died
On the way back to London
His Excellency's wardrobe fell into the water, like a dagger in
    your heart
You died in Switzerland in the Saint-Aubain insane asylum
Your last wits
Your last rites
And that's where I saw you for the third time
It was snowing
Walking behind your hearse I was arguing with the ushers
    about their tip
You loved only two things in this world
A cockatoo
And the pink fingernails of His Excellency

There's no hope
And we have to work
Shut-in lives are the densest
Steganic tissues
Remy de Gourmont lives at number 71 Rue des Saints-Pères
Cartridge thread or twine
"One man can encounter another man, but a mountain can
    never encounter another mountain"
Says the Hebrew proverb

Precipices meet
I was in Naples
1896
When I received the *Little Illustrated Journal*
Captain Dreyfus being stripped in front of the army
My fifth uncle:
I'm head cook at the Club Hotel in Chicago
I have 400 kitchen-boys under me
But I don't like Yankee cooking
Please note my new address
Tunis etc.
Regards from Aunt Adèle
Please note my new address
Biarritz etc.

O uncle, you're the only one who never felt homesick
Nice London Budapest Bermuda Saint Petersburg Tokyo
    Memphis
All the great hotels fought to get you
You are the master
You invented a number of sweet dishes that bear your name
Your art
You give yourself you sell yourself you are eaten
No one ever knows where you are
You don't like to stay put
It seems you own a *History of Cuisine down the Ages and
    throughout the World*
In 12 vols. octavo
With portraits of the most famous cooks of all time
You knew about everything that was going on
You were always everywhere anything was happening
Maybe you're in Paris.
Your menus
Are the new poetry

I left all that behind
I'm waiting
The guillotine is the masterpiece of plastic art
Its click
Perpetual motion
The blood of bandits
The songs of the light shake the towers
The colors crash over the city
Poster bigger than you and me
Open mouth that cries out
And in which we are burning
The three hot-blooded young people
Haniniah Mishael Azariah
Adam's Express Co.
Behind the Opera
We must play leapfrog
Froggy went a-courtin'
Springboard woman
The pretty toy in the advertisement
Let's go!
"Siméon, Siméon"
Paris goodbye

It's a riot
There are hours that chime
Quai-d'Orsay-Saint-Nazaire!
You go under the Eiffel Tower—looping the loop—to come
    down on the other side of the world

Then you go on

The catapults of the sun lay siege to the irascible tropics
Rich Peruvian owner of a guano business in Angamos
Acaraguan Bananan is launched
In the shade
The hospitable mulattos
I spent more than a winter on those islands of the blessed

Denver, the Residence City and Commercial Center

DENVER is the capital of Colorado and the commercial metropolis of the Rocky Mountain Region. The city is in its fifty-fifth year and has a population of approximately 225.000 as indicated by the U. S. Census of 1910. Many people who have not visited Colorado, believe Denver is situated in the mountains. This city is located 12 miles east of the foothills of the Rocky Mountains, near the north central part of the state, at the junction of the Platte River and Cherry Creek. The land is rolling, giving the city perfect drainage. Altitude one mile above sea level. Area 60 square miles.

Ideal Climate, Superior Educational Advantages Unequalled Park System

DENVER has the lowest death rate of the cities of the United States.

DENVER has 29 parks; total area 1,238 acres.

DENVER has 61 grade schools, 4 high schools, 1 manual training school, 1 trade and 1 technical school.

DENVER has 11 playgrounds — 8 in parks, 3 in individual tracts.

DENVER has 209 churches of every denomination.

DENVER has 56 miles of drives in its parks.

Commercial and Manufacturing City

Annual Bank C l e a r i n g s, $ 487,848,305.95.

Per capita clearings, $ 180.00.

Annual manufacturing output, $ 57,711,000 (1912).

Eighteen trunk lines entering Denver, tapping the richest agricultural sections of the United States.

DENVER has 810 factories, in which 16,251 wage earners were employed during 1911. The output of factories in DENVER in 1911 was valued at $ 52,000,000. The payroll for the year was $ 12,066,000 — OVER A MILLION DOLLARS A MONTH !

DENVER, COLORADO, BERLIN, GERMANY and MANCHESTER, ENGLAND, are cited by Economists as examples of inland cities which have become great because they are located at a sort of natural cross-roads.

For detailed information, apply to the *Denver Chamber of Commerce.* *Prospectus free.*

The secretary-bird is dazzling
Beautiful buxom women
You have iced drinks out on the terrace
A torpedo-boat burns like a cigar
A game of polo in the pineapple grove
And the mangroves fan the studious young girls
My gun
A shot
An observatory on the side of a volcano
Big snakes in the dried-up riverbed
Cactus hedge
A donkey trumpets, tail in the air
The cross-eyed little Indian girl wants to sell herself in Buenos
    Aires
The German musician borrowed my silver-handled riding
    crop and a pair of suede gloves
That fat Dutchman is a geographer
People play cards waiting for the train
It's the Malaysian woman's birthday
I received a package with my name on it, 200,000 pesetas, and
    a letter from my sixth uncle:
Wait for me at the trading post until next spring
Have a good time take your drinks straight up and don't spare
    the women
The best electuary
Dear nephew . . .
And there was still something else
Sadness
And homesickness.

O uncle, I waited a year for you and you didn't come
You'd left with a group of astronomers who were going to
    study the sky over the western coast of Patagonia
You were acting as interpreter and guide
Your advice
Your experience
No one could sight the horizon with a sextant better than you

The instruments balanced
Electromagnetic
In the fiords of Tierra del Fuego
At the edge of the world
In the glow of electric fish you gathered protozoic moss adrift
    between two oceans
You collected meteorites made of iron peroxide
One Sunday morning:
You saw a mitred bishop emerge from the waters
He had a tail like a fish and he sprinkled you when he made
    the sign of the cross
You fled into the mountains screaming like a wounded lemur
That same night
A hurricane destroyed the camp
Your companions had to give up all hope of finding you alive
Carefully they packed up their scientific instruments
And, three months later,
The poor intellectuals,
They came up on a campfire one night where gauchos were
    talking about you
I had come to meet you
Tupa
The beauties of nature
The stallions screw each other
200 black bulls bellow
Argentine tango

So?
So there aren't any more beautiful stories?
Lives of the Saints
Das Nachtbeuchlein von Schuman
Cymbalum mundi
La Tariffa delle Putane di Venegia
Navigation by Johann Struys, Amsterdam, 1528
Shalom Aleichem
The Crocodile of Saint-Martin
Strindberg demonstrated that the earth is not round

Already Gavarni had abolished geometry
Pampas
Disk
The Iroquois women of the wind
Hot sauces
The propeller of gems
Maggi
Byrrh
Daily Chronicle
The wave is a quarry where the sculpting storm cuts away
    chunks of dressed stone
Quadrigas of foam that take the bit in their teeth
Eternally
Since the creation of the world
I whistle
A shudder of wreckage

My seventh uncle
No one ever knew what happened to him
They say I look like you

I dedicate this poem to you
Mr. Bertrand
You gave me strong drink to immunize me against the fevers
    of the canal
You subscribed to the Press Argus to get all the clippings
    about me
Last Frenchman in Panama (there aren't even 20)
I dedicate this poem to you
Bartender at the Matachine
Thousands of Chinese died where the blazing Bar now stands
Your own distillery

You got rich burying the victims of cholera
Send me the photograph of the forest of cork-oaks that grow
  on the 400 locomotives abandoned by the French under
  taking
The living dead
The palm tree grafted in the loading bucket of a crane over-
  grown with orchids
The cannons of Aspinwall gnawed by toucans
The tortoise nets
The pumas that nest in the caved-in gas tank
The locks punctured by swordfish
The pump pipes clogged with a colony of iguanas
The trains stopped by invasions of caterpillars
And the Louis XV coat of arms on the gigantic anchor whose
  presence in the forest you were never able to explain to me
Every year you replace the doors in your bar, encrusted with
  the signatures
Of everyone who comes through
Those 32 doors what a testimony
The living tongues of that damned canal you cherish so

This morning is the first day on earth
Isthmus
Where you see simultaneously all the heavenly bodies in the
  sky and all the forms of vegetation
Unparalleled equatorial mountains
Unique zone
The Amidon Paterson steamer is still there
The colored initials of the Atlantic & Pacific Tea Co.
The Los Angeles Limited that leaves at 10:02 to arrive on the
  third day and is the only train in the world with a beauty
  parlor
The Trunk the signals and the toy cars

To teach you how to spell the ABC of life beneath the ruler
    of departing whistles
Toyo Kisen Kaisha
I have some bread and cheese
A clean collar
Poetry dates from today

The Milky Way around my neck
The two hemispheres on my eyes
At top speed
There are no more breakdowns
If I had time to save a little money I'd fly in the airplane races
I've reserved a seat on the first train through the tunnel be-
    neath the English Channel
I'm the first flyer to cross the Atlantic in a monocoque
900 million

Earth Earth Seas Oceans Skies
I'm homesick
I follow every face and I'm scared of mailboxes
The cities are wombs
I don't follow the roads anymore
Lines
Cables
Canals
Nor suspension bridges!

Suns moons stars
Apocalyptic worlds
You all still have a good role to play
A seltzer bottle sneezes
The literary tittle-tattle keeps moving
Very low
At the Rotonde
As if at the very bottom of a glass

I'm waiting

I'd like to be a fifth wheel
Storm
Noon at two PM
Nothing and everywhere

— PARIS AND ITS SUBURBS: *Saint-Cloud, Sèvres, Montmorency,
Courbevoie, Bougival, Rueil, Montrouge, Saint-Denis, Vin-
cennes, Etampes, Melun, Saint-Martin, Méréville, Bar-
bizon, Forges-en-Bière.*

June 1913-June 1914
— translated from the French
by Ron Padgett

Carolyn Kizer

Twelve O'clock

At seventeen I've come to read a poem
At Princeton. Now my young hosts inquire
If I would like to meet Professor Einstein.
But I'm too conscious I have nothing to say
To interest him, the genius fled from Germany just in
time.
"Just tell me where I can look at him," I reply.

Mother had scientific training. I did not;
She loved that line of Meredith's about
The army of unalterable law.
God was made manifest to her in what she saw
As the supreme order of the skies.
We lay in the meadow side by side, long summer nights

As she named the stars with awe.
But I saw nothing that was rank on rank,
Heard nothing of the music of the spheres,
But in the bliss of meadow silences
Lying on insects we had mashed without intent,
Found overhead a beautiful and terrifying mess,

Especially in August, when the meteors whizzed and
zoomed,
Echoed, in little, by the fireflies in the grass.
Although, small hypocrite, I was seeming to assent,
I was dead certain that uncertainty
Governed the universe, and everything else,
Including Mother's temperament.

A few years earlier, when I was four,
Mother and Father hushed before the Atwater-Kent
As a small voice making ugly noises through the static
Spoke from the grille, church-window-shaped, to them:
"Listen, darling, and remember always;
It's Doctor Einstein broadcasting from Switzerland."

I said, "So what?" This was repeated as a witticism
By my doting parents. I was dumb and mortified.
So when I'm asked if I would like to speak to Einstein
I say I only want to look at him.
"Each day in the library, right at twelve,
Einstein comes out for lunch." So I am posted.

At the precise stroke of noon the sun sends one clear ray
Into the center aisle: He just appears,
Baggy-kneed, sockless, slippered, with
The famous ravelling grey sweater;
Clutching a jumble of papers in one hand
And in the other his brown sack of sandwiches.

The ray haloes his head! Blake's vision of God,
Unmuscular, serene, except for the electric hair.
In that flicker of a second our smiles meet:
Vast genius and vast ignorance conjoined;
He fixed, I fluid, in a complicit yet
Impersonal interest. He dematerialized and I left, content.

It was December sixth, exactly when,
Just hours before the Japanese attack
The Office of Scientific R & D
Began "its hugely expanded program of research
Into nuclear weaponry"—racing the Germans who, they
    feared,
Were far ahead. In fact, they weren't.

Next night, the coach to school; the train, *Express*,
Instead pulls into every hamlet: grim young men
Swarm the platforms, going to enlist.
I see their faces in the sallow light
As the train jolts, then starts up again,
Reaching Penn Station hours after midnight.

At dinner in New York in '44, I hear the name
Of Heisenberg: Someone remarked, "I wonder where he is,
The most dangerous man alive. I hope we get to him in time."
Heisenberg. I kept the name. Were the Germans, still,
Or the Russians, yet, a threat? Uncertainty. . . .
But I felt a thrill of apprehension: Genius struck again.

It is the stroke of twelve—and I suppose
The ray that haloes Einstein haloes me:
White-blond hair to my waist, almost six feet tall,
In my best and only suit. Why cavil?—I am beautiful!
We smile—but it has taken all these years to realize
That when I looked at Einstein he saw me.

At last that May when Germany collapsed
The British kidnapped Heisenberg from France
Where he and colleagues sat in a special transit camp
Named "Dustbin," to save them from a threat they never
    knew:
A mad American general thought to solve
The post-war nuclear problem by having them all shot.

Some boys in pristine uniforms crowd the car
(West Pointers fleeing from a weekend dance?),
Youth's ambiguities resolved in a single action.
I still see their faces in the yellow light
As the train jolts, then starts up again,
So many destined never to be men.

"The Paris Review remains the single most important little magazine this country has produced."

—T. Coraghessan Boyle

Save 20% off the newsstand price by subscribing Order Paris Review Books directly. . . .

THE PARIS REVIEW

Bill me for:

☐ $20 for 1 year (4 issues)
☐ $40 for 2 years ☐ $60 for 3 years
(All payment must be in U.S. funds. Postal surcharge of $6 per 4 issues outside USA)

☐ $1000 to be a Paris Review Associate (lifetime subscription included).
Bill this to my Visa/MasterCard:

_____
Card number   Exp. date

☐ New subscription ☐ Renewal subscription
☐ New address

Name _____

Address _____

City _____ State _____ Zip code _____

Please send gift subscription to:

Name _____

Address _____

City _____ State _____ Zip code _____

Gift announcement signature _____

Please send me the following:

☐ *Twice Told Tales* by Daniel Stern   ($18.95)
☐ *Imaginary Paintings* by Charles Baxter   ($7.95)
☐ *The Paris Review Anthology*   ($25.00)
☐ *The Writer's Chapbook*   ($19.95)
☐ Other _____
_____

Name _____

Address _____

City _____ State _____ Zip code _____

☐ Enclosed is my check for $ _____
☐ Bill me for $ _____
☐ Bill this to my Visa/MasterCard:

_____
Card number   Exp. date

No postage
stamp necessary
if mailed in the
United States

BUSINESS REPLY MAIL

FIRST CLASS   PERMIT NO. 3119   FLUSHING, N.Y.

POSTAGE WILL BE PAID BY ADDRESSEE

THE PARIS REVIEW
45-39 171 Place
FLUSHING NY   11358-9892

No postage
stamp necessary
if mailed in the
United States

BUSINESS REPLY MAIL

FIRST CLASS   PERMIT NO. 3119   FLUSHING, N.Y.

POSTAGE WILL BE PAID BY ADDRESSEE

THE PARIS REVIEW
45-39 171 Place
FLUSHING NY   11358-9892

In Cambridge the Germans visited old friends
Kept apart by war: Austrians, English, Danes,
"In a happy reunion at Farm Hill."
But then the giant fist struck—in the still
Center of chaos, noise unimaginable, we thought we heard
The awful cry of God.

Hiroshima. Heisenberg at first refused
To believe it, till the evening news confirmed
That their work had lead to Hiroshima's 100,000 dead.
"Worst hit of us all," said Heisenberg, "was Otto Hahn,"
Who discovered uranium fission. "Hahn withdrew to his
    room,
And we feared that he might do himself some harm."

It is exactly noon, and Doctor Einstein
Is an ancient drawing of the sun.
Simple as a saint emerging from his cell
Dazed by his own light. I think of Giotto, Chaucer,
All good and moral medieval men
In—yet removed from—their historic time.

The week before we heard of Heisenberg
My parents and I are chatting on the train
From Washington. A grey-haired handsome man
Listens with open interest, then inquires
If he might join us. We were such a fascinating family!
"Oh yes," we chorus, "sit with us!"

Penn Station near at hand, we asked his name.
E.O. Lawrence, he replied, and produced his card.
I'd never heard of him, but on an impulse asked,
"What is all this about the harnessing
Of the sun's rays? Should we be frightened?"
He smiled. "My dear, there's nothing in it."

So, reassured, we said goodbyes,
And spoke of him in coming years, that lovely man.
Of course we found out who he was and what he did,
At least as much as we could comprehend.
Now I am living in the Berkeley hills,
In walking distance of the Lawrence lab.

Here where Doctor Lawrence built the cyclotron,
It's noon: the anniversary of Hiroshima:
Everywhere, all over Japan
And Germany, people are lighting candles.
It's dark in Germany and Japan, on different days,
But here in Berkeley it is twelve o'clock.

I stand in the center of the library
And he appears. Are we witnesses or actors?
The old man and the girl, smiling at one another,
He fixed by fame, she fluid, still without identity.
An instant which changes nothing,
And everything, forever, everything is changed.

Margaret Atwood

Frogless

The sore trees cast their leaves
too early. Each twig pinching
shut like a jabbed clam.
Soon there will be a hot gauze of snow
searing the roots.

Booze in the spring runoff,
pure antifreeze;
the stream worms drunk and burning.
Tadpoles wrecked in the puddles.

Here comes an eel with a dead eye
grown from its cheek.
Would you cook it?
You would if.

The people eat sick fish
because there are no others.
Then they get born wrong.

This is not sport, sir.
This is not good weather.
This is not blue and green.

This is home.
Travel anywhere in a year, five years,
and you'll end up here.

SAS
INTERNATIONAL HOTELS

Fly with SAS. Stay with SAS. Pay with Diners Club. It couldn't be simpler.

Ⓓ *Diners Club International*®
An SAS company in Scandinavia.

Ask the hotel concierge for information and reservation.

Hertz

Hertz rents Ford and other fine cars.

The manuscript of "Frogless," a poem which appears in this issue, by Margaret Atwood. Ms. Atwood wrote the poem on an SAS Hotel's bedside notepad while she was in Gothenburg, Sweden, last September for the Nordic Book Fair. "I've written quite a lot under those circumstances. Perhaps it's being in a hotel room or a plane with no ringing phone and no supervision. Also, there's something about jet-lag that breaks down the barriers."

The Art of Fiction CXXI
Margaret Atwood

Margaret Atwood was born in Ottawa, Ontario, in 1939. As a child, she lived in the wilderness of northern Quebec, and also spent time in Ottawa, Sault Sainte Marie and Toronto. She was eleven before she attended a full year of school. In high school Atwood began to write poetry, inspired by Edgar Allen Poe, and at sixteen she committed herself to a writing career, publishing a collection of poems, Double Persephone, *six years later.*

Her second book of poetry, The Circle Game, *earned her the Governor General's Award — Canada's highest literary*

*honor—and from that time forward she has been a dominant
figure in Canadian letters. In 1972 Atwood sparked a hot de-
bate when she published a controversial critical study of Canadian literature,* Survival: A Thematic Guide to Canadian
Literature. *In it she claimed that Canadian literature reflects
the submissive as well as survivalist tendencies of the country,
born from its being a subordinate ally to the United States,
a former colony and a country with vast stretches of untamed
land. Following the publication of this volume, Atwood
retreated from Toronto, where she had been working as an editor at the publishing house Anansi, to a farm in Alliston, Ontario, where she began to write full time.*

*Atwood has published nineteen collections of poetry, in-
cluding* The Circle Game *(1964),* The Journals of Susanna
Moodie *(1970),* Power Politics *(1971),* You Are Happy *(1974),*
True Stories *(1981) and* Interlunar *(1984), but she is best
known for her novels, which include* Surfacing *(1972),* Lady
Oracle *(1976) and, most recently,* Cat's Eye *(1988). Her most
widely read novel is* The Handmaid's Tale *(1986), a chilling
account of a puritanical theocracy, which won Atwood a second Governor General's Award, and which was recently made
into a motion picture. She is also the author of two children's
books,* Up in the Tree *(1978) and* Anna's Pet *(1980) and two
collections of short stories,* Dancing Girls *(1977) and* Blue-
beard's Egg *(1983). She has edited Oxford anthologies of
Canadian verse and Canadian short stories and, with Shannon
Ravenel, the 1989 volume of* The Best American Short Stories.

*The question of women's status has frequently been an issue
in Atwood's work, and feminists have seized upon her writing
as a product of the movement. Atwood has also made other
political and philosophical issues themes in her work, such as
Canada's struggle to create an identity and in recent years, her
concern for human rights.*

*This interview was conducted in a house near Princeton
University, where Atwood had gone to give some readings and
lectures. In person, Atwood is much as one might expect from
reading her work—incisive. For many hours over a period of
two days during which teenage boys bounced basketballs and*

played music outside, people walked in and out, and football games played on the television in the next room, Atwood sat, attentive, answering each question without hesitation. She never strayed from her point, never seemed to tire, and remained, like a narrator from any one of her books, unflappable.

INTERVIEWER

Has the theme of survival always been intrinsic to your work?

MARGARET ATWOOD

I grew up in the north woods of Canada. You had to know certain things about survival. Wilderness survival courses weren't very formalized when I was growing up, but I was taught certain things about what to do if I got lost in the woods. Things were immediate in that way, and therefore quite simple. It was part of my life from the beginning.

INTERVIEWER

When did you make the leap from considering survival to be a physical battle to considering it to be an intellectual or political struggle?

ATWOOD

When I started thinking about Canada as a country it became quite evident to me that survival was a national obsession. When I came to the States in the sixties I felt that nobody knew where Canada was. Their brother may have gone there to fish or something. When I was at Harvard I was invited as a "foreign student" to a woman's house for an evening for which I was asked to wear "native costume." Unfortunately I'd left my native costume at home and had no snowshoes. So there I was, without native costume, with this poor woman and all this food, sitting around waiting for the really exotic foreign students in *their* native costumes to turn up—which they never did because, as everybody knew, foreign students didn't go out at night.

You've written about the theme of foreignness a good deal.

Foreignness is all around. Only in the heart of the heart of
the country, namely the heart of the United States, can you
avoid such a thing. In the center of an empire, you can think
of your experience as universal. Outside the empire, or on the
fringes of the empire, you cannot.

In your afterword to *The Journals of Susanna Moodie* you
write that if the mental illness of the United States is
megalomania, that of Canada is paranoid schizophrenia.
Could you say something more about that?

The United States is big and powerful; Canada is divided
and threatened. Maybe I shouldn't have said "illness." Maybe
I should have said "state of mind." Men often ask me, "Why
are your female characters so paranoid?" It's not paranoia. It's
recognition of their situation. Equivalently, the United States'
feeling that it is big and powerful is not a delusion. It *is* big
and powerful. Possibly, its wish to be even bigger and more
powerful is the mentally ill part. Every Canadian has a complicated relationship with the United States, whereas Americans
think of Canada as the place where the weather comes from.
"Complication" is a matter of how you perceive yourself in an
unequal power relationship.

How do you view Canada and its literature within this political relationship?

Canada is not an occupied country. It's a dominated country. Things are more clear-cut in an occupied country—the
heroes and the villains are obvious. One of the complicating

things, of course, is that the United States will eagerly swallow anything. It's very welcoming in that way. Canadian writers often find that they have a better time in the United States than they do in Canada, because living in Canada is to some extent like living in a small town. They will rally around you when you break your leg, but on the other hand, if you get too big for your britches, well, they perceive it as exactly that. Alice Munro's book, which is titled *The Beggar Maid* in the United States, is called *Who Do You Think You Are?* in Canada . . . as in, "Who do you think you are, behaving like that—the Prime Minister?" The U.S. loves success, the American dream that anybody can be president of the United States or get into *People* magazine. But with Canadians, it's much more likely to be: "You know, people might not like it if you did that." There are a lot more snipers in the bushes.

INTERVIEWER

Where have you been treated better as a writer, would you say?

ATWOOD

I suffer more vicious attacks, more personal attacks, in Canada, because that's where I'm from. Families have their most desperate fights among themselves, as we know. However, if you look at per capita sales figures, people recognizing me in the street, of course it's more in Canada. If I sold as many books per capita in the United States as in Canada, I'd be a billionaire.

INTERVIEWER

Is it more difficult for women to get published than men?

ATWOOD

I'm afraid the question is simply too broad. Do we mean, for instance, in North America, or in Ireland, or in Afghanistan? There are categories other than gender. Age, class and color, for instance. Region. National origin. Previous publication. Sexual orientation. I suppose we could rephrase the question and ask, is it more difficult for a first novelist who is female than for her male counterpart, of the same age, class, color, national origin or location, and comparable talent, whatever that may be. Judging from the experience of Latin American female writers—of which there are many, though few are known in translation—the answer would be, yes. Women in many countries find it difficult to get published at all—consider the Middle East, for instance. Or black women in South Africa. In fact, they find it difficult to write. Or difficult to become educated. The barriers to women writing are often put in place at a very early age and in very basic ways.

But if we're just talking about, say, North America, obviously commercial publishers want to publish things they can sell. Whether such publishers will publish a given book—whether by a man, woman or turtle—depends a lot on what they think its reception will be. I don't think there's an overt policy against books by women, or an overt quota. Much depends on the book, and on the intuition of the publisher. It's true, however, that the majority of books that do appear are still written by men and reviewed by men. Then there's the subject of reviewing. That's where you're most likely to see gender bias, bias of all kinds.

INTERVIEWER

Is it difficult to write from the point of view of a male?

ATWOOD

Most of the "speakers" or narrative points of view in my books are those of women, but I have sometimes used the point of view of a character who is male. Notice I try to avoid saying "the male point of view." I don't believe in the *male* point of view, any more than I believe in the *female* point of view. There are a good many of both, though it's true that there are some thoughts and attitudes that are unlikely to be held by men on the one hand or women on the other. So when I do use a male character, it's because the story is about something or someone that can't be otherwise conveyed, or that would be altered if it were to be conveyed through a female character. For instance, I recently published a story in *Granta* called *Isis In Darkness*. It's about the relationship — the tenuous relationship, over the years — between a women poet and a man who has, I guess, a sort of literary crush on her and how the woman affects the man's life. If I'd told it through the woman herself . . . well, you can't tell such stories about romantic infatuation from the point of view of the object of the infatuation without losing the flavor of the emotion. They would just become "who is that creep hanging around outside the balcony" stories.

INTERVIEWER

Can you tell the gender of a writer from reading the text alone?

ATWOOD

Sometimes, certainly, but not always. There's a famous case in England of an Anglican vicar who said he couldn't get anything published. So he wrote under the name of an East Asian woman, and got a novel accepted by Virago. There's a certain amount of opinion around that says, for instance, that women can't or shouldn't write from a male point of view, and so forth. Men are very sniffy about how they're portrayed by women, but the truth is that most of the really vicious, unpleasant male characters in fiction or theater have been written by men. The ethnic joke principle seems to be at work: it's okay to say a man has smelly feet, no ethics and bad table manners if the writer is a man, but if it's a woman saying exactly the same thing, then she somehow hates men. The male *amour propre* is wounded. And if she writes nice male characters, they're seen as "weak" by other men — though if a man puts a man in the kitchen, that's realism. And on and on.

We have fallen very much into the habit of judging books by their covers. "Authenticity" has become a concern. I tend to side with creative freedom. Everyone should write as she or he feels impelled. Then let's judge the results, not the picture of the author on the back flap.

Your question also assumes that "women" are a fixed quantity and that some men are "better" at portraying this quantity than others are. I, however, deny that the quantity is fixed. There is no single, simple, static "women's point of view." Let's just say that good writing of any kind by anyone is surprising, intricate, strong, sinuous. Men who write stereotyped women or treat them like stuffed furniture or sex aids are portraying something—their inner lives, perhaps—and that's interesting to know about, up to a point. But it should not be mistaken for life outside the author's head.

INTERVIEWER

How do the activities of writing poetry and writing prose differ for you?

ATWOOD

My theory is that they involve two different areas of the brain, with some overlap. When I am writing fiction, I believe I am much better organized, more methodical; one has to be when writing a novel. Writing poetry is a state of free float.

INTERVIEWER

I have the feeling that you work out problems in your poetry, but that you hold onto the metaphors and dramatize them in your novels.

ATWOOD

The genesis of a poem for me is usually a cluster of words. The only good metaphor I can think of is a scientific one: dipping a thread into a supersaturated solution to induce crystal formation. I don't think I solve problems in my poetry; I think I uncover the problems. Then the novel seems a process of working them out. I don't think of it that way at the time; that is, when I'm writing poetry, I don't know I'm going to be led down the path to the next novel. Only after I've finished the novel can I say, well, this poem was the key. This poem opened the door.

When I'm writing a novel, what comes first is an image,

scene or voice. Something fairly small. Sometimes that seed is contained in a poem I've already written. The structure or design gets worked out in the course of the writing. I couldn't write the other way round, with structure first. It would be too much like paint-by-numbers. As for lines of descent—that is, poem leading to novel—I could point to a number of examples. In my second collection of poems, *The Animals in That Country*, there's a poem called "Progressive Insanities of a Pioneer." That led into the whole collection called *The Journals of Susanna Moodie*, and that in turn led into *Surfacing*. Or, another line of descent: the poems in parts of *True Stories* have obvious affiliations with the novel *Bodily Harm*. It's almost as if the poems open something, like opening a room or a box, or a pathway. And then the novel can go in and see what else is in there. I'm not sure this is unique. I expect that many other ambidextrous writers have had the same experience.

INTERVIEWER

Do writers perceive differently than others? Is there anything unique about the writer's eye?

ATWOOD

It's all bound up with what sorts of things we have words for. Eskimos, the Inuit, have fifty-two words for snow. Each of those words describes a different kind of snow. In Finnish, they have no "he" or "she" words. If you're writing a novel in Finnish, you have to make gender very obvious early on, either by naming the character or by describing a sex-specific activity. But I can't really answer this question because I don't know how "others" observe the world. But judging from the letters I receive, many others recognize at least part of themselves in what I write, though the part recognized varies from person to person, of course. The unique thing about writers is that they write. Therefore they are pickier about words, at least on paper. But everyone "writes" in a way; that is, each person has a "story"—a personal narrative—which is constantly being replayed, revised, taken apart and put together again. The significant points in this narrative change as a person ages—

what may have been tragedy at twenty is seen as comedy or nostalgia at forty. All children "write." (And paint, and sing.) I suppose the real question is, why do so many people give it up? Intimidation, I suppose. Fear of not being good. Lack of time.

INTERVIEWER

Do you ever feel struck by the limitations of language?

ATWOOD

All writers feel struck by the limitations of language, all serious writers.

INTERVIEWER

Why is there so much violence in your work? *Bodily Harm*, in particular.

ATWOOD

Sometimes people are surprised that a woman would write such things. *Bodily Harm*, for instance, was perceived as some kind of incursion into a world that is supposed to be male. Certainly violence is more a part of my work than it is of Jane Austen's, or George Eliot's. They didn't do it in those days. Charles Dickens wrote about Bill Sikes bludgeoning Nancy to death, getting blood all over everything, but if a woman had written that, nobody would have published it. Actually, I grew up violence-free, and among people who were extremely civilized in their behavior. When I went out into the wider world, I found violence more shocking than would somebody who was used to it. Also, during the Second World War, although there was not violence in my immediate vicinity, the *angst* — you know, the anxiety about the war — was ever-present. Canada went into the war in 1939, about two months before I was born. The per capita death rate was high.

INTERVIEWER

Yet you write as if you've lived through violence.

ATWOOD

But I write as if I've lived a lot of things I haven't lived. I've never lived with cancer. I've never been fat. I have different sensibilities. In my critical work I'm an eighteenth-century rationalist of some kind. In my poetry I'm not at all. There's no way of knowing in advance what will get into your work. One collects all the shiny objects that catch the fancy—a great array of them; some of them you think are utterly useless. I have a large collection of curios of that kind, and every once in a while I need one of them. They're in my head, but who knows where! It's such a jumble in there. It's hard to find anything.

INTERVIEWER

Is sex easy to write about?

ATWOOD

If by "sex" you mean just the sex act—"the earth moved" stuff—well, I don't think I write those scenes much. They can so quickly become comic or pretentious or overly metaphoric. "Her breasts were like apples," that sort of thing. But "sex" is not just which part of whose body was where. It's the relationship between the participants, the furniture in the room or the leaves on the tree, what gets said before and after, the emotions—act of love, act of lust, act of hate. Act of indifference, act of violence, act of despair, act of manipulation, act of hope? Those things have to be part of it.

Strip-tease has become less interesting since they did away with the costumes. It's become Newtonian. The movement of bodies through space, period. It can get boring.

INTERVIEWER

Has motherhood made you feel differently about yourself?

ATWOOD

There was a period in my early career which was determined by the images of women writers I was exposed to—women writers as genius suicides, like Virginia Woolf. Or genius reclusives like Emily Dickinson and Christina Rossetti. Or doomed people of some sort, like the Brontës, who both died young. You could fall back on Harriet Beecher Stowe or Mrs. Gaskell; they both led reasonable lives. But then George Eliot didn't have any children; neither did Jane Austen. Looking back over these women writers, it seemed difficult as a writer and a woman to have children and a domestic relationship. For a while I thought I had to choose between the two things I wanted: children and to be a writer. I took a chance.

INTERVIEWER

In much of your work, love and power seem to be intricately connected — love as a power struggle in *Power Politics*. Do you see any other way between men and women?

ATWOOD

Love relationships between men and women do involve power structures, because men in this society have different kinds of, and more, power than women do. The problem for a woman in a relationship is how to maintain her integrity, her own personal power while also in a relationship with a man. Being in love with somebody is an experience that breaks down ego barriers. The positive part of that is a feeling of "cosmic consciousness," and the negative pole is a feeling of loss of self. You're losing who you are; you're surrendering — the fortress has fallen. But is it possible to have an equal exchange in a society in which things aren't entirely equal? *Power Politics* is fourteen years old. People tend to put it in the present tense. Each of my books is different — presenting different situations, characters and involvements. My most domestic novel is *Life Before Man*. In it, there's an equilateral triangle. There are two women and one man, and viewed from any one point in the triangle, the other two are not behaving properly. But you can go around the triangle and look at it from all sides. To be asked what I think as a person is a different thing. I have a very good relationship with a man, and I've had it for some time. The novel is not merely a vehicle for self-expression, or for the rendition of one's own personal life. I'm quite conservative in that way: I do see the novel as a vehicle for looking at society—an interface between language and what we choose to call reality, although even that is a very malleable substance. When I create characters in novels, those characters aren't necessarily expressing something that is merely personal. I draw observations from a wide range of things.

INTERVIEWER

How do you work? Can you describe how you write your first draft?

ATWOOD

I write in longhand, and preferably on paper with margins and thick lines with wide space between the lines. I prefer to write with pens that glide very easily over the paper because my handwriting is fast. Actually, I don't churn out finished copy quickly. Even though I have this fast handwriting, I have to scribble over it and scratch things out. Then I transcribe the manuscript, which is almost illegible, onto the typewriter.

INTERVIEWER

Do you have a time, a day, or a place for writing? Does it matter where you are?

ATWOOD

I try to write between ten in the morning and four in the afternoon, when my child comes home from school. Sometimes in the evenings, if I'm really zipping along on a novel.

INTERVIEWER

Do you write a novel from page one through to the end?

ATWOOD

No. Scenes present themselves. Sometimes it proceeds in a linear fashion, but sometimes it's all over the place. I wrote two parts of *Surfacing* five years before I wrote the rest of the novel:

the scene in which the mother's soul appears as a bird, and
the first drive to the lake. They are the two anchors for that
novel.

INTERVIEWER

What is the most difficult aspect of writing?

ATWOOD

That would be book promotion — that is, doing interviews.
The easiest is the writing itself. By "easiest" I don't mean
something that is lacking in hard moments or frustration; I
suppose I mean "most rewarding."

Halfway between book promotion and writing is revision;
halfway between book promotion and revision is correcting
the galleys. I don't like that much at all.

INTERVIEWER

Do you work closely with editors?

ATWOOD

I used to be an editor, so I do a lot of self-editing. I rewrite
a lot before I show things to people. I like to have a manuscript
in more or less its final shape before anyone sees it.

That doesn't mean I can spell. There's that, and the fiddley
things like punctuation — everyone has different ideas about
that. So I work with an editor to improve that aspect of the
text, of course. Ellen Seligman of McClelland and Stewart was
devoted and wonderful when we worked on *Cat's Eye*. Things
like, "You have "soggy" twice on the same page." Meticulous.
And I've had great fun doing some stories by phone with certain magazine editors — Bob Gottlieb of *The New Yorker* and
Bill Buford of *Granta*, for instance. These sessions always take
place when you're in Switzerland or about to get into the bath,
and they have to have it done right away. Bargaining goes on,
horse-trading. "You can have the dash if I get the semi-colon."
That sort of thing. But an editor doesn't just edit. She or he
sees the book through the whole publishing process. I have
close and long-standing relationships with, for instance, Bill

Toye of Oxford, Canada; Nan Talese, who's been my U.S. editor since 1976, and Liz Calder of Bloomsbury in the U.K. One of the things you want from an editor is simply the feeling that he or she understands your work. Money is no substitute for that.

INTERVIEWER

I've noticed that money is a very important factor in your thinking. Have you always seen things in such sharp economic terms?

ATWOOD

When you're poor, you do. I went through a period of being quite poor, of having to really watch it in order to buy myself time to write, and indeed in order to eat. My poverty wasn't the same as real poverty, in that I had some sense of direction. I didn't feel trapped. Actually, because my family lived in the woods, it was rather difficult to tell whether we were rich or poor, because none of those things applied. It didn't matter. We had what we needed—we grew a lot of our own vegetables and things. So I grew up outside of that. I wasn't in a social structure in which it mattered at all. Then I was out on my own quite early. I was brought up to believe that I should support myself. I had a bank account quite early on and learned how to use it. I was taught to be financially independent, and I always have been. Money is important for women, because you'd be amazed how it alters your thinking to be financially dependent on someone. Indeed, anyone.

INTERVIEWER

Have you ever thought of writing a novel in which a woman had an extremely important job?

ATWOOD

Yes, I have thought of doing that. But I've shied away for the same reason that George Eliot never wrote a novel about a successful English nineteenth-century woman writer, although she was one. It's still so atypical as to be a social exception. Besides, I'm not a business person. I'm a self-employed person. I don't have to deal in a power structure in the same way. I don't have to claw my way up through the corporate world. There is a successful woman in one of my books. She's the young, female judge that Rennie interviews in *Bodily Harm*. She's just so perfect. She has modern paintings, a wonderful husband, children; she loves her work—remember her? Rennie interviews her and can't stand it. A woman interviewer—of the "lifestyles" variety—once got very peeved with me because she felt I wasn't telling her the real dirt. She wanted the inner guck. I finally said to her, "If you had your choice, what would you like me to say to you?" She said, "Well, that you're leaving Graham, right now, and that I've got the scoop on it, and that I can come home and watch you pack."

INTERVIEWER

Have you always questioned institutions?

ATWOOD

Well, I grew up in the woods, outside of any social structures, apart from those of my family. So I didn't absorb social structures through my skin, the way many children do. If you grow up in a small town you instinctively know who is who and what is what, and whom you can safely be contemptuous of.

INTERVIEWER

How do you come by your titles?

ATWOOD

I like "come by," because that's about the way it is. I "come by" them, much as you "come by" some unexpected object in a junk store or lying beside the road. Sometimes the title arrives almost at the beginning of the writing of the book: *The Edible Woman* and *Lady Oracle* are cases in point. Sometimes you've been looking very hard in other directions, and the right title will just leap at you from the side. *Bodily Harm* came while I was doing some unrelated reading of a legal nature. Several books have gone through a number of working titles: for *Surfacing* there were two serious previous titles and about twenty possibilities—some of them variations on the final one. *Cat's Eye*—I think that came early on, and was very necessary in view of the central physical object in the book. *The Handmaid's Tale* was called *Offred* when I first began it. It changed by page 110. I know this because I kept a sort of working diary—not notes, but a running total of pages written—to encourage myself. I've read and continue to read the Bible a lot—partly as a result of being in all those hotel rooms, partly a long-standing habit—so the final title really did come from Genesis 30. I think too that it was one of those words that puzzled me as a child. "Hand-maid." Like "foot-man." It's a very odd word.

INTERVIEWER

Is the Bible a literary inspiration to you? I know that you've spoken of having "the gift" in almost religious terms.

ATWOOD

That's not an analogy I'm particularly comfortable with because it is religious. But "the gift" is real. Along with it goes a sense of vocation and dedication. You get the call.

INTERVIEWER

At the end of *Lady Oracle*, Joan says, "I'm not going to write Costume Gothics anymore. Maybe I'll write science fiction. Maybe I'll write about the future." In a sense you have done this in *Handmaid's Tale*. There is an evolution in your work toward a larger focus on the world.

ATWOOD

I think the focus has become wider, but surely that happens with every writer. What you do first is learn your craft. That can take years. In order to do that, you have to pick subjects that are small enough for you to handle. You learn how to do a good job with that. Of course, in the larger sense, every novel is—at the beginning—the same opening of a door onto a completely unknown space. I mean, it's just as terrifying every time. But nevertheless, having made the journey a few times, you have little guideposts, little signposts in the back of your mind. One of the most salutary things is writing a novel that fails, doesn't work, or that you can't finish, because what you learn from these failures is often as important as what you learn from doing something that succeeds. The prospect of having it happen again isn't so terrifying because you know you got through it.

INTERVIEWER

Can you look over your past work with pleasure; would you change it if you had the chance?

ATWOOD

I don't look over my past work very much. I would not change it anymore than I would airbrush a photo of myself. When I do look at my work, I sometimes don't recognize it immediately, or I'm indulgent, as one is towards the work of the young. Or I wonder what I could possibly have been thinking about, and then I remember. I suppose when I'm eighty I'll have a good old pig-out on my past productions, but right now I'm too preoccupied with what's on my plate. What a lot of food metaphors!

INTERVIEWER

Have Canadian critics been hard on you lately?

ATWOOD

My Canadian critics haven't been any harder on me than they usually are. If anything, maybe a bit easier; I think they're getting used to having me around. Growing a few wrinkles helps. Then they can think you're a sort of eminent fixture. I still get a few young folks who want to make their reputations by shooting me down. Any writer whose been around for a while gets a certain amount of that. I was very intolerant as a youthful person. It's almost necessary, that intolerance; young people need it in order to establish credentials for themselves.

You seem to know a great deal about visual art. Does this come from research or first hand experience?

ATWOOD
All writers, I suspect—and probably all people—have parallel lives, what they would have been if they hadn't turned into what they are. I have several of these, and one is certainly a life as a painter. When I was ten I thought I would be one; by the time I was twelve I had changed that to dress designer, and then reality took over and I confined myself to doodles in the margins of my textbooks. At university I made pocket money by designing and printing silk screen posters, and by designing theater programs; I continued to draw and paint in a truncated sort of way, and still occasionally design—for instance the Canadian covers of my poetry books. It's one of those things I'm keeping in reserve for when I retire. Maybe I can be a sort of awful Sunday painter, like Winston Churchill. Several of my friends are painters, so I've witnessed the difficulty of the life. The openings with the bad wine and drying-up cheese, the reviews with the perky headlines that don't quite get it, and so forth.

INTERVIEWER
Is there anything that sticks in your mind as having been your greatest reward as a writer?

ATWOOD
The first poem I ever got published was a real high. Isn't it funny? I mean, all the other things that have happened since then were a thrill, but that was the biggest.

INTERVIEWER
I mean something more personal, though.

ATWOOD
Alright, yes. I was in Copenhagen, and just walking along, you know, window shopping in a crowded mall. Denmark has

a historical relationship with Greenland where a lot of Inuit live. Along the street came some Inuit dancers done up in traditional Greenland dress. They had their faces painted, and they had furry costumes on, impersonating beasts and monsters, spirits of some kind. They were spirit dancers, growling and making odd noises to the crowd. They had clawed hands and face-distorters in their mouths — pieces of wood that made their cheeks stick out in a funny way. One of these furry spirit-monsters came over to me, took his face-distorter out of his mouth, and said, "Are you Margaret Atwood?" I said yes. He said, "I like your work." And then he put his face-distorter back in his mouth and went growling off into the crowd.

— Mary Morris

Watching Her Die

Reynolds Price

My father's last aunt moved in with us when I was ten and she was a thousand. Eighty-three, to be truthful, and virgin pure but sadly broke down. She'd lived near us, in her family home, all her life and mine. Only when she tried to rise one morning, stepped through a wormy board by her bed and stayed there trapped till my father found her just before supper, did she even consider giving up the old house.

Pure as she was, she'd raised my father when his own mother died; but once he got her foot unstuck, even he had to put the truth to her plain. "Old Lock, time's up. You've outlived your house. We offer you ours."

Aunt Lock knew *we* did no such thing. Not if *we* included my mother, which it had to. Mother had dreaded Lock's arrival from the moment my father proposed. She always said "He popped the question, then showed me the fly in his ointment—he was duty-bound to see Miss Lockie to the grave in kindness, assuming he or anybody outlived her." To explain that my mother was known, statewide, as loving to a fault and a martyr to kindness is a quick way to say what Lock was like, by then anyhow, that far gone in time.

Her short legs were bowed as any hoop. She stammered every word; and she understood less than any two geese, though she didn't know it. She thought she specialized in God and healing. You'd run in the house with a bleeding hand; she'd seize your wrist and say "Lick it, son!" When your mother protested that spit might infect it, Lock would tell her "Child, watch the animal kingdom. They lick everything that hurts and it *heals*." She'd of course known several people who cured the last stage of cancer with timely licks from a warm wet tongue, preferably their own.

With all the facts Lock knew about God, she was oddly silent in public with adults. It was mainly with me that she let them slip, when my parents were absent. I had the standard childhood way of avoiding my parents when I felt unhappy. Like other children, I'd walk off alone or seek out somebody neutral but kind—like a maiden aunt in the dim back room of the busy house. I'd lie on the hooked rug Lock set by her bed and let her pour what dammed up in her when my parents wouldn't listen. It was frequently memories of my father's boyhood. I asked for them often, not understanding I was near the age when I'd start being a man myself and would need to know how another boy managed to grow and make his own son.

I doubt Lock comprehended that, having changed so little through the length of her span. But something would make her tell a brief story about Dad's mischief and then let a quick strange moral appear in the empty air, like a quirky motto stitched on a sampler. She'd tell about the time he stripped the setting from the supper table, plates and all, hid them in the sideboard and ran for the woods while the family were coming from the porch to eat. Once she described the empty table and the ten baffled faces, she might draw a feeble breath and say "God showed him tricks like that every day."

She'd never explain but move back to telling how warts were cured by words alone, in new-moon light. I doubt she expected me to think for an instant about God's purpose in teaching Dad tricks, but of course I'd think of little else for the rest of that day. And the several times she let me know how

"God has promised I will not die"—no explanation—I turned
the promise over all ways from there on out, for her life and
mine. I'd seen a child die on the street beside school, and I
felt no need to share the fate.

Those words about death were almost the strangest, except
for the time I confessed to torturing a boy with a withered arm
at school—I twisted it hard and watched his face. Lock heard
me tell the whole miserable act; and when I expected at least
a scolding, she almost smiled, looked far out the window and
said "Keep it up if you need to—worse, if you must. You're
making him better than you by far." So altogether from the
day she joined us, Lock became even more a part of my mind
than the rest of my family (I've acknowledged my parents, plus
I had two sisters older than me.).

In addition, more than anyone else I knew, I could always
find her. Her room was behind a dark brown door right off the
kitchen; she was generally there in a green rocker or—on a dry
day, when her asthma let up—she'd be on a walk through the
deep back yard that passed through carefully tended grass into
thick ranks of scarlet sage and then into pines, far as any strong
boy could hope to walk, much less an old woman on miserable
legs.

It was such a day, I'm recalling now. Mid-October, a spotless
sky and air as dry as a bona fide desert, though mercifully cool.
Despite all that, I'd had a miserable day at school. Because of
the strange way Lock responded to my old confession of cruelty, I'd left the crippled boy alone. He'd even started bringing
me gifts of dried fruit from his father's store on the edge of
town where white-trash houses shaded into black with no firm
line, except in blood when a trespass occurred. Peaches,
apricots, pears and figs. I didn't care for them but I didn't say
so, just gnawed them at recess along with the boy and watched
him grin.

Yet on that grand October day for no discernible human
reason—a day for brave deeds—I suddenly saw my hand reach
out, take that boy's arm and wrench it behind him till I heard
a serious crack on the air. The boy said not a word of com-

plaint, though silent tears rolled down his face; and his eyes
never blinked. Then I watched him walk to the edge of the
playground, by himself, and slowly test if his arm was broke.
His back was turned but, just by the slowness of how he
moved, I could guess the pain and the tears still rolling. His
arm moved finally, straight out beside him like the school pa-
trol; and then he just walked down the sideline and turned
at a street and headed home, a quarter-past noon. As it turned
out, he stayed gone four more days.

By three forty-five on the guilty day, as I walked home, I
knew I should climb to my white room, fall down on my back
and beg the Lord, who'd memorized my meanness, to pardon
me some way without demanding I find the boy and beg him
first. His name was Zollicoffer Phipps, called Zollie. But since
my path led through the back woods, I was deep in the cool
shade, stroking through twigs and abusing my soul, when —
Lord! — I heard my name out loud.

"Dalton Burke" in a high soft voice but keen as a sunbeam.

I stopped cold and tried to guess was it human. I'd had more
than one communication from the unseen world, years before
I was ten; so I had some grounds for judging the matter. But
in five more seconds, I couldn't decide.

"Dal? Answer me."

I'd also been asked to answer before, by unseen voices that
never spoke the question. But something made me guess it
was a woman, even a girl — where the hell was she? (I'd started
to cuss.) I turned every way. Just thicker leaves and deeper
shade, on every side. All my life, what I can't see, I seldom address; so I held my tongue.

"D-*Dal.*"

Aunt Lockie, out this far alone?

Exactly that, though it took awhile to find her. Ten yards
away in a neat clearing I'd never noticed, Lock sat on a huge
uprooted oak. It looked freshly killed. The roots were still
damp, but we'd had no wind or lightning for a month. Anyhow it had landed at the right height for Lock. She was firmly
seated, holding a limb and for once her small feet touched the

ground—in chairs they tended to dangle useless. She was cool as the day and not even panting, so I figured she'd been back here a good while. That, and the distance she'd covered, made me think she'd wrangled with Mother, badly this time. So I moved on closer. "You waiting it out?"

Lock even smiled and refused the question. "I'm 'fust-rate,'" she said, one of her numerous old-time replies that gave me a fit when school friends were near, though many of them had similar antiques in their own back rooms. In general back then, children knew many more old people than now. Living near them, having to kiss and greet them, we learned far more about the speed and goal of life than children today. But I honestly doubt it made us gladder to know them or kinder. Anyhow there was nothing Aunt Lock had done that was really first-rate—or so I thought then—except raising Dad, and that was behind her.

That opened a path for me to say "I'm worse off than I've been, in living memory."

Mother would have laughed at the solemn phrase; but Lock took me, as she'd taken my father, dead-earnest at all times, even when we teased her. So now she pointed to the dry ground below; and when I sat, she said "What's your plight?"

I told the whole story, in her own way. Lock couldn't just say "It happened one afternoon last week." She had to back and haul a good deal to establish the day, the hour and weather. Then she'd dress whatever rooms were involved and give you descriptions of everybody with such precision that, years ahead, you could pick them out from an angry mob. I told her every fact she didn't know, since I left her at breakfast—the disappointment I'd had in reading class and all the other extenuators. Then I painted my crime in grim detail and said "I've mentioned excuses, Lock. They don't count, do they?" I hadn't looked straight at her eyes for a while; and even when she started, I couldn't look.

She said "Very much to the contrary, Dal, th-they all count against you." From then on she never stammered again. She'd given me lengthy thumbnail sermons before, on a lot more subjects than the powers of spit; but nothing had prepared me for what came next. She said two or three more sentences on the no-count nature of childhood meanness. Then she took a brief silent pause.

I risked a glance at her; but she was faced straight out beyond me, at nothing but leaves, far as I could see.

Then still looking off, she seemed to take a wide left turn in her mind. She said "Now I'm asked to die for you, son.

She'd long since learned not to call me *son*; it riled my mother. So trying to grin, I said "I'm Dalton, your favorite great-nephew. And Dalton's asking for no such thing." Jokes from Lock were scarce as snow, but I thought somehow she was teasing me. Young as I was, I knew about Jesus dying for the entire human race; but I couldn't think Lock was meant to follow him. Bad as I felt about Zollie's arm, I didn't quite see myself in Hell. So I said "Lock, I've been died for, remember?"

At first she nodded. Then she thought awhile longer. By now she'd all but proved she was listening, so I watched her closely. She was not watching me; she still faced the woods. And with every second, her face got paler and her skin got thinner. Soon a thousand hairline veins stood out in her spotty brow and down her throat. They turned dark purple as if her blood was desperate for oxygen, dying fast. In the space of two minutes that seemed like a month, I had to believe my great-aunt was dying because she was asked.

She was somehow dying because of me and the cruel acts I couldn't stop doing, young as I was. Strangest of all, the change didn't scare me, though I finally said "Aunt Lock, hold back. You said God promised you'd never have to die." If she heard, it made no difference at all. So I finally made the painful offer I'd tried to shun. I said "I'm to blame." Still no good; she was past my reach.

By then her eyes had drifted shut, and soon they also started to die. The lids, that were always paper thin, went nearly transparent till I could see the ghost of her pupils gazing through—thank God, not at me. And her lips, that had also thinned, drew up in a thorough smile of a sort I seldom saw on Lock unless my father bent to kiss her on Christmas morning or at the supper he always cooked for her birthday. More than once Mother said "Miss Lock's never known a whole happy day; and she means for us to share her discontent." So while I estimated that her death was less than a minute ahead of us now, I asked "Are you happy?"

Any other time, she'd have stammered badly at that big a question. And she did wait so long I thought she was gone. Then a voice, from farther out than she'd gone before, said plainly "Happy? No. But I'm honored, yes, and glad to serve." Another long wait while every cell of her skin went still as the dead oak she sat on.

I thought "Any second, she'll pitch over on me." And I braced to catch her.

But one more time, that far voice spoke. "Shut your eyes now, son, and count to a hundred."

I not only shut my eyes; I bent way down and hid my face in my folded legs. I figured when she fell, I could roll her aside. Then I counted slowly. As always, I got confused in the sixties and backtracked some; but from ninety-five on, I spoke the last numbers. I thought if Lock was hearing me still, she'd say what next when I got to one hundred. But no word came, no sigh, no breath. Even the leaves all sounded dead. I shouldn't have been the least surprised since I almost never prayed anymore. I kept the decision a private fact; but at nine, I decided God had more work on his hands than my slim business. But that October afternoon, again I spoke out loud once more, "Sir, help me please." Then I looked.

I've said Lock never played tricks on us, but even the greatest actor on Earth couldn't have imitated death this well. I'd seen two old great-uncles dead and a friend of mine, in the wreck of his bicycle, near our school. Lock was dead all right; and I still wasn't scared or thinking ahead to what I'd tell my mother now, not to mention Dad, when he got home. I put one finger out toward her, waited in midair to see if she'd flinch, then went the whole way and touched her wrist where it still gripped the limb.

Up till today she'd kept a steady heat, lukewarm and weird, like standing oatmeal; so I'd always shied off feeling her skin except when she absolutely required it. Now though she was cool and not weird at all, peaceful really. My finger stayed on her flesh so long, I felt her go maybe five degrees cooler, with not a trace of pulse or twitch.

I stood up finally and stepped well back. No way on earth I could get her home now, with my schoolbooks and lunchbox. But I should stretch her out, or she might fall—any breeze would tip her down in a heap. That's when I suddenly thought I should listen, listen at least as hard as Lock. Whatever voice had spoken to her might have some useful advice for me. Children, this side of the early teens, are still smart enough to know such things. I put both hands down calm at my sides, shut my own eyes and tried to slow my heart. It obeyed so soon that, for one cold instant, I thought it was stopping too. But I stayed in place; and next I heard it thudding onward, slow but trusty.

Then a voice, the same old voice I'd heard in early years, said "Leave her here, boy. She's where I want her." I held on a good while, hoping it would offer some word on where I should go next, who I should hunt down and what I should say.

And eventually, once a crow had called, the voice said "Now you are free again; she saved your skin."

My mind was suddenly clean as a washed slate. I tried to think of my name but couldn't. I knew just one thing, *Haul your rusty ass* out *of here*. So, young as I was, I hauled it home.

Mother was out, my sisters were on a field trip to Raleigh, the cook wouldn't be back till five o'clock. Dad, being a doctor, might come in early or not till past bedtime. For once I hated the house being empty, but I still wasn't what you could truly call scared. I believed the voice. I knew not to worry now about Zollie. He'd been repaid already by whoever ran the show, this peculiar day. Someway tomorrow, or by Thanksgiving, I'd make my amends. He and I would be friends for life; I'd be his protector.

In my own room though, my private belongings began to wake me. Familiar objects, like a Barlow knife and a silver dollar from the year I was born, stared back at me and saw my shame and my wild rescue. An actual human being, just now, had volunteered to be my scapegoat and pay some debt I owed to justice. I had felt bad enough, just on my own; but nothing had made me understand how hard the sky, or the voice behind it, viewed my cruelty and all such acts, here and elsewhere always. Being not just young but normally human, I hoped the voice would let me lead my parents to Lock and say no more than that I'd discovered her, coming from school, dead there in the woods. And since the last place I'd said a prayer was in my bed, I lay down there, got still again and asked if I could take my father to the woods and not explain why Lock died on me.

I thought the voice was ready to speak, but no word came that I could hear.

I told myself the answer was *Yes*. I still think it was.

The cook came in a while later and worked on, singing so high she woke the local bats before sundown. Soon after five, Mother was suddenly downstairs with her, laughing and saying "No, no, *no*." I stayed in my room and finished my homework, praying that Dad would turn up shortly, then would climb up to take his evening leak and check on me. I honestly think, till the day he died, he thought I'd evaporate some unannounced morning between the time he left me at breakfast and touched me upstairs again when he got home. I'd known forever he prized me more than both my sisters, I understood my disappearance would ruin his life, I mattered that much in all his plans. But I wouldn't know why till I had one satisfactory child of my own, the gray-eyed daughter who rewards me still.

When I heard Dad finish washing his hands, I was still on the bed. I rolled to the wall and balled myself up to look like sleep.

He came in anyhow, sat on the edge and tapped my hip. "Sarge, you sick?"

Just before I had to respond, I suddenly wondered if that was it. Was this whole afternoon some kind of sick dream? Was I laid up now in a hospital bed with a record fever, a puzzle to science? Was I the dead person and this was eternity? Had

Zollie gone home and prayed for justice and all I was going through now was just my strange but fair deserts? I'd been saved though; I still trusted that. So I turned to face Dad and said "No, tired."

Dad studied me to test my honesty. Then he nodded. "*School*-tired." He had disliked school as much as me, and he always said how amazed he was that he spent thirty years on something that bitter. Whatever, it had made him a first-rate surgeon, widely sought. Next he sat on quietly, watching his hands. He had told me, more than once lately, how much he was hoping they'd last him out till he had to retire. He thought sometimes they'd begun to quiver.

So I whispered clearly "Stop looking; they're *still*." It made me think of Lock dead of course, but I kept my secret.

He searched my face again and then laughed. "You know too much."

I said to myself *He's righter than ever* but I laughed too.

"How's Lockie feeling?" That was nothing strange. He knew how Lock and I, most afternoons, listened to the radio from four to five—"The Lone Ranger," "Terry and the Pirates." Lock's favorite was "The Phantom," who knew "what evil lurks in the hearts of men." Every day without fail, Dad would see me first and ask about Lock—had we liked our programs? If I said yes and that Lock was normal, he could put off paying a before-supper visit to her back room and risking Mother's temper.

With him, I always knew I could reach for the truth at once, no fooling around. I told him "You need to see something right now; but don't ask questions, not yet at least. Let's get downstairs, quiet as we can, and out to the woods."

The way he replied was the reason I'd loved him all my life and honor him still, long past his presence. He said "Then lead me."

Silent as braves, we got outdoors, on through the yard and into the trees without so much as a yell from Mother, though she had to be watching at the kitchen window.

When we were a good ten yards into thicket, and our backs were hid, I stopped and faced Dad. I even asked him to step back a little. "I need to tell you something hard."

He'd after all had people die in his hands, his literal hands; so his face didn't frown, and he stepped well back.

When he pulled a red dogwood leaf to chew, I suddenly thought I'd spare him the mystery, Lock's awful merciful words before leaving. I said "Aunt Lockie has passed away. I found her body, back deep in here, when I came home from school. Her heart just stopped, no sign of blood. I couldn't lift her. She was peaceful and safe, so I didn't tell Mother but waited for you."

My father was strong on the order of iron, strong but ready to love what he loved. I'd seen him cry only once till then, when a girl child died as he touched her heart to repair a valve. He climbed to my room that terrible evening, not stopping for Mother, and sat on my bed and said "This one finger *touched* her heart—for the first time, son, to give her the life she ought to have—and it stopped, stock-still." Here in the woods though, dusk coming down, he let my news pass into his eyes. Then he looked back awhile.

I thought he was hiding his grief this time—Lock was his mother, to all intents—and I said "Don't mind. I won't tell a soul."

But he faced around and was smiling a little. He said "Have you told me the real truth, Sarge?"

I must have looked troubled.

"She's not been killed? You said no blood—"

I raised my hand in the standard boy's oath. "Sir, she's peaceful." That much was true.

Dad was no sunny-sider; he tended to frown. Till now I'd never heard him say any death was a blessing. I thought he meant Mother; it would finally lift the load of poor Lock off her mind and back. I nodded. "That's why I didn't tell Mother, I saved it for you."

Dad shook his head and waved me off; I'd misunderstood. What came next was the hardest thing he ever told me. "I've waited for this through long years now." He looked inward past me and stepped on forward to take the lead for maybe five yards. Then he recalled he didn't know where she'd be. I would need to guide him.

He'd never conceded that job to me, not till that moment;

but I stepped forward proudly. As I passed him I touched his arm for an instant. "It's not bad, I told you—not one scratch or bruise."

As we went, it suddenly dawned on me some dog might have found Lock and mauled her face. So I moved on faster than he usually walked, to get there soon enough to warn him back if her body was changed. For at least five years, I'd forged alone through these same trees, trying to imagine I was threatened by Indians and vicious beasts, all barely hid an arm's reach off. And I always tried to imagine *bravery*, how to walk toward what might be my death without the hair of my neck rising cold. Finally that dusk—with Dad behind me, trusting my knowledge—I was truly fearless. My blood ran warm and steady and smooth as an August river, and the hundred-yard trip seemed longer than Lewis and Clark's whole cross-country trek.

By the time I reached the edge of the clearing, the evening light could barely get through the circling pines. But right away I felt relief. Lock was still upright on the fallen tree, her eyes were still shut, one hand was holding the small limb for balance. I knew a single gust or a hard footstep might tip her forward in a heap on the ground, so I waited in place till Dad caught up.

Faced with a problem, he mostly reacted speedily. Now though he waited silent, on my left.

I looked to his profile, and at first he wouldn't face me.

Then he relented and his gray eyes were calm. He all but whispered "Sarge, you're wrong."

I quickly tried to guess his meaning—what else was this old lady but frozen in *rigor mortis* by now? What had I misunderstood?

Dad reached across the gap between us, took my hand and slowly walked toward her.

In my eyes anyhow Lock seemed to quiver as fast as a hummingbird's wing, a visible blur. I figured the force of our gentle footsteps was reaching her body, but it hurt to see, and I must have pulled back on Dad's hand a little.

Anyhow he turned me loose and went on.

I stayed where I stopped, maybe ten feet back.

Dad slowed his pace but went right to her.

She was dead as ever, to my mind at least. Even the bird's-wing blur was still. For the first time, I saw what you see on death masks—whatever fears and pains they knew, the dead faces of famous men, like Napoleon, are smooth as children. Maybe death is that easy. Or more likely maybe, before they can mix the plaster and make your mask, the pull of gravity eases the lines of age and dread, leaving you young and hopeful again. My great-aunt didn't look young or glad; but she did look tranquil, a whole new thing in the years I'd known her. I saw Dad's hand reach out toward her hand; and I thought *Lord God, she'll powder to dust*. I'd read about ancient maidens who powdered when their perfectly lovely corpses were touched. Nothing happened though, that I could see. He'd only laid two light fingers on her, and soon I figured he was hunting a pulse.

The fingers rested gently on her wrist for a good long while. Then he seemed to shake his head in sadness. But next he drew back and almost whispered "Dear Lock, it's me."

I'd never heard him say *dear* till now. Mother told me once "He'd die for us both, but he won't say *darling* like everybody else." All I could think was *If he's glad she's gone, why's he trying to wake her?* I thought he was trying to pay his respects, to show he was there and honored her body. Then I knew we would have to call for help, strong men with a stretcher. I stepped on to Dad and quietly said "Before much later, we need to get help."

He waited a moment and said "We may have the help we need." With his hand still on her, he whispered "Dear Lock, now answer me." Then he said "Please. This moment."

And over what felt like the next ten years, Lock came on back. Almost no daylight was reaching us, but I thought I could see the color of blood creep back through her face. I knew I could hear the creak of her breath till finally her eyelids quivered fast, and then she was looking up at Dad.

He didn't speak but offered his other hand.

At first she didn't take it. Her eyes searched round till they located me. She didn't quite frown, she surely didn't smile, she gave a slight nod. Then she took Dad's other hand and gradually stood. He looked and acted like the olden beau she never had or the ideal son she claimed he'd been from the day he was born. They passed right by, touching me nowhere, and walked till they reached the thicket again. Lock stopped there, and facing just the woods, she spoke out plainly "Are you taking me home?"

Dad said "I am." They both moved on and I fell in behind them.

But I stayed close enough to hear that, every few yards, Lock would speak—short phrases about the leaves, the light, the weather. I'd never heard her say so much when she and I walked; her breath was too precious.

It seemed her breath was sufficient now, though she stammered some. We were all the way out the far edge of the woods, with the house there before us—the kitchen lights— when Lock stopped once more and said a whole sentence. "It's bound to be time to eat and I'm hungry."

Till then I'd never heard Lock mention hunger; she ate a lot less than a hand-sized bird. So I stood in place and watched Dad lead her on to the house and up the back steps, slow as ever.

I was baffled beyond description of course. But I had the bare minimum of sense to wait and fix their picture deep in my mind—a son and his mother somehow alive and certainly changed. At the time I wasn't thinking I'd need the picture ever again. I didn't plan to store it buried in hopes it would bloom someday with news and hope. But here this instant I could take up a pen and draw them for you—Lock and my father—clear as I saw them, though full dark had very nearly fallen between us. All these years later, I bring it up on the screen of my eyes more times than most memories.

Whatever happened, what changed in Lock from that night onward was seen by nobody else but me. All her worrisome traits stayed with her right on—the stammer, the ugly marks of age, the draining worship she paid my father were strong as ever. With all the strangeness of those dim hours in a single day, neither Dad nor Lock ever brought it up in conversation, public or private. It might just have been a long dream I had, to punish myself for the vicious mad dog kenneled inside me, hot to lunge. Did Lock really suffer some brand of death? I had no medical implements with me of course, but even now I'm ready to swear that she wasn't breathing when I left her upright that afternoon. Or was she merely fooling to curb a boyish tendency in me?

Was it all Lock's idea, or was she truly driven on by an unseen judge? If it was some brand of practical joke, it was the first and only such in a long solemn life. If death truly seized her, the way I saw it, then who brought her back—my dad with a touch and one loving word or the unseen judge maybe changing his mind? Dream or fact, it serves Lock's purpose of punishing me, to this minute now when I tell the story; and I've had maybe more occasions than most men to punish myself, again and again for common meanness, by simply calling back to mind the sight of a woman dying for me.

There is one fact I can still bring forward to prove that afternoon's story true, a chain of actions and deeds that happened to sane human creatures other than me. From that time forward, though she'd talk with me as before in public—at meals, in rooms with my parents or sisters—Lock never addressed me in private again, not so much as a *yes* or *no*. Even in public, where she often addressed me as before, she never spoke my name, not once. I'd come home every day from school at four, turn on the radio and lie on the rug. Lock would hear the sound and come in from her room—slow and creaky, rolling on her bowlegs like some old sailor—to take her chair and hear our shows with no single word. She'd smile, laugh or frown in accord with the story. She'd meet my eyes as often as ever, always kindly. She'd darn any wornout sock I brought her; she'd still lean down and scratch my scalp as the plots tensed up in our radio shows.

But that was the only way we touched, from then till her second and last departure. I was never again compelled to kiss her powdery whiskers; never smelled her musty neck again, for all our laughter—and we laughed a lot. At first I thought of ways to scare her—to call the firetruck or claim my head had burst into pain like a gasoline fire and would split any instant and scald us both. I held back though and learned to respect her, the way you'd trust a St. Bernard that saved your life but was naturally mute.

That much of my great-aunt was dead to me, shut up and gone. It made me think of a thousand questions only she could answer. They all pertained to my father's youth, things he'd never tell me—what he was weak at, ways he failed before he got so strong and fearless. Finally though I had to believe Lock had told me the last hard thing to know. And she'd told it plainly in real daylight in actual woods the final day I was outright fierce. *You can somehow choose to pay the debts of a needy boy or other grown soul, if you have that much to give and are willing.*

Lock died again, for what I assume was the final time, eight quick years later when I was away—my first year of college. Dad's letter said she went in her sleep, no trace of a struggle, ninety-one years old. At first I thought it was the worst kind of death; no living soul could truly mourn her. For years the thought seemed perfectly sound. But then I got my adult life and the ones I cherished, my daughter chiefly.

And the year I was fifty, a business trip took me back to my hometown for several days. The last evening, with time to spare, I found our house. We'd sold it fifteen years before, when Mother died. Still it was in better shape than me, fresh-painted though empty—a weathered sign *For Rent* in the yard. I had the good sense not to look in the windows, but I found myself walking straight for the woods.

For whatever reason they were very much changed. Contrary to the general rule of memory, the trees were a good deal taller than before with serious girth way past my reach and a thickness above that shaded out the old thicket and briars and left a clean floor. My legs at least recalled the path; and dead though it seemed those forty years since, Lock's fallen oak was

still where she left it the night Dad roused her. Some of the
bark had peeled away, but the sturdy trunk was hard as ever.
And the small limb that Lock's hand gripped was waiting still.
I'm no great keeper of souvenirs; but suddenly there in the
quickening dusk, I thought I'd snap off the limb and take it—
my great-aunt's anchor in a world she surrendered. And I
made two tries, but the limb refused and then I was glad.

Lock Burke blazed up there instantly before me—in my
mind, understand—and the sight of her vanishing face and
life repeated, clear as the long-gone voice that counseled me,
a truth I hold ever close to my heart and mean to enact when
my own chance comes.

I've doubted an awful list of things in my long life—the
truth of my wife, my friends and God, even my all-but-flawless
daughter. I've doubted that the Earth itself should last or my
tragic race, all humankind. But since Aunt Lockie paid all for
me, alone in dark woods with night coming down, that she
couldn't navigate if we hadn't saved her, I've never since
doubted my place in the world or my endless duty to find at
least the needful heart for whom one day I lay my own life
down and depart.

John Tranter

Rain

I

'We went to New York,' Kathy said.
'Colin was painting well then, and he was
on the edge of a breakthrough, he said.
Breakdown was more like it. He was drinking,
smoking a lot of dope. He'd sit on the floor
and stare at his work, and talk about his soul.
Why are men full of shit? He painted
big canvases, twelve feet across,
red, black and purple zigzags,
then he'd blacken them with a blowtorch—
trying to face up to the Americans,
he said. The way he talked about it,
it was like a boy's competition
down at the bottom of a schoolyard,
kids punching each other on the arm,
proving they could take the punishment.
You know, with Jackson Pollock, that
investment in the ego—prove yourself,
throw your soul onto the canvas,
one false step and you're a phoney.
But that's bullshit. You can make
as many false steps as you want;
if a piece doesn't work, you just
throw it out, or scrape it back
and paint something better over it.'

It was a lovely spring morning. We were
enjoying the breeze at the front of the ferry.
The light went down into the water
then it reflected off the sandy bottom
and glinted pale green through the waves.

'We were going to cafés in the Village,'
Kathy was saying, 'and reading books—
Action Painting, poetry, the Beats,
the Existentialists—popular philosophy
seemed to be obsessed with the arts then—
apart from the native consumer philosophy
that polished every American artifact
and made it glow with reflected money—
and every trend had a capital letter.
Colin said he had to get drunk to paint,
to see his own soul truthfully,
so he could wrestle with it, he said,
late into the night. You know, he slept
eight hours just like any office worker,
except he organised it so he slept
ten in the morning through to six at night.
People thought he was so full of fire
that he went without sleep. Huh!
Well, he liked to give that impression.

What did I feel about New York?
I can't sort it out. It broke me.
It made me into an artist. I don't know.
I still have a lot of hostile feelings.
It's like advertising—of course it's
necessary, and often it adds flavour
and colour to things, but at the same time
it's obviously made up of greedy lies.

I'd been fascinated by photography,
how a snapshot can freeze a scene
and turn a piece of three-dimensional
coloured, moving reality, full of sound,
into something flat and motionless,
silent, permanent, like an art print,
and show you things you couldn't really see,
tiny details, the blur of frozen movement,
an expression that flitted across a face.

That had been my major project
at art school, before I met Colin
and dropped out. I took it up again
in New York, just photographing people
on the street. I rigged up a darkroom
in the bathroom; everybody does.
It never gave me the results
I wanted — solid tone, clean prints —
I was always having to pack it up
so we could use the bathroom, and the air
was full of dust. In a darkroom
it's not the light that gets to be a problem;
you can work at night. No, it's the dust;
lint from towels, dust in the air,
dandruff, grit — it gets on the negatives
while you're printing, and the prints come out
with big white spots all over them.
But I managed. The work kept me sane
when things got bad — and they got bad —
and it reminded me of who I was.
I was disintegrating, otherwise.

I drank a lot at first. I think
it helped me to cope, or at least
that's what I believed at the time.
Some of the people you meet — artists,
dealers, artists' wives — those people

were competitive. That was their style.
New Yorkers have a tendency to see
their worst faults as virtues—I guess
if you were one of those piranhas
and had to look in the mirror every morning
you'd gas yourself. So they'd developed
elaborate theories about how vital
competition was—competition, the essence
of petty capitalism, for God's sake,
not even monopoly capitalism, let's get
our focus set at the proper level,
we're dealing with the *petty* bourgeoisie—
how it separated the sheep from the goats,
artists from weaklings, men from boys—
they didn't mention women or girls—
and you'd hear them talking late at night,
high on speed, smoking the cigarettes
that Albert Camus actually used to smoke,
or so someone said who'd been to Paris,
arguing that the spotlight of fame
lit up the peaks, that fashion helped us all
to focus on the very best work,
without wasting time ploughing through
all that second-rate stuff. The critics
would do that. Shark eat shark, it was
a kind of Darwinism they were advocating.

I had the kid to worry about—a big city
is no place to bring up a five-year-old.
But we found a school that Timmy liked—
at that age you adapt, he made friends,
and I'd take him early every morning—
I had to be up at six to do that,
get him ready, take the bus uptown,
so I had regular hours, of a sort.
And I'd shop, and work from nine to two
in a typing pool. We needed any money

I could bring in. I wasn't paid well.
I couldn't get a work permit,
so I wasn't officially supposed to work
at all. I was being exploited,
but we had to eat. What the hell.

In the afternoons I'd collect Timmy
and take him to a park uptown
for a glimpse of grass and the ducks—
he used to love the ducks—then I'd
bring him home, and clean and get dinner.
Colin would be out at the Cedar Bar
drinking and arguing, or asleep,
or just away somewhere in the jungle.
We called New York the Jungle.
Timmy would tell me about the things he'd done
at school. In a way it was a peaceful life,
if I'd been able to step back from things.

We were young, and we certainly weren't rich.
Colin had just won a landscape prize,
and it seemed a lot of money at first.
But things are so expensive in New York.
He gave himself a year to make it
in the States, and it grew clear
as the last few months leaked away and
the bills mounted up, and the money went,
that he wasn't going to make it at all.
I felt terrible—for all the phoney talk
he really suffered, and he went through hell.
He'd swallowed the whole competitive myth,
and now he was at the bottom of the pile,
eating shit.

      About that time
an art dealer took to calling around.
He liked Colin's work, and my photographs,
he said he'd arrange a show in the Spring.

He advanced us some money. Then some more.
He bumped into me in a bookshop one day,
and bought me lunch. And another time
at the laundromat, and we lunched again.
He was a nice guy, I thought; intelligent,
he read books, he was on the artist's side,
and he had that glow success brings.
I started seeing him from time to time.

Well, don't look at me like that,
what was I supposed to do? Colin,
he was hardly speaking to me any more,
sunk in his drink and his marijuana
and his late-night painting binges.
I was as lonely as hell—America
can make you feel like you don't exist.
And Trent was so intelligent, so . . .
sophisticated, so full of enthusiasm.
You've got the same kind of optimism,
you know who you are, that's why
I like you.'

              I didn't disillusion her.
Sure, my life was falling into a pattern.
I'd finished a degree in architecture,
and I'd spent two years in Thailand
working on a rural housing project.
I'd married recently—unhappily at first,
as it turned out, but that was my fault
for being headstrong about my career,
and I figured I could adjust and adapt.
In a month I was to start work with
a city firm, designing office blocks.
Yes, I should have known who I was.

'That's what I missed,' Kathy went on.
'Colin used to have it—that belief
in your work, in yourself, a zest—but

it got kicked out of him, worn away,
eroded. There's always someone else
better than you, younger than you,
someone with more energy, newer ideas,
more fashionable cigarettes, better
contacts, willing to compromise an inch
more than you. It really eats you up.
Colin was worn down to nothing. And
I must admit Trent was very generous.
We were broke, and he advanced us money.
And it was more or less understood
that if Colin made it, had a big show,
sold out, the money would be repaid.
If not — it was a casual arrangement.

One night things turned out really bad —
Trent and I had gotten into the habit
of using cocaine from time to time,
at his place, when I'd put Timmy to bed.
He'd invited this other couple over,
and we drank some scotch, and did some coke,
and we all got pretty well stoned,
and the next thing I know I was involved
in this group sex thing, very unpleasant.
Don't look shocked; that was long ago.
Believe me, I was a different person. Jesus,
when I think of those manipulative bastards . . .'

Kathy was pretty, and when she was angry
a slight flush stole up her throat
and spread across her cheeks. Her eyes
were deep green with hazel flecks,
and they enlarged slightly as though
she were staring at something remarkable,
but she was only staring at her hands
as they slowly clenched and unclenched.
I noticed her skin was slightly freckled —

it seemed to match the eyes and auburn hair.
The unhappy emotions she described
made me feel close and somehow special.
Perhaps she had the gift of making anyone
she spoke to feel special, I don't know.
Her voice dropped perhaps half an octave
and an air of shared intimacy grew.
For no real reason, I remembered
taking my first puff of a cigarette—
you go dizzy, and your fingertips tingle.
Her arms were goosepimpled in the breeze,
and I felt an irrational urge to touch her
bare skin—just to brush her arm
lightly, with the back of my hand.
I felt myself go red suddenly,
and I turned away to look at the water.

Kathy had noticed nothing. 'Those
manipulative bastards,' she said again.
'When they left I got angry. I saw clearly
how I'd been used all along, set up—
even when he met me in the laundromat—
hell, Trent had his laundry sent out,
he was vain, such a pain in the neck,
he wouldn't be seen dead in a laundromat!
We had a fight, we were always fighting,
I asked him to drive me home—it was freezing,
a storm, and the rain had turned to sleet—
I remember the wipers on the windscreen
scraping back and forth through the mush—
Trent always drove fast—he had a Porsche,
what else?—I was crying and yelling,
he was laughing at me, I got mad—
I guess I must have hit him in the face.
We were doing sixty, at least, maybe more,
and in the wet the car skidded and rolled,
and kept rolling. I blacked out. Sometimes

I still have this dream, we're skidding,
the screech of metal scraping on the road,
and I'm reaching out for him, screaming—

when I came to we were upside-down,
we'd gone through a metal fence and fallen
twenty feet into an excavation site.
My face was pressed against the roof,
the seat-belt holding me up, and Trent—
a metal pole had speared through the door
and through Trent's chest near the neck.
He was hanging there in agony,
clawing at it. He could hardly breathe,
and he made this horrible gulping noise,
over and over, trying to get air.
There was a stink of gasoline everywhere.

Well, the ambulance, they cut us out
with jacks and metal cutters, they were wonderful.
They had to work fast, and they did.
I was just bruised, but they had Trent
full of drugs and serum while they worked.
By the time they got him to the hospital
he was in a coma. A lung was punctured
in the crash, the skull damaged, and the spine.

I remember he said once the Porsche
wasn't quite up to his style, they just
didn't make a car flash enough. Well,
his style from then on was a wheelchair.
He couldn't remember anything at all,
not even me. Me! Jesus!
Can you believe that? Six months
we'd been seeing each other every Monday,
I thought I meant something to him,
and now I'm a zero, I don't exist,
he couldn't even remember my face!

The cops found cocaine in his jacket,
traces, and searched the apartment,
and found more cocaine wrapped in foil
in the freezer, and marijuana under the bed.
He got six months in prison, a light sentence,
but it was the end of his art dealing days.
Finally his parents came and wheeled him back
to some hick town in Minnesota,
and no one ever saw him again.

O God, look, we've arrived.'

I'd been so engrossed in Kathy's tale
I hadn't noticed where we were. I felt
quite light-headed and confused —
how was I supposed to react
to her story? Did she want sympathy?
She'd been working on her prints all night
getting ready for an exhibition,
and she'd taken lots of coffee and methedrine,
so maybe her emotions were a little skewed.

Jack and Colin joined us on the wharf.
We stopped off at a local shop and bought
bread and cheese and fresh ham for lunch
and walked around the shore to the houseboat.

It was moored in the shade of some trees
close in to the eastern side of the island
in the shelter of a small bay. It was old,
but large and roomy, with a sundeck at the back.
The name 'Pequod' was painted on the bow;
a joke of Masterson's. He had money,
he often lent the boat to his friends,
and he'd fitted the place out comfortably —
there was a hi-fi with lots of records,
mostly jazz from the late fifties,

an old wind-up gramophone,
hot running water, plenty of books.
We had some lunch, and then a long nap.
Later we took a walk around the foreshore,
then wandered back to the houseboat
and played gin rummy on the deck
until it started to drizzle, and we went inside
for some hot rum and sandwiches.

Towards evening a storm came up
with a thrashing of leaves and heavy rain.
The six o'clock ferry failed to appear,
so we made up our minds to stay the night.
As dark came on it grew worse,
the wind knocking branches off the trees.

Jack opened a bottle of old bourbon
and we all had a drink before dinner.
I noticed Colin was drinking rather fast,
gulping it down quickly, and pouring another.
He knocked up a good sauce for the spaghetti
Kathy cooked, a kind of bolognese
heavily flavoured with garlic and black pepper
and some fresh basil he found growing in a pot
on the front deck of the boat. There was wine—
Masterson was proud of his well-stocked cellar.
We chose a strong burgundy-style red,
and ended up drinking half a dozen
between the four of us. It was a good meal,
with lots of talk and spirited argument.

After dinner Jack wound up the gramophone
and asked Kathy politely for a dance.
They circled gravely in the lamplight.
The rain had passed, and the night was still.
I had a coffee on the deck, and thought
how soon all this would be over;

the late nights, the talk, the drinking.
Soon I'd have a career to think about.
The music was plaintive country and western —
a blend of steel guitar and violins.
I recognized the 'Tennessee Waltz.'

We'd just organized ourselves for the night
and I was having a quiet drink with Kathy
on the deck, when Jack came out and said
that Colin had complained of feeling unwell.
We went inside. Colin looked awful.
'I should have left the drink alone,' he said,
articulating his words awkwardly. 'I'm sorry.
It was that last bottle of gin.' He laughed.
His face was grey. 'It's the tablets I'm taking.
You're not supposed to mix them with alcohol.'
Kathy gave me a look, and went to the kitchen.
I followed her. 'He's taken too much,'
she whispered angrily. 'It's morphine. I didn't
want to bring it up, but that's the problem.
What do we do? Keep him awake, I suppose.'
I couldn't think of anything to say.
I think I was shocked: about the drugs, or
about Kathy treating it so casually,
the two things were confused in my mind.
We went back into the living room.
'Keep him awake,' Kathy said. 'Just
walk him around a bit. He'll be right.'
'Did you hear that?' Jack said.
'Just keep awake, old son.'
I had a feeling he knew what was wrong.
Colin didn't reply. He'd fallen back
in his chair with his mouth open.
A string of spittle hung from his lips.
'I'll make some coffee,' Kathy said,
and went to the kitchen, tying on an apron.
'Let's get him up and moving,' I said.

I took one side, and Jack took the other,
and we began walking him around the room.
His legs didn't seem very strong,
and he buckled at the knees once or twice.
Then he stumbled into one of the chairs,
so Jack rearranged the furniture
to give a clear passage through the room.
'Open the door,' I said, 'and take him
out onto the deck, then back again.'
'Oh dear, wait a minute,' Colin said,
and lurched for the railing. He threw up.
'Good idea, old son,' Jack said.
'Clear the stomach out. You'll feel better.'
He seemed to vomit forever, groaning
and heaving for breath between spasms.
Finally he wiped his mouth with his hand
and stumbled back into our arms.
'A touch of dry retching. Better now.
It's freezing, let's light a fire,' he said.
I don't think he knew where he was.
We took him back into the bathroom
and splashed cold water on his face.
'This is no good,' Jack said.
'We've got to think of something better
to keep the bugger awake. Hey, Colin,
how are you? Are you awake?'
Colin mumbled. 'Listen,' Jack said.
'I'm going to tell you a story. A true story.
I want you to remember it, okay?
I'll ask you to repeat the main points,
so wake up and start listening. All right?'
'Sure, I'll listen. I'll remember.
My legs are wrong, they feel all rubbery.'
'Never mind your bloody legs. Just walk,
and listen.' Jack started talking;
and this is what he told us, as we stumbled

back and forth through the houseboat
from the kitchen to the half-lit living room
to the cool dark outside on the porch.

II

'When I came back from Korea,' Jack said,
'I looked around for things to do.
I didn't seem to fit in, somehow.
I tried selling trucks, then security work,
then I went to night school for a while.
I had a talent for journalism then,
taking photos, and writing up stories,
but nothing much ever came of that.

Beth and I got married. The first year or so
was okay, but we got on each other's nerves
after a while, living in a small flat.
I had a feeling I was hemmed in,
my life was going around in circles.
I couldn't get a decent job, Beth
was thin and nervy. She was a city girl
originally, from Chicago, and she seemed
to suffocate in Sydney—though she said
it reminded her of home—it was the Harbour.
The only time she ever brightened up
was when we went for a picnic to a beach,
or for a weekend camping or fishing.
She was interested in intellectual issues,
but she liked to read about them alone.
She didn't make friends easily, I guess.
Finally she got a job writing stuff
for a magazine, a women's publication.
That brought in some money, but not much.

Anyway, I hadn't done as well in Sydney
as I thought I might, so when I heard about
a job offer in Ashford, the country town
where I'd grown up, I jumped at it.
The local paper had changed from metal type
to photo-litho offset reproduction,
and the guy who'd made the photo blocks
was taking the chance to retire. He couldn't
cope with the new technology, he said.
He was just too old. They needed someone
to manage the darkroom and shoot the film
and develop the printing plates for the press.
I'd done some darkroom work, and I reckoned
I could learn the rest, so I took the bus
to Ashford and went straight to the owner,
a fellow called Bartlett. My dad had known him,
and old Bartlett remembered me as a kid.
'I'll take a risk on you, Johnny,' he said,
'for your dad's sake.' So Beth and I
packed our things and moved to the country.

We rented a small house out the back
of the print shop, built from local rock,
a warm, honey-coloured sandstone.
Beth made it cosy in no time.
The first year there was no electric power
for one reason or another, but we had a stove,
an old wood-fuel thing—at six every morning
I used to get up and light it,
and put on a pot of coffee. For light
we had kerosene lamps that gave out
a soft yellow glow. Of an evening
Beth would sit at the kitchen table sewing
or working at a course she was taking,
in modern history and the labour movement.
Her cooking—her family was Polish originally—

she'd cook dumplings, and potato cakes,
and beef stews, rich and full of spices.
I'd study up on my darkroom work,
but that never took much time.
Then I'd read — westerns, fiction, anything.
I was a great reader then — voracious.
I'd remember the flavour of a book — dry
and sharp, say, or heavy and simmering — but
the plot and what happened to the characters
would go right out of my head like smoke.

For the first year my hands were full
picking up the trade. Old Bartlett
taught me all the photo-litho stuff.
He was well-read, and sharp as a pin.
He wasn't sentimental about type,
or the old Linotype machine.
'Noisy, poisonous bloody thing,' he said,
when the truck came to take it away.
'Good riddance', he said, and that was that.
Once I had the job under control
I eased off a bit, and looked around.

Ashford was a nice little town
a few miles inland from the coast;
small enough to be personal and friendly,
large enough to have a sense of activity.
People went to Sydney now and again;
there was a good high school and a branch
of a technical college, and a decent library.
Most of the money was in dairy farming.
There was an old sawmill outside of town.
A Bob Kingston owned the mill, a big man.
He had four brothers who worked there;
it had always been a family concern.
He owned the main hotel, and a hardware store.

I had some money, from my dad's estate —
he'd died soon after I was born —
and I started looking around to invest it.
I wanted to be part of the place again,
to feel I had a home, that I belonged.

Beth told me she was expecting a baby,
and the news gave me a bit of a shock.
I'd been used to weighing things up
with just my own fate in the scales;
now I saw things in a different light —
more long term. I saw how you had to
lay things down so they'd come into fruit
for someone else, miles down the track.
I bought some land on the outskirts of town,
and sold it six months later for a profit
to a fellow called Redding, an Englishman,
who set up an agricultural feed depot.
With the money I'd made I looked around
for something more substantial to invest in.
I soon saw Kingston was in my way.
Not deliberately, though he'd done things
against my father in the old days,
at least that's what Bartlett told me.
No, there was no reason, that was just
the way he was — arrogant, pushy.
If he saw that you were in his way
he'd just push you over, he wouldn't
ask you politely to step aside.

There was a block of land behind the pub
I wanted to develop as a garage.
I knew I could make some money on it,
and I knew it would work as an investment
for whoever set up shop there.
There were always trucks and tractors

needing to be fixed, and the other garage
was owned by a fellow who drank too much
and didn't seem to be that reliable.
When I put it up to Council for rezoning,
Kingston blocked it. No reason, he just
got the numbers up and blocked it.

Then he went around behind my back
and bought the land off old Willoughby.
He must have had some pressure there,
to push the old man around like that.
I had a contract and everything set up,
ready to sign, but Willoughby went yellow
and slithered out of it and sold the block
to Kingston, who left the land to rot
with weeds and Mexican castor-oil plants
growing up through the derelict cottage.
That really pissed me off, to be honest.
He didn't get any benefit out of it.
I faced him about the matter one day,
and he just laughed at me. He said
he didn't even want to talk about it.
'That's just business, young fellow,'
he said. 'I'm bigger than you, that's all.'
And that was the end of the matter
as far as Bob Kingston was concerned.

I'd been playing around a little — hell,
the pressures of a new job, a new town,
my wife getting pregnant like that
without having planned anything properly —
well, there's no excuse, but there it was,
I was having this affair, with Paula,
she stayed in the hotel, the big one
on the riverbank, that Kingston owned.
She worked as a barmaid, during the week.

In the summertime she flew a plane
doing joy-rides at country shows,
stunt flying, that sort of thing.
She said she had some college diploma,
what she thought she was doing behind a bar
serving beer to farmers I don't know.
She had a kind of sulky air about her,
as though life hadn't treated her well,
but as far as I could see she'd done all right.
We met at the local dance — they had one
most Friday nights, a dinner dance,
you got to know people that way.
One night I gave her a lift home —
it was raining — it was late — well,
I don't have to explain how these things
happen — it's chemical, the scientists say,
the slightest perfume, some affinity,
I don't know — I parked behind the pub,
the rain was running down the windscreen,
that mournful song "Good Night Irene"
playing on the car radio —
when I hear that song I get the shivers —
I just turned to say good night to Paula,
there were raindrops on her eyelashes
and on her lips, and the next thing I know
we were kissing — that's all that happened
then, but it was magic, it was like a drug,
I had to see her the next day, and the next.
I was avoiding Beth — I felt terrible.
I made excuses to drink at the pub,
I got jealous if she spoke to other men —
God, it was Paula's job, to be friendly
with the customers, she was a barmaid, after all —
I had to see her, look at her hair, her lips —
not that anything happened, anything serious,
it was just a passion, we were acting
irrationally — I felt like a kid,
stupid, head over heels, ashamed.

Then Beth was killed. I killed her.'

Jack stopped here. 'Let him sleep,'
he said, and we dropped Colin on a sofa.
I was dizzy from walking in circles,
and bruised from bumping into furniture.
'I'm all right, Jack,' Colin said.
'A slight problem with the medication.'
He was awake by now. 'Ask me a question,'
he said. 'I remember everything.'
No one spoke. Had Jack killed his wife?
That's what we were all thinking.
'You got a job in Ashford,' Colin said.
'And there was a Kingston fellow, a bad type.'

'Help me bring in the coffee,' Kathy said,
and I went with her to the kitchen.
'What's this about his wife?' Kathy asked
in a whisper. 'You know him pretty well,
what's it about?' I knew him, but not well.
'How would I know?' I said. 'A wife —
I didn't even know he'd been married.
I don't understand what's got into him.'
Perhaps Jack was making it all up,
a kind of game to keep Colin awake.
I could see Kathy was still worried
about him — her mouth was drawn tight
and her green eyes were flicking about the room
in a distracted pattern. 'Hey, relax,'
I said, and put my arm around her shoulder
and gave her a hug. 'It's all right.'
'Sure,' she said, but she was still frowning.

We took the coffee out to the deck.
Colin was sprawled on a cane lounge.
'There's a giant fruit bat out here,'
he muttered, 'in the branches of that tree.'

'He'll be all right now,' Jack said,
and poured some bourbon into his coffee.
We sat there in silence for a while.
'I didn't kill Beth deliberately,'
Jack said. 'That's not what I meant.'
And—minus a listener, Colin
had dozed off—he went on with his story.

'One day I rented a small boat,
with an outboard motor, and I took her out
to a reef a mile or so offshore
where I knew we'd get good fishing.
We took a picnic basket—sandwiches,
cold lemonade, a bottle of beer.

Beth was the happiest I'd ever seen her;
she was expecting a baby, her courses
were going well, I had a job I liked.
Of course I was thinking of Paula, but what the hell.
There was a heavy swell from a storm
the day before, and the boat was moving a bit.
We caught a few nice bream, but
after an hour or so I could see
Beth was starting to feel unwell.
'My dad owned a boat,' she said,
'and he used to take us out fishing
on Lake Michigan, in the summertime.
I'd always get seasick from the movement,
but he never noticed, or seemed to remember.
Can we go in now?' A squall had come up
from nowhere, the sky had gone black
and the waves were getting bigger and bigger.
I started the motor and we went back in,
and coming in over the bar, where the river
runs over a sandbank into the ocean,
the propeller caught in a patch of floating weed—
the outboard died, and the boat turned

side on to the waves. It was growing dark.
The water was very rough, green water
from the ocean churning with yellow mud
from the flooded river. It was pouring,
a cold, stinging rain. I grabbed the oars
and tried to turn the boat, but a wave
swamped us half full of water.
Beth was afraid, and for some reason
she stood up just as a big wave hit—
the boat tipped up and went over—
Beth took a terrific knock on the head,
and that's the last I ever saw of her.
I dived again and again—there was a rip
where the currents crossed, and I was swept
a mile down the beach. I woke in hospital.
It was two days before they found the body.

It knocked me around, I'll admit that.
But I kept going. I drank a bit,
for a while, but I kept going. I had to.
Old Bartlett put up with a lot,
but in the end I pulled myself together.
I moved to of the house. I couldn't sleep;
everything I looked at—the kitchen,
the table where she'd worked at her studies,
the bed we'd slept in together—all that,
it gave me the horrors and I couldn't sleep.

Then I began seeing Paula again.
I was lonely, you wouldn't believe how bad
the nights were, walking the streets
till the sun came up, talking to myself.

'Let's go out to the silver mines,'
Paula said one day. I had a Jeep,
a four-wheel drive, and we took that.
It was a lovely day, dry and clear.

We stopped halfway there for lunch,
and splashed in the river—it was cold,
flowing down from the high country,
water so cold it chilled your bones.
We had a beer, and ate some sandwiches.
It reminded me of my picnics with Beth,
and that got me down somewhat.
I'm not usually prone to depression.

We drove further into the hills—
Paula knew her way around the bush,
and she'd grown up in those parts.
The mines were in a god-forsaken valley
in the high ranges miles from anywhere.
It was rough country, cut through
with creeks and gullies and thick
with stringy-bark scrub. The buildings—
sheds, an office, huge milling machines—
they'd been abandoned thirty years ago,
and they were standing silent in the heat.

The office was unlocked, and we went in.
Dust lay over everything, but otherwise
it was exactly as it used to be—
chair, desk, pens, blotting paper,
a set of balance scales weighing the dust,
bottles of dried purple and green ink,
rubber stamps. It gave me a strange feeling.

'Did they get much silver out of here?'
I asked. 'Sure, lots,' Paula said.
'Then it got scarce and uneconomical.
So they closed the mines. There are tunnels
you can get into, though they're boarded up.
I used to come here when I was a kid.
Go down deep enough and there's a river
that runs underground from the mountains

and leads into a limestone cave.'
We looked into one of the tunnels.
A light rail track went down
into the darkness at a steep angle.
We climbed down about a hundred yards
till the rails disappeared in a pool
of water. I threw a stone, plop! My lighter
wasn't strong enough to show the other side.
Something about the colour of the water—
stained a dirty brown, dark and still—
reminded me of when Beth died,
the flooded river, and the muddy waves.

'And there's silver down there?' I asked.
I was thinking of my father's money.
'Yes, but not in rich veins,' Paula said.
'It's kind of diluted, dispersed,
mixed up with lots of rock and stuff.
In the end it cost more to mine it
than they could get for it on the market.'

I was thinking—in thirty years
mining technology must have improved.
They would have more efficient machinery
now. And this mine had been forgotten.
Paula was watching me. 'Well,' she said,
'Bob Kingston owns the mining rights,
if you're thinking of starting it up again.'

Kingston? That was a blow. Like a dreamer,
I'd already begun planning how I'd
start the mine. A friend called Bellamy—
a hard drinker, I'd known him in Korea—
was now a mining engineer in Queensland.
And I had that money of my father's,
so I had cash to invest. But Kingston—
he wouldn't share anything with anybody.

We drove back. I was silent, thinking.
My mind was whirling around and around.
'I'm not sure that showing you that mine
was such a good idea,' Paula laughed.

'Let's have a swim,' I said. I felt hot.
We swam awhile, then lay on the warm rocks.
I could feel an animal strength in Paula,
and a subtlety of mind. She seemed to know
what was going through my mind, and she was
one step ahead of me at every turn.
We made love there, for the first time.
I suppose it had to happen—we were
alone together in the heat of the bush,
the silence, not a soul for fifty miles.
Her eyes were a tiger-stone colour—
gold flecked with brown and green—
and she had a strange stare: it looked
right into you, deeper and deeper.

On the drive back to town she drew away.
Perhaps she wanted to keep our intimacy
hidden in the bush, in the back country.
That was fine by me. I didn't
want anyone getting too close.

The months went by, and I sank into my work—
the darkroom was a perfect place to brood,
lit by the dim red safelight.
You could just make out the shapes
of the plate camera—it filled half the room—
and the developing tanks along the wall.
The sound of running water rippled
like an underground spring. I had
an old valve radio tuned in
to the ABC—symphony concerts,
the Country Hour, Blue Hills, and

late at night—it was always night in there—
—the American Dance Band, and their smooth
unceasing optimism. Weeks went by
and I slowly came back to myself,
floating along on the rivers of sound,
absorbed by work, developing my plates.

Paula called me one day. She was
getting her plane ready for the show.
'I'll give you a joy-ride,' she said,
'for free.' We met out at the airfield.
I didn't tell her I'd done some flying
in Korea. I think she wanted to test me.
It was a sports biplane, single motor,
and she threw that thing around the sky
like she was trying to break it in half.
Luckily I hadn't eaten any breakfast.
After a while she put the plane down
out by Devil's Lake, near the coast.
She'd brought a picnic basket, and some beer,
and we had a swim and then ate some lunch.
And then . . . one thing led to another.

I felt strange about her, almost tender,
yet she was tough as nails underneath
and there was something in her manner
I distrusted, something not right.
She was too much like me—hard, driven.
What did she have to be hard about?

'The weather got a bit rough up there,'
she said. 'I hope you didn't mind the bumps.'
'The weather was fine,' I said. 'No problem.
I'm looking forward to the trip home.'
She laughed, and we dropped the subject.
'I talked to Kingston,' she said. 'He'll let you
open the mine. He's busy with the mill

and hasn't any time to spend on it, so
you'll have to do it alone: finance,
engineering, hiring men, administration.
He'll put in half the money, up to
eighty thousand; you find the rest.
He'll go fifty-fifty on the profits.
Okay?' I didn't know what to say.
How had she swung it? It didn't matter,
as long as I could get on with it
and make something useful of my life.

I told Bartlett — I often dropped by
in the evening, and usually stayed to dinner.
For a bachelor, he was a good cook.
That night I was so excited
by the plans buzzing around in my head
that I shovelled the food down. Bartlett listened,
but he didn't say anything. He looked awkward.
'It's not my business,' he said in the end,
'but I'd stay clear of Bob Kingston
and Paula. People say — this is gossip,
I don't know why I'm repeating it — but
they reckon she's his daughter, illegitimate,
not that that matters these days,
and as far as I'm concerned it never did.
But to keep your daughter as your mistress,
that's too much for my stomach.
So I'd just keep a little distance
if I were you. But who wants advice?
Forget I said anything. Eat up.'

But my appetite was gone. Another blow.
Perhaps it was just malicious gossip —
small towns are poisonous like that —
but yes, there was something about Paula
that was wrong — I'd felt it from the start.

For a week or two I did nothing, then
I rang Bellamy, my engineering friend
in Queensland, and talked about the mine.
He was game, and the idea intrigued him.
He came down and took a good look.

'Some of the shafts are half flooded,' he said,
'but a few pumps will soon fix that.
The ore looks to be medium grade,
but easy to get out. The market's firm.
You could break even in a few years.
From then on it should be steady profit.'

And with those profits I could buy
shares in the name of a dummy company,
a few here, a few there, then
push Kingston out into the cold.

We were in action three months later.
We had a year of dry weather—drought,
was what the farmers called it. The pumps
had the tunnels dry within a month.
The mine had a lot more silver in it
deeper down, and with the new equipment
we were soon getting a good yield.
We broke even by the end of the year.

Then Kingston sent a note demanding
cash for his share of the investment.
Nothing formal, just a note scribbled
in pencil on an old piece of paper.
His mill was going bad, he said, and
he needed the money to shore it up.
I went to the pub and asked to see him,
but he wasn't there. I found Paula
in a back room, changing into a frock

she often used to wear when she worked,
dark blue, with tiny pink flowers.
There was a plate of food on a side table—
a half-eaten chop, some vegetables—
and a cup of coffee, and a cigarette
smeared with lipstick stubbed in the saucer.
We'd hardly spoken in the last year.

He was away up the back country,
she said, scouting timber for the mill.
'Tell the bastard he'll get his money,'
I said, 'in a year or two, if he wants it. But
I can't just tear half the investment
out of the mine. The bank would close us up.
Bellamy's broke. I've got nothing else.
Tell him he must understand that.'

'Oh, he understands,' Paula said.
There was a sad, flat tone to her voice.
She had a hairpin between her teeth
while she fixed her hair in the mirror.
God, she was lovely. 'I'm beginning to
regret I ever got you into this,'
she said. 'Kingston has the legal right
to get his cash now, or take the mine.'
Of course I knew how he operated—
unrealistic behaviour, inhuman demands.
There was no joy in it, just
a sick satisfaction in destruction.

There was an old cot in the corner.
I pushed Paula onto the bed, and kissed her.
We made love. It was quick and desperate,
more anger than love, and I felt cheated,
as though Kingston was in the room, watching
and laughing in that thin voice he had.

I drove back to the mine—the drought
had broken, it had rained for a week,
and all the pumps were working day and night.
Barry, the supervisor, said that Kingston
had turned up an hour before, soaking wet,
and had gone down Number Two tunnel
to poke around. He'd never been before,
and didn't know the safety regulations.
'Frankly, I'm worried,' Barry said.
'He was yelling, and I couldn't stop him.
After all, he owns half the mine.
But Number Two's starting to fill with water,
and the river's rising up from below.'

I didn't want to lose a major partner,
so I took a helmet and a piece of rope
and went in after him. A mile down
I came to a ford flooded with muddy water
washed down the underground river
from the hills and gullies up above.
Kingston was out there in the darkness
clinging to a crate. The rising water
had jammed it up against the tunnel roof.
'Hurry up,' he said. 'I'm bloody cold.
The water rose up and cut me off,
I can't swim. Hurry, throw a line.
He was too far for that, and the water
was deep. I tied one end of the rope
to a piece of track, and let myself
into the water, holding the other end.
It was freezing. 'What were you doing?'
I had to yell above the sound of the river.
'You little shit,' he said. 'You're cheating!
There's no silver here. You and your mate
are milking me. I want my money back.'

'There's nothing much here in Number Two,'
I said. 'It's limestone. Number One's good;
and Number Three is full of bloody silver.
You got the assay reports. Can't you read?'

'And stay away from Paula,' he yelled.
His voice was screeching, he was in a rage.
'I look after her, nobody else.
Understand?' I laughed. Here he was,
on the edge of the pit, and giving orders.
'Bring the rope here, for Christ's sake!'
But I couldn't; it wasn't long enough.
I'd have to let it go and swim to him,
and I wouldn't get back against the current,
not pulling the weight of both of us.
Kingston was being sucked into the dark.
He was finished, and I think he knew it.

My helmet lamp was fading, but the beam
picked out his eyes in the gloom.
His mouth was working, and he blew out
gasps of air. He was going under,
inch by inch. 'Son,' he said hoarsely,
'Help me. You bastard. Help me.'
He was gasping between every word.
I couldn't let go of the rope,
we'd both die. 'I can't,' I said.

'Ah, fuck it!' he said, and he went under.
Where he'd been, there was just a bubble,
then nothing. My lamp was fading.

I climbed up out of the tunnel,
in the dark, up to the windy evening.
The light was strange, dim and luminous,
heavy clouds were blowing out of the west.

I was so glad to breathe the air,
to feel the rain on my skin, I thought
I'll go on, I'll make money,
I'll climb up out of this shit.

They never found Kingston's body.

Paula left, she went to Singapore
with that plane of hers, and no one
heard from her again. She took up
with some French aviator, and got lost
in the war they had there, in Indo-China.
The mine? It petered out in the end,
just like it had years before.
I locked up the shop and walked away.
Oh, I got some money out of it,
but not much. I ended up in Sydney,
like I'd begun. Older. Alone again.

What does it all mean? You tell me.
I've had it. I'm going to bed.'
Colin had stumbled off long ago;
I could hear him snoring faintly somewhere.
Jack stretched, and finished his bourbon,
and wandered inside. It was late;
I could hear a night-bird on the shore.

I went in and got a drink. Poor bugger,
I thought; all that struggle for nothing.
Then I remembered a pair of drug runners
I'd met in Thailand — middle-aged men
but full of energy, heavy drinkers,
flying a light plane up to Burma,
taking risks to make a lot of money
to take home to their families in Marseilles —
one had proudly shown me a photo

of his blonde young wife and baby son—
both now in jail in Bangkok,
for life. Maybe twenty young lives
had been saved; but when I turned them in,
had I really done the right thing?
And Kathy, struggling too, and in the end
losing—what had she lost—her promise?
But she still had a kind of faith,
going on with her life and her work.

III

When I came out Kathy was standing
by the railing, looking up at the sky.
You could see a few stars, here and there,
glinting through the patchwork cloud.
I lit cigarettes for us both
and we leant on the rail, side by side,
just as we had on the ferry on the way up.
She was wearing slacks and a silk blouse,
grey, with tiny yellow polka-dots,
and a perfume, something soft and delicate.
After a while Kathy broke the silence.

'Do you ever think,' she asked, 'that there's
some pattern in things, a kind of balance?
The Indians have this idea of karma,
where everything is added up, and you pay
for bad things, and do well if you're good.
But that's just childish, isn't it?
I don't know what the pattern is.
Maybe there isn't one, just the law.

When Trent was crippled in the crash
I felt responsible—well, I was,
in a way, but the drugs, the setup,
that other couple, the whole evening—
it was a rotten game that went wrong.
In America everything has a ticket.
Trent fumbled the deal, and paid the price.
Do you think that's why it happened?'

I shrugged my shoulders. She went on—
'After that little episode
I tried to make things work with Colin.
You can imagine I felt shaken up,
but Colin was at the bottom of the pit.
The big show he'd been working on,
it fell through when Trent was convicted
and went to jail. Trent's name was poison.
No New York gallery would touch him.
Anyone who'd been connected with him
was the same. They all took drugs,
it wasn't that—it was getting caught.
Colin's paintings were good—well,
looking back on them, they weren't
earth-shattering, but they were as good
as most of the rubbish being shown then.
But it was no use, no one wanted it,
they wanted the new thing then,
the post-abstract thing from Germany,
that wet Romantic landscape stuff,
West Coast Realism, other fashions,
and Colin had lost the strength to keep
making it new every goddamn day,
so he never made it in the States,
and New York was just a nightmare,
a bad dream that cost us a fortune.

And then the accident happened.
Colin was minding the kid, but
he was drunk again, I should have known
it wasn't safe to leave him with Colin
but I had to get out of the place
once in a while. I'd go to a bar
on Tenth Street and drink a bit.
Timmy ran out onto the street—
he was chasing a kitten, someone said—
and a truck full of fur coats hit him.

Poor little kid—he lived for a week,
a week doesn't seem long, does it?
But it was a lifetime for Timmy.
After that, nothing mattered. Nothing.
Not Colin, not his bullshit painting,
not that rotten business with Trent.
My whole life looked like a bad road
that led up this week of torment,
and yet it meant nothing. Maybe—'
she seemed to find it hard to speak—
'maybe if I'd gone mad; or into a convent,
to devote myself to God; maybe if I'd
written it all down like a novel,
and learnt how to become a great soul
with significant things to say about pain,
how the most innocent are made to suffer—'
Kathy was sobbing at last, the tears
running down her cheeks onto her blouse—
'but no, my life wound up in a heap
at the side of that wretched little cot
in a New York slum hospital, and
it all ended in a tiny, painful death,
and I can't find any meaning in it.'

I let her cry. What could I say? People
don't live and die for a purpose,
like a character introduced in a movie
and done away with in the final scene
so the plot will turn out right.
Life was a mystery, with no explanation.
How can you talk about that? The water
and the clouds and the starlight had been
just like that for a million years,
and a hundred million lives had come and gone.
If you dwelt on those things, you'd go mad.
I looked down into the water. I could see
sheets of phosphorescent plankton rippling
deep down under the boat, shimmering
electric veils, pale green and blue.

Kathy leant against me. 'It's getting cold,'
she said, and I put my arm around her shoulder.

When we went inside we found
Colin fast asleep on the bed
I'd meant to use, in the living room.
Jack was snoring on the other bunk.
'We'll just have to share a double bed,'
Kathy said. 'Is that all right with you?'

We took the bourbon into the bedroom
and undressed with our backs to each other
and slipped in between the sheets. Her leg
lay against mine. A street lamp
from the footpath on the shore outside
made mottled pools of light dip and
ripple on the ceiling above our bed.
I let my hand rest on her arm, just

touching. 'Tell me about Colin,' I said.
'He wasn't into morphine when you left.'
'Oh, you don't want to hear all that.
I've been boring you. You must be tired.'
'Go on,' I said. 'I'm not, if you're not.'
Her skin was cool. I felt my fingers must be
burning her arm. Why didn't she pull away?

'Colin got drunk at a party,' she said.
'He was drunk, and he got into an argument
about masculinity and action painting
at a party this rich painter was holding
on a boat out on the East River.
Klassky was his name, and he'd made it.
Oh, there were rich painters, and then
there were painters who weren't rich at all.
The argument got violent, and Klassky
pushed Colin—he didn't mean to hurt him,
but Colin tripped sideways down a ladder
and his head slammed against a winch fitting
and he injured the side of his face. He got up
and knocked Klassky down with one hit.
Colin thought he'd killed him at first,
but he hadn't—he'd knocked him out,
and when Klassky fell he struck his head
on the railing, and the skull was fractured.
It caused a blood clot on the brain.
It took a few days for all this
to come out, and the waiting was awful.
They kept them both in hospital for weeks,
but very different ones, believe me.

When Colin's face had been patched up
he went to apologise to Klassky.
He was anxious about it, and jumpy.
They'd given him morphine in the hospital
because of the fractures in his facial bones.
By the time he got out he was addicted,
shaky, and going through withdrawal.
Klassky had a reputation for violence.
He'd broken a woman's nose once at a party
after an argument about Picasso, and
he'd knocked out an art critic's teeth.
But when he went to visit, Colin found
a changed man. The doctors had him on sedatives,
and he kept the curtains drawn against the light.
He was in a wheelchair, and he dozed off
from time to time. Friends would read to him.
He liked religious books, the lives of the saints.
I guess he'd developed a fixation of some kind—
his mother was religious, from the old country,
always going to church and praying a lot.

When Colin said he was sorry, Klassky
burst into tears, and hugged him. Colin
came back to sit with him again,
and offered to read to him, and in the end
he became a regular visitor, and a friend.
Colin was painting less, drawing a little,
maybe a watercolour or two of an evening,
tiny sketches in ink and sepia wash.

He started taking Klassky out for walks
every day, and always at dawn—
there was less traffic, it was easier
with the wheelchair, and Colin said
the peaceful atmosphere seemed to help—
he'd calm down and focus on his drawings
through the rest of the day. The jungle
showed a different side then, I guess.
I'd go with them some mornings,
when I'd finished in the darkroom.

There was no one to take to school.

Klassky didn't seem to mind being
in a wheelchair. He'd made a lot of money,
and invested it well, so he had an income.
His sense of smell had grown more acute.
When we wheeled him past a bread shop—
he always asked to go by the bakery—
you could smell the hot fresh bread,
and Klassky used to rock back and forth
and laugh excitedly, and make us wait
while he drew in great breaths
of that lovely warm scented air.
Sometimes he'd be laughing and crying
at the same time, and I'd have to
wipe the tears from his face with a tissue,
and his beard would be all wet.
Then there was a place on Second Avenue
that made chocolates on Friday mornings,
and he really liked to smell that.

And on Sundays he'd go to church,
the Serbian Orthodox on Twenty-Fifth,
and he'd sit there for maybe an hour
inhaling the incense, murmuring to himself.

In the end he became a convert
to the Catholic Church. He sends us postcards,
scenes of martyrdom, that kind of thing.
We heard he went to Rome last year,
and had a private audience with Guess Who.

Well, the money ran out, eventually,
and that was the end of our American Dream.
We came back to Sydney, we separated.
We're still friends, we went through
too much together not to be.
Colin got a job at the hospital,
helping kids with colour therapy.
And of course he brought back his problem.

And I have my photography. As you know
there's not much money in that.
Oh, I could do corporate accounts,
but can you imagine me shooting
some advertising fuckwit in a Porsche?
And keeping a straight face? Not likely.
I do what I have to do, and I survive.'

Kathy finished her drink, and lay back.
'I think that's enough bourbon,' she said.
'And you?' I could feel she was looking at me
in the dark. 'What were you up to,
while I was going crazy in New York?'

I thought about California,
my brother dead on his motor bike,
studying for my degree, Thailand,
a marriage that hadn't turned out well.
'I can't start all that,' I said.
'You don't want to hear about buildings,
and the personal stuff is too complicated.
Let's go to sleep.' I didn't want to sleep,
I wanted to make love to Kathy, but
it all seemed confused and impossible.

'You can tell me some other time,' she said.
She kissed me on the lips, and her voice
came murmuring into my mouth. 'Oh Sandra,'
she said, and she was moving in my arms.

My Mirage

Jim Shaw

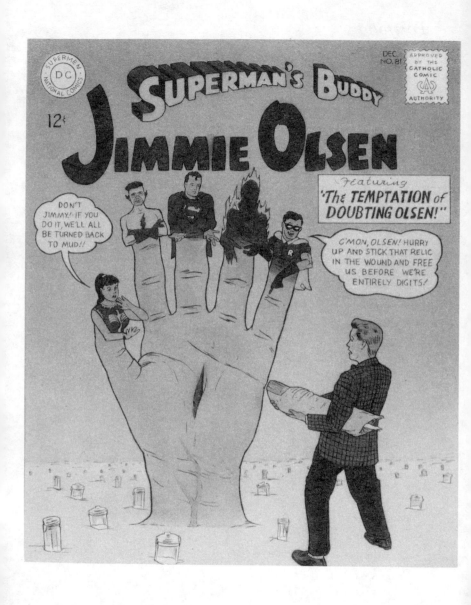

The Temptation of Doubting Olsen

Bubble Gum Cards (Fronts)

Blue Cross

Devotional Art

Girls in Billy's Class #4

Europe (Repeated)

Donald Revell

Last: 1991

The unsigned architecture of loneliness
is becoming taller, finding a way farther
above the horizontal flowering
of the Cold War, the peonies
and star asters of wild partisanship.
I have a shambling gait and lonely
hysteria, but no Terror. I am free
to shamble past the vacant lot of my son's
conception, to shamble past the bar where I
conceived adultery as a Terror
that would be endless, flowering
in great waves through air striated like chenille.
I walk for a long time and try to conjure
elsewhere in its early isolation.
I cannot. It is all redestinated
by the future like the loose balloons
a janitor recovers at 6 AM
from cold light fixtures. The Cold War is ending.
Buildings are taller and have no names.

1

The romance of every ideology
torments the romance of another. How
beautifully, in the beginning, in
the gale and embrace of isolation, boys
capered over a shambles and swore oaths.
The scent of urine in the hall at home
was righteousness. The beautiful nude
obscured by dust in a paperweight
was righteousness. Neglectful townships coming
into steep flower just as boys were flowering
needed the correction of righteousness,
the horizontal slag of government
by children. Only the insane allegiances
endure. The mad counterparts are lovers
passion cannot explain nor circumstance
restrict to the dead zones of irony.
A counterpart of the end of the Cold War
is adultery. A counterpart
of loving a divided Berlin
unto death is fatherhood, the doting
maintenance of sons in vacant lots
continuing the wars of rubble
for righteousness' sake and for the sake
of nudes obscured by dust and vulgarity.

Romance torments romance. The most beautiful
moment of the twentieth century
galed and embraced the acrid smoky air
as the Red Army entered Berlin
as Hitler shrivelled in the gasoline fire
as Red Army flags opened above Berlin
safeguarding the ruins of a changeless future.
Townships blackened even as they flowered.
Loose balloons cluttered the low sky and sun.
I walked for a long time and tried to conjure
the form of kindness. It was domestic
animal confused in the tall grass.
Boys set fire to the grass. History
that opens flags opened the fire,
and Berlin, divided from Berlin,
began to love its children past all reason.

2

A daughter carries a flag inside her voice.
A son reads the sermons of pain and writes on walls.
I have only a son. He starves the ground
he walks upon, preparing a dead city
to be worthy of his sister's flag, to shine
as exploded windows shine, raining down
for hours after the wrecking crews have gone.
I have a lover now who hates children.
The hatred floats inside of her, a weightless
sexual pavilion of perfect form and perfect
emptiness, nothing like my wife. I thought
by making love to her I would conceive
nothing but Terror, outrage upon outrage,
a violence that would last my whole life
and free my son. I was ignorant as a balloon.

Across the luminous expressway, I see
the shapes of charred tenements castellated,
fading into the more tender shapes of night.
It may be the last night in history. Tomorrow
pulls down the Berlin Wall, pulls down my marriage,
and I return to my lover's bed to float
in a white condom, no longer my son's father.
Tomorrow describes everything in detail.
It explains nothing. It does not teach my boy
that tenements are better than the future,
better than peace, more likely to produce
a sister than are the glassy hands of mornings
without end or walls denuded of their wire.
In the dead zone of irony before dawn,
only the cats cry, like martyrs in the flame.

3

Gates everywhere. The Brandenburg. The Great
Gate of Kiev beneath which children stride
onto an invisible crescendo
disappearing into gasoline fires,
emerging as the new shapes of righteousness
in slow vans through the Brandenburg Gate.
Oaths are secret because none suspects
that they are kept. They thrust themselves towards us
unashamedly, like the insane homeless,
and we do not see them. In our loneliness,
we see a chance for love in betrayal,
not death. In our loneliness, we see the happy
triumph of glassy hands in free elections,
not the denuding of Berlin or wanderings
of children in vans reduced by fire
to black transparencies in the morning shade.
When Joan of Arc surrendered to the flames
she cried out "Jesus, Jesus." Some years later,
a failed magician who had loved her cried out
"Joan, Joan" as the flames mocked him with a sortilege
too easy to be unreal or profitable.

I walk for a long time and try to conjure
the form of loneliness without Cold War.
It is ash upon ash, a chiaroscuro
aloft and on the ground, completely still.
Oaths are secret because none suspects
the desperation of every object, the child
in every atom of the misused world
thrust towards us, crying out whatever
sacred name it witnessed put to death
on the ascending music of a wall.
Our buildings are tall and have no names.
The parks grow grassy hands instead of flowers.

4

Afterwards, the calm is piteous
but insubstantial as a smell of burn
that does not rise in smoke or die with the fire.
Imagine walking out of a house at sunrise
and having to invent air, invent light
from nothing but untriggered memory.
All things beloved are recalled to pain.
Air recollected from the wrists of girls
braceleted for Confirmation, crossed.
Light recollected from between the cars
of night trains in a deep river valley
where islands in the river glowed like swans.
Air recollected from a ditch in flower.
Light recollected from the sex of flowers
in bare rooms, the grainy light of blondes.
Air recollected from religion.
Light recollected from the incensed clutch
of bodies before sunrise in the oaths
of a great and ignorant lost cause.

Imagine walking out of a house at sunrise
having spent the night in bed with a stranger.
Aloft and on the ground the calm
unfurls like flags without device or slogan.
The inconsequence of the day ahead
stirs airless atmospheres in darkness
visible as daylight but without shade.
Without Cold War, without the arbitrary
demarcation of cause from cause, of light
and air from the unsexed improvisations
of memory, I cannot see to walk
or breathe to breathe. Sex becomes applause.
Sex becomes television, and the bastard
avant garde of lonely architecture
breaks ground at the unwired heart of a city
that marks the capital of nothing now.

5

A scratchy, recorded call to prayer crosses
the alley from one new building into mine.
The consolations of history are furtive,
then fugitive, then forgotten like a bar
of music that might have been obscene or sacred
once, in another city, in the days
before today. My son is well. He works
the public ground and needs no Antigone.
My wife writes pamphlets in the next room.
My lover sits beside her at the table,
sharing the joke, unmapping the tall future
and its unbiased children, reinventing
the sexual pavilion to accommodate
plague wards. Romance forgives romance.

The early isolation of this gorgeous
century disappears into good works.
The future is best. To put a final stop
to the grotesque unmercy of martyrdom
and to the ruinous armies of mad boys
whose government is rape, whose justice
is a wall, revoke all partisanship,
adjourn the Terror. The future is best.
It unobscures the dusty nudes. It protects
the river islands and their glowing swans.
But when I need to die, who will light the fire?
What name shall I cry out and what music
burn to a black transparency in my heart?
No fire is terrible enough to be my daughter.

Woman Found Dead
in Elevator

Ruth Tarson

I really hate these readings, the famous author comes and reads from his book and then there's a discussion afterwards, and you can ask questions, I was the first to raise my hand, and he said, you have a question? And then he goes home and reads his bank books, and you go home and stare at the blank piece of paper in the typewriter, and the laundry was really piling up in my apartment. Thus, in the middle of the night, mysterious knocks on my door, a voice hissing, do your laundry, bitch! I called the police, but the police said, do your laundry, bitch! too. And a message left with my answering service: Landlord called, understands you have a big pile of laundry in your apartment, wants to know if you are going to do the laundry or what, suggests you read the terms of the lease of your low rent and still rent-controlled apartment which you still occupy after all these years and which does not provide for the piling up of laundry.

I think the mysterious knocks on my door, etc., may be from

the laundryman who lives in the basement with the laundry machines and he's very hostile towards me, or maybe it's Marcos, the super, who has a sperm problem, but will he listen to me, no. And he said, you have a question, he said, the famous author, not Marcos. He was here to do a reading from his major new novel soon to be a major motion picture and all that garbage, and starring Meryl Streep, no doubt, I said. And he said, you have a question, he said. And I said, how about that *Out of Africa*, I said, it was not one of your better readings by an author from a new work, you could barely hear him, it was such a lousy sound system. But as the psychiatrist said, who listens. And he said, you have a question, he said. And I said, yes, I had a question, I said. They have this big telescope now, I said.

The audience rustled, restless; the place was crowded, standing room only, they hated my question about the telescope, and someone yelled, go home and do your laundry, bitch! and he said, you have a question, he said. I popped a calcium pill into my mouth and chewed quickly to prevent further bone loss. The question about the telescope seemed to have aroused his interest, aroused something; he sat there scratching at his zipper; perhaps he saw the telescope as a phallic symbol, his writings were filled with the phallic. This from a man who may not even have any real sperm, I'm not saying he does, I'm not saying he doesn't, what am I, his sperm bank?

Marcos, the super in my building, was always scratching, he wore these incredibly tight jeans, which is where the problem with the sperm came in, but will he listen to me, no. Marcos was always down there in the basement with the laundryman, the laundryman who did not scratch; he wore a metal crown on his head with six points, each point a different color, red blue gold green, etc., and he was just too elegant to scratch. He just sat there looking at me, hostile, that was because he didn't like my laundry. This feeling about my laundry frightens me sometimes, he frightens me, but what can I do, live my life for the laundryman; excuse me, it's enough trying to live my life for myself, and the common good, to vote, to support public television, not to wear fur, and lest we forget, the woman in the elevator, the dead one, which was an integral part of my question about the telescope, and he said, you have a question, he said, and I said, yes, I had a question, I said. I stopped for a moment to listen to the gentle snore of my immune system asleep on the job. They have this big telescope now, I said. That was the question, I said. I could hear the sound of brain cells dropping away in my brain pan, millions of cells a day, all irreplaceable, I really hate these readings.

They'll probably create an award for it soon, for Best Reading by an author from a new work, and the winner is, you have a question, he said. The winner is definitely not me, I said. I had no new work. Excuse me, I said, what I had was a pile of laundry in my apartment waiting to be cleansed of pizza stains and coffee and soy sauce and some brown blotchy stuff I couldn't name. And he gave out such a yell.

The Stain Remover! he cried, and immediately he stopped scratching at his zipper and pulled out his note pad and began to write furiously in it, excuse me, he said, he's a modern day Jack the Ripper, he said, who haunts laundries in search of women with terrible laundry, and especially the one with the brown blotchy stuff, not even she knows what it is.

They have this big telescope now, I said. This telescope is so big, I said, they can look all the way back in time to the very first nanosecond of time just before the big bang, and the birth of the universe, pow! A star is born, Meryl Streep, no doubt, I said. You have a question, he said. You want to call a policeman, he said. You want to write a letter to your congressman, he said. Excuse me, I said, but very soon they may be able to look back beyond that first nanosecond of time to a time before time began, I said, to a time, I said, when there was no time.

Oh, I knew that, he said, and he pulled out his little pad and began to write furiously in it, again. And I said, excuse me, I said, this is my question, I said, stay out of my question, I said. You have a question, he said. Yes, I have a question, I said. And my question is this. I've been working on a story, Woman Found Dead in Elevator, it's a great title, I think, but

I've been having a lot of difficulty with it, and my question is, should I continue to work on it, and try to finish it, or should I put it aside and start on something else.

Excuse me, he said, but before you do anything, shouldn't you take your laundry down to the laundryroom where that funny laundryman is. Excuse me, I said, but are you talking about my laundryman. Are you talking about the funny black man who wears a metal crown on his head with six points, each point a different color, red blue gold green, etc., and he just sits there, hostile, looking at me, and he never helps me with the laundry or anything, and he said, that's the one, and I said, excuse me, I said, but I wish you would stay out of my laundry. I really wish that you would get your own laundry, I said, then we could talk about your laundry for a change, instead of always talking about my laundry. Well, excuse me! he said, I'll go out and buy some laundry right now if it'll make you happy. And I said, I'm just saying, leave my laundry alone, and he said, well, you can just bet I'll leave your laundry alone from now on! and he slammed the door on the way out. And the laundryman gave me a dark look and went over to check the machines to see if they were okay and he took off his crown and checked each point of the crown, red blue gold green, etc., to see if they were still okay and he placed the crown back on his head and sat there looking at me the way he always did, and he said, excuse me, he said, you have a question, he said.

Maybe I should ask him my question. It was a question that had been on my mind ever since I had seen the show about the big telescope on public television, Channel Thirteen. I hardly ever watched the commercial channels these days. Woman Found Dead In Elevator. Who was she, that was the question. Who was that bag of bones and hank of hair so recently alive and full of hope. Or was it despair. Or was it fear. Was it Meryl Streep? It's Meryl Streep! Excuse me, said the famous author, returning with a small bag of laundry, a few towels and some socks, and a couple of t-shirts, excuse me, he said, but it's not Meryl Streep! You can't make it Meryl Streep! Excuse me, but I certainly can, I said. It's Meryl Streep, and she's come to this building to do some research for the character she's playing in the new billion dollar movie based on the billion dollar book written by the famous author of the world. She went into the elevator and there she met with Foul Play, a famous theatrical agent of the world, who was there to discuss her billion dollar contract with her.

Excuse me, he said, but there is no such thing as a famous theatrical agent named Foul Play, you've gone too far now, and I said, oh, yes, there is, excuse me, I said, it's short for Fowler, Fowler Playson, a wealthy son of old money, who changed it to Foul Play when he joined a rock group against his family's wishes and got on drugs and wrote songs about how great drugs are and then he went to the Betty Ford clinic and came out and wrote songs about how bad drugs are. Maybe it's Betty Ford who was in the elevator. Woman Found Dead In Elevator May Be Betty Ford! And you call that laundry, I said, a few towels and some socks, and a couple of t-shirts. Excuse me, I said, but that is not laundry in this building, and the laundry-man knocked on the door and told us to stop making so much noise, we were disturbing the laundry machines, one of which, he said, had stopped right in the middle of the last rinse cycle, and would we, excuse me, he said, please, put a sock on it.

Time was running backwards. Pretty soon there would be no more time. We would have come to the place before time began. And that was the basement where the laundryman lived and ruled. And where Marcos, the super, whose sperm was somewhat questionable, also hung out. Ah, Marcos! Marcos! I said. The light was out in my kitchen, I said.

The bulb had burned out all the way up there in the ceiling, and excuse me, but how was I supposed to get up there and unscrew the white glass dome, I had no ladder. And it was hot up there, and there were those three tiny little screws, and excuse me, but what if I dropped the white glass dome. And it smashed on the floor. And I got a sliver in my foot and the three tiny little screws rolled under the refrigerator. And I ran out and pressed the button for basement. Marcos would help, I would offer him money, he could buy some sperm with it. Ah, Marcos! Marcos! I said, they have this big telescope now, Marcos, I said.

Marcos looked at me and scratched at his zipper, he wore these incredibly tight jeans. I had warned him of the dangers to his sperm count, but he just patted his bulge, I don't need you to count my sperm, he said, I count my own sperm, he said. They have this big telescope now, Marcos, I said. Marcos said, he couldn't do it now, he was too busy. I'll pay you, Marcos, money! I said, I'll borrow from my money market fund! I said, and Marcos said, never mind, he had his own money market, but if I wanted the ladder, I could take it. Do it yourself, he said, it's just a couple of screws, he said, and I said, all of your sperm are going to die, and he said, don't worry about my sperm, I got plenty, he said, and he patted his bulge proudly, and I said, excuse me, I said, but they will never make it up the canal. And the laundryman just sat there looking at me, he didn't help, nobody helped, did the famous author help, no. I'm going to stop watching public television, it's too much for me.

You have a question, said the answering service. Yes, I have a question, I said. Did any publishers call, that was the question. Did any agents call, that was the question. And the big telescope. And the burned out bulb in my kitchen. And my laundry. I paid a fortune every month for an answering service that never had any answers. Excuse me, said the answering service, there were some calls, and these calls had no answers, but they did raise some new questions, and the answering service laughed, and said, do your laundry, bitch! and pay your bill, you're way overdue.

Landlord called, there may be a dead woman in the elevator, do you know anything about it. Says he will not have any dead women in his elevator. Suggests you read terms of lease of the ridiculously low-rent apartment you occupy, and which is, unbelievably, still rent-controlled.

Marcos, the super, called, he had his sperm count taken and it's very low, says you should have told him sooner about the tight jeans, says you just don't want him to have babies. Says you hate Latinos.

Laundryman called, says you left your laundry in the washing machine, you'd better come and get it out, it's turning sour, and other people need to use the machine, do you think you're the only one.

Landlord called, says, yes, there is a dead woman in the elevator, it's not Meryl Streep, it's not Betty Ford, says woman looks a lot like you, and if so, would like you to vacate the apartment immediately, and no, you will not get your security back, you made a mess of the apartment, and it will cost him much more than that to repair the damage.

Marcos, the super called, says the dead woman in the elevator is definitely you. Laundryman called, says the dead woman in the elevator is you and you have blood stains all over your clothes and those stains will never come out, he may try putting some wet salt on them, it works sometimes, and can he have the jar of quarters you left in the basement.

Famous author called, wants to do script on story of your life, understands you were found dead in the elevator, doesn't think Streep can play it, maybe Cher, says script need not be exploitative simply because you were found dead in elevator. Says you have many deep aspects in your nature, witness your question about the big telescope. Also wants to know the status of his laundry.

Excuse me, I said.

You have a question, he said.

Yes, I have a question, I said.

I slipped a sheet of paper into the typewriter and typed Woman Found Dead in Elevator across the top of the page, what a great title for a story. But before I did anything, I should go down to the basement and pour some Final Touch into the last rinse, I always missed the fabric softener cycle, and as a result my laundry was full of wrinkles and had a lot of static. And he gave out such a yell, again.

Final Touch! he said, the story of Tiffany Sterling, who led her lover into the vengeful waters of the last rinse that flooded them all in the fatal, final touch! and he pulled out his pad and began to write furiously in it, one more time! Excuse me, I said, but once again I have to point out that this is my laundry, and I ran out and pressed the button for basement, and he came running after me, waving the note pad, I love you!

he cried, I want to mix your laundry with mine! he cried. And we both cried then and went down to the basement together, and there was the laundryman sitting there and looking at me, hostile, as always, the metal crown, each point a different color, red blue gold green, etc., on his head, and the washing machines, all of them with better laundry than I would ever have, thrumming away, and I could see that he was definitely agitated tonight, I could see that he hated me, and I said, oh, why do you hate me so, I said.

He took the metal crown off his head, each point a different color, red blue gold green, etc., and for a minute I thought he was going to stab me with it, and he said, excuse me, he said, I could take this crown and stab you with it, I could plunge it into your heart, each point a different color, red blue gold green, etc., and it wouldn't make a difference, you won't change. You said it was Meryl Streep, and it wasn't, you said it was Betty Ford, and it wasn't, and today you mixed your colors in with your whites, and your laundry is one big mess, it is the worst laundry I have ever seen, and the famous author said, right! he said, I told her it couldn't be Meryl Streep, he said, and yet she complains about my laundry, and the laundryman said, she don't deserve to have no laundry, and the other one, the famous author of the world said, but first I have this gig in Vegas, I'm writing some special material, and there's going to be a line of girls behind me, and they said, the two of them, you have a question, they said. Yes, I had a question, I said. Excuse me, I said, did I leave a jar of quarters down here, that was the question.

And then Marcos came barging in, sneering at me, and scratching at his zipper as usual. *In vitro* fertilization, said Marcos, they take the sperm and they take the egg, and they put them together in a little dish, and they make love together in this little dish, he said, and I got a baby, he said. I'm also taking some food supplements, zinc, he said. I don't need you, he said. Mind your own business, he said.

So ends my laundry. Thanks a lot, Marcos, I said. Thank you all, thank you, laundryman, and thank you, famous author of the world, and I pressed the button for up. Excuse me, I said, stepping gingerly over the dead body in the elevator, but I'm going up and continue work on my story, God knows if I'll ever finish it, I said. God, I said, who just might be standing there at the end of the big telescope in that place before time began, in that time when there was no time. I could ask God the question. God would say, you have a question, God would say. It occurred to me that even with God there might be questions that had no answer. I sat down at the typewriter and stared at the paper. And I said, excuse me, I said, yes, I have a question.

Jorie Graham

Who Watches from the Dark Porch

1

   Is it because of history or is it because of matter,
mother Matter—the opposite of Interpretation: his consort: (his purple body lies
shattered against terrible
   reefs)—matter, (in it
a shriek or is it
   laughter)
(a mist or is it an angel they strangle)—
   that we feel so sure we lied
or that this, here, this thing
   is a lie, a
sound, a
   vibration? Thing

so beautifully embalmed in its syllables,
   the orchard of them, sprouting up quick because of the sunshine.
   Don't blink and your looking will be the same as
their sprouting.
   Don't blink and your looking will go barehanded one on one
with the slippery, wrinkling, upslanting *it*, don't

   blink ruddy impersonator in your gothic selfhood,
fringed with lashes,
   trying to match your stare to the orchard,
even as the possibilities (blink) begin to exfoliate,
   suitors surrounding her the one and only,
right version and more right versions,
   each one stripping the next layer off her,
her casting a look your way you catch and yet
   you too, because there is no choice,
starting in on the strip,
   her stillness suddenly not stillness anymore but the ser-
                                                    pentine

flecked winking of the instant replay
   repeating endlessly the one idea
which seems now lord like each time it's different,
   each blistering instance orphaned,
each impersonation, veil after veil, whirring
   —or is it *her* whirring?—
the brainfever like a shriek but inaudible, inaudible,

   and translating now into the mercury lights
through which the surgeons
   bend.

2

Blink. There. It's just the body. Put it on.
  Down on tight, yes, like that, it is somewhat elastic.
No hiss—no shame or crime. Monoxides, plasma.
  The carbon molecule like a great seaweed through it.

Hands, a lap.
  A sense of peril caked with a rubbery
forgetfulness.
  Waxy foliage all round for the glance to tap.
Inside, something angular, a memory of utmost
  rectitude—

  but far away, inside, like the reason that persuaded one,
                                                  long ago,

drowned in the plump debut.
  So. Sit down, here is a chair.
Later there will be bureaucracy, heredity, doctrine,
  the "perfect" day,

but now, sit, here is a soft wood seat
  in the screened-in porch. Nightime in summer. Hum.
Swarm of nocturnal intelligence.
  Cicadas unceasing in the confectionary air.
The leavening of milliseconds.
  Scurry of something in the leaves.
Laughter? TV through the neighbors' screen?

  Sit. The latticework and on it your gaze now.
Swank greens for your eyes to root in.
  Spores filtering in.
Green dust and the glance it's in, mixing.

Green dust and the breath it's in, mixing.
Sit.

There. It's just the inflammation — purr. Blink again.

3

Now I will make a sound for you to hear.
A sound without a mouth.
No face.
From across the fenceline, there in your neighbor's house.

A child's sound. Maybe laughter — no — maybe a scream.
The sound of a carnivore at the end of the millenium.
The listening also that of a beast, listening.
For all intents and purposes a shriek. The air sucks it up.

A riddle. The air is riddled.
It seeps through the green the cicadas derange.
The light from the neighbor's windows waxing the magnolia
leaves.
Neighborlight glittering like gasoline over one side of
the big tree.

Now I will make it again, this sound,
from somewhere inside the small girl next door,
punctual, a scream, of monoxides and carbons,
a piston to what distended machine — a shriek? no? a laugh? —

lung-stuff, flinty, diamond-backed, floating out through
the layer of flesh, the layer of house, prickly light, pleated
greens, cicada scream, wooly creepers over the
veranda screen—a scream?

                    —isn't that laughter,
isn't that the cadence of crackling laughter? no—
isn't that too high-
pitched, guttural? what is he doing, our neighbor, in the
                                cicadas, under the

green, mossy, under the mercy, under the swank duplex?
Now I will make it spill again
under the milliseconds. Oh but she's giggling now?
She's playing with her father? It's hot. The end of the
                                weekend.

Now I will make it impossible to tell the difference.
Now I will make it make no difference.
Now I will make there be no difference.
Now I will make it. Just make it. Make it.

How do you feel?

4

If I am responsible, it can't be for everything.
May I
Close my eyes for a minute?
It is so sleepy here and green, green,
                    the neighborlight golden-headed, slender,

stepping sidelong across the yard —
spice from his passage,
the lozenge of light over the treeflank and the greensward
   trembling,
where the flatfooted luminosity dawdles, substantial.
It is so sleepy here in the green.

Let the cry stay in the air like one more speckled creature,
interesting.
Let the pestilence add its color, no?, let the cry
float with its sharp metal wings
out into what it can't cut,

let it buzz out into the branches of the spangly
magnolia that will not refuse it,
let it be buoyed by the applelimbs, by the dayglo
apples, let it rub their skins, see how they

receive it, acid consonant
lofting in the spore-stunned air, magnified, slid under the
                                      wing
of the cicadas and helped to eternal life there,
pronged cry, wedged into the laminate grassy eternity,

locked in, the missing piece, the mistress of the scene,
let it coat me, let it be my irridescent sticky
stare — emptiness, green, and on it, instead of a face,
that cry
floating.

5

Maybe if I turn the TV on?
   Let's graze the channels? Let's find the

storyline composed wholly of changing
   tracks, click, shall I finish this man's phrase with this

man's face, click, is this the truest news—how true—what are

the figures
   and is this authorized—a spill? a leak?—whose
face is the anchor,
    who's that moving papers on the desk behind him

    there, below the clock, a woman? a map that
moves?, when the lights blink is it *now* there
   or are those troop movements? where day is
breaking? precincts reporting in?—
   whoosh—see how even you can't hear it

anymore, the little shriek, below
   this hum: hum of the set,
refrigerator in the summer heat,
   steel wings (the fan),
snarl of cicadas winding
   down,

whine of the bus,
   of the all-night safety light on the
garage (somewhere in here the

   problematic sound) hum of the anchor's voice
giving us figures now
   over the square where
chanting picks up, hum
   of the close-up where the infant's legs glow

gripping the father's neck—
   the lower mouth screaming,
the upper face squealing,
   a banner near them, and when the wind shifts,
a banner slapped over them,
   disappearing them,
beautiful!—
   cursive over their seeing—
black demands, serpentine—
   Then features pushing something facelike back through—
eye-pits, jawbone—
   Where is this we've awakened,
the crowd is not satisfied, you feel the camera, the

pilgrim,
   slip as the reporter wonders
what to do, what's next?, the image suddenly elastic as he
   ducks—gunshot?—
horizon of stockinged legs, screams,
   close-up on a
sleeve,

then
   shape back in place, sky back in place,
point-of-view, having gorged itself, back,
   single point-of-view as if dumbstruck, back,
then the voice-over recovers, taut, its singleness

   so thin,
green,
   like the bullet's path without the bullet,
a tendril, waving in the
   stunned air,

stringy, ar-
   ticulate, rising up, up, and looking back,
words its vertigo,

    all round it the hum of the crowd, windy, without

    consequence, a wheeze a snarl, dawdling, rapacious,

    the voice rising up, slender, no immunity,

    trellissed on our looking, trying to root in our beastly
                                    listening,

then the image back, there, under the voice,
   moblike,
trying to push-up under the voice,
   trying to suck the voice-over down—
pictures, *the matter*,
   swelling under the quick
voice—

   —the facts? spores?—flecks of
information,
   fabric through which no face will push,
proof,
   a storm of single instances,
confetti tossed at the
   marriage of

now to now: dots, dots
   roiling up under the golden voice—

Now: connect the dots, connect the dots,
connect the dots, connect the dots,
   connect the dots, connect the dots,
connect the dots, connect the dots—

Feeling ok?

6

Said Moses show me Your face.
   Not the voice-over, not
the sound track (thou shalt not thou
   shalt not) not the interpretation—buzz—
the face.
   But what can we do?
Call the

7

        policeman, the surgeon?
Who's the boss, what's the right number?
   I sit in the rocker, back and forth, back and forth.

Let's consider the dark, how green it is.
Let's consider the green, how dark, with the rocker at its
                      heart.

Forwards, forwards, the sirens shriek past.
Into this they go: thick sound of the rocker rocking: wood on
                                                          wood:
so compact there underneath their going,
a footnote, no messy

                          going
anywhere,
          rocking,

erasing each forwards,

erasing, a sound like dice being incessantly retossed.
So it adds up in the end to stillness?
This the immaculate conception, the heart of the matter,

the great white heart,
pile-up of erasures—play, reverse play—
the runners laying their equal sign down
onto the dry floorboards

till it's this clot, this white opening,
the scene of the accident,
part feather part scales—

                          —thwack, thwack—the marriage

hymn,
what the god said to wait for He'd be back,
here in the place where it's all true so why move,
here in the nuclear-free zone, everyone in it for

capital gains, don't move, we can all fit, narrow place, He

said keep going I'll be back, you're on the
right track, keep rocking, forwards, then the other forwards,
the lovers in each other's forwardness,
facing each other,
both *forwards* absolutely

true—one of them death the other one
not but who can tell, they can't unwrap now, it seems like
it's love or at least a
private matter, they have the right

number, so sit still sit still the lively understandable
spirit said,
still, still,
so that it can be completely the

now, center stage, this your kind's
victory, the mind in
apogee—said *still*, said
don't wait, just sit, sit—Said

no later, no matter.
There, you got it now. You got it.

A manuscript page from an essay on Albert Camus by V.S. Pritchett.

The Art of Fiction CXXII

V.S. Pritchett

V.S. Pritchett was born on December 16, 1900. Over the past two years he has published a collection of six decades of travel essays, a biography, and his ninth volume of literary criticism. At ninety he continues to be a prolific writer, and has completed a new story collection, A Careless Widow, *even in the wake of the publication of his* Complete Short Stories *(1990). Although he has worked in many literary genres, he is best known for his short stories and travel writing.*

While his stories have been compared to those of Joyce and Chekhov, Pritchett claims it was Irish writers such as Sean

O'Faolin, Liam O'Flaherty and Frank O'Connor who taught him what a short story could be. Eudora Welty has said, "Any Pritchett story is all of it alight and busy at once, like a well-going fire. Wasteless and at the same time well-fed, it shoots up in flame from its own spark like a poem or a magic trick, self-consuming, with nothing left over. He is one of the great pleasure-givers in our language."

At his father's insistence, Pritchett left school when he was fifteen to work in the leather trade—an experience which provided him with material for his early novel Nothing Like Leather *(1935). At twenty Pritchett went to Paris, where he "lived an abysmal bohemian life and wrote a terribly pretentious and mannered prose." He supported himself working as a salesman in shops, and later as a correspondent on the Irish rebellion for* The Christian Science Monitor *and a journalist in Spain. His first book,* Marching Spain, *published in 1928 and like many of his works long out of print, was a travel book about his tour of that country.*

Along with eight volumes of critical essays, many written at the rate of one a week for The New Statesman, *where Pritchett eventually became literary editor, he has written critical biographies of Balzac (1973), Turgenev (1977), and Chekhov (1988). He has no interest in scholarly doctrines—his aim is to illuminate a writer—and in the end, his biographies send one back to the authors' books themselves.*

Pritchett, a former president of English PEN and International PEN, is the president of the London Society of Authors, and was knighted in 1975. He lives with his wife of fifty years, Dorothy, near Primrose Hill, London, in a narrow Georgian house. His drawing room overlooks the green canopy of Regent's Park. It was here that this interview was conducted on two separate occasions in 1990. In person V.S. Pritchett is a small, energetic man, with a lively luminous face and a lop-sided grin that makes him seem years younger. Words come out of him quickly, easily and precisely. He has about him the eagerness and intelligence of a man who enjoys talk and enjoys people. When, at the end of one rainy-day meeting Pritchett began to recount a story he was working on, he stood up in

his book-lined sitting room and was transformed into a ven-
triloquist. Chortling as he spoke, hands in the pockets of his
cardigan, he suddenly took on the voices of all the characters,
and brought his story to life. Irving Howe once said of him
that "no one alive writes a better English sentence," and at
ninety, V.S. Pritchett is still making his sentences into stories.
As he puts it: "Intervention invents itself."

INTERVIEWER

Your career as a writer has been so long and distinguished
that we could spend hours on every aspect of it. But let us start
from the beginning: you are the first member of your family,
which you have classified as lower-middle class, to become a
writer. Where do you think your talents come from?

V.S. PRITCHETT

I don't really know. My father was a businessman but artis-
tic. He designed textiles and sold them to Liberty's. I remember seeing him feel and stroke silk, and wondering what he
was doing—he was assessing its quality. My mother was a
Cockney and a good storyteller and mimic. She used to go out
shopping and come back imitating people she had seen, with
their different voices and accents. She read me stories by the
humorists of the time. One of her favorite books was *The Tales
of The Night Watchman* by W.W. Jacobs. They always started
with "Well, as I was saying the other day, said the Night
Watchman," and went on from there. They had very good dialogue and were wildly funny. My mother used to be hysterical
with laughter. My grandfather was a Congregationalist minister working up in Yorkshire. He was a good working-class boy,
but in those days—towards the end of the nineteenth century—
there was a feeling that you could rise in the world through
education. He had a good voice and spoke with precision and
eloquence. Some lady in the neighborhood sent him to theo-
logical college for a year at her own expense, and he became
a Congregationalist minister. I was often sent to stay with him
for holidays and enjoyed his company. He was an ardent walker
over the fells and moorlands of Yorkshire, and he took me with

him. He would say to me, "But you haven't learnt Greek and Latin?" then take a coin out of his pocket, show me the Latin inscription on it and try to initiate me. Or he would say, "You must read Macaulay at once!" or "Have you not read Ruskin? You must start straight away!" I was about nine or ten.

INTERVIEWER

You have also mentioned a W.W. Bartlett, your school teacher. How was he an influence.

PRITCHETT

I went to a state primary school in Dulwich, where we lived. Mr. Bartlett was very unconventional. He never kept to the curriculum, and he broke all the rules and regulations of the educational authorities. He disorganized us very well. He used to spend a whole day on history, for example, instead of the regulatory forty-five minutes, or send us out into the surrounding countryside to draw wild flowers. This was perfect for a future writer, but not for ambitious boys who wanted to pass exams and get good jobs. Eventually Mr. Bartlett left and became an important figure in the world of education; he was replaced by a woman teacher who was also very good. She once told us to go the Horniman Museum nearby and draw something, anything we liked. I brought back a picture of an amulet, which she liked, and for which she gave me a prize—a pocket edition of Ruskin in three volumes! I still have it. I had been to the Dulwich Art Gallery and looked at pictures by David and Poussin and so on, not knowing anything about those artists. And there they all were in Ruskin. I was about twelve, and it was a struggle reading him, but I got to volume three, of which the first fifty to seventy pages are on the pathetic fallacy in literature. He argued that it was incorrect to assign human feelings to inanimate objects. He picked on Homer and showed where he had gone wrong. The book was about how to write criticism, and I worked hard to understand it.

INTERVIEWER

What were your very earliest influences?

PRITCHETT

My first passionate reading, I suppose, was Walter Scott, which I started reading when I was five. I was picking my way through "Scottland" a long time, until the old lady next door came over and said, "Why waste your time on all this trash?" I was a tremendous prig.

INTERVIEWER

You have said that from the age of ten you knew you would be a writer. Did you start writing then?

PRITCHETT

There was a children's encyclopedia in our house, and I read an article on the Alhambra in it and decided to write a novel about the war between the Castilians and the Arabs, full of battle scenes and romance. I sat down and wrote a hundred pages of it; then my father found it and mocked my use of pretentious words and made me burn it. For a long time I harbored a great resentment against him for that.

INTERVIEWER

You left school at fifteen, presumably because you could not afford it. But there were scholarships for bright pupils like you. Did you try to get one?

PRITCHETT

With his eccentric teaching method, Mr. Bartlett had ensured that I would never get one! The scholarship exam questions were on Noah's Ark, and what they wanted was historical knowledge, with facts and figures and dates. I thought the story was rather dull, but the voyage was thrilling, and I made up a fantastic account of the voyage—what people were doing on the boat, with animals and the dove coming in and all of that. Naturally I failed the exam. So I was sent to work in the leather trade.

INTERVIEWER

Why leather? What kind of work did you do?

PRITCHETT

Someone told my father there was a future in leather. At first I was an office boy, but soon I became a messenger, taking documents to the docks and the warehouses and so on. This was tremendous, because instead of being cooped up in an office all day I could get out. At the same time, people in the higher echelons of the trade were very well-educated. They read a lot and were intrigued by the idea that I really wanted to be a writer. That's when I began to write little sketches. But what encouraged me particularly was going to some local lectures; one of the subjects was Milton, and as it happened I had read *Paradise Regained*, though not *Lost*. I wrote an essay on it and the lady lecturer publicly proclaimed it to be the best. This was marvelous! I sent it to two papers in the country, and although no one published it, I had got the fever.

INTERVIEWER

So how did you get out of the leather trade?

PRITCHETT

At school I had started learning German and French, and I was good at them. Afterwards I worked on my French fairly hard and read a great deal. So after four years the firm gave me money to take a year's leave of absence to go to Paris—I think it was about twenty pounds. The money was soon finished, and I got a job in a photographic shop. It was very boring, but I met all sorts of people, artists and photographers, who were not big names, but interesting. They all wore hats and scarves and colorful clothes. At the same time, I began writing. I had formed the notion that if you want to write, you should write about what you know and what you are doing, exactly. So I wrote a sketch about living on the fifth floor of a cheap hotel in Paris, and sent it to the *Christian Science Monitor*. To my delight it was accepted and published.

INTERVIEWER

What made you choose an American paper over an English publication?

PRITCHETT

My father was a Christian Scientist and subscribed to it. It was an important paper, with a huge circulation, like the *Times* of London. Famous American writers wrote for it, as it was well-edited and paid handsomely. I was thrilled to be published by them, and sent them other sketches, which they also published. When Mrs. Eddy, the founder of the paper, died, however, a religious dispute arose among her successors resulting in a huge loss of money, and suddenly they couldn't pay the contributors. I nearly starved, and would have if my landlady had not noticed that I never ate, didn't go out in the evenings and was getting skinny. She gave me some money to go back to London, which I did, and I went to see the London editor. He was a cultivated man, and he thought it was terrible that I hadn't been paid. What could he do? He sent me to Ireland to write a series of articles. It was during the troubles of 1921–1924, and he asked me to travel all over the country and write, not about the war, but about how ordinary Irish people lived and coped with the situation.

INTERVIEWER

Ulysses was published in 1922 when you were in Paris. Did you read it? What did you think of it?

PRITCHETT

Oh yes, I read it. Although it was an expensive book and I couldn't afford it, someone loaned me a copy and I struggled through it. I thought it was frightful! The first chapters, written in that staccato, adjectival manner were especially offputting. It was on later readings that I realized how important a book it was. It is a study in style, and some of the later chapters are marvelous — the famous one about the old woman sitting on a chamber pot and having a stream of consciousness, for example.

INTERVIEWER

You were in Ireland at the time when Yeats and Lady

Gregory had a literary coterie around the Abbey Theatre. Did being a journalist give you an entrée to them?

PRITCHETT

It did. I wrote to Yeats and went to interview him. He was very impressive — tall, handsome, with dramatic gestures and a fine voice. I was having tea with him one day, and I remember he picked up a pot of tea and, finding that it was already full of old tea, he opened the window of his Georgian house and flung the contents into the square! Rhetoric poured out of him all the while.

INTERVIEWER

Did you meet other members of his group?

PRITCHETT

I did. Fortunately, Dublin is a small city, and it was not difficult to seek people out and see them, but I never went to their salons. There was a hotel by the sea where James Stephens used to go and watch the boats come in, and I went there often to see him. He was a very good talker — they all were. I saw Sean O'Casey many times. I remember he had written above his desk, "Get on with the bloody play!" Apart from writers, I met a number of interesting people just traveling around the country, including my first wife. That marriage was short-lived.

INTERVIEWER

Another member of the group was George Russell, the Irish poet AE, who published your first short story, I believe?

PRITCHETT

AE was a mystic and a comfortable old chap. He was immensely talkative, and he was then editing the *Irish Statesman*. I sent him my first story which was about a gypsy who gets into a fight and accidentally stabs his own donkey and kills him instead of his adversary. It was over-written and florid — I had never been with gypsies — and oddly enough AE accepted it. He kept it for two years and finally didn't publish it. He said it got squeezed out by Irish politics! Later he did publish a story of mine, but he never paid me!

INTERVIEWER

After Ireland you were sent to Spain as the *Christian Science Monitor*'s correspondent, which was the beginning of a life-long relationship with Spain. Reading your books about that country, one gets a great feeling of understanding and affection. What was it that attracted you to Spain?

PRITCHETT

Ireland hadn't changed my mind about life, but Spain did. I learned Spanish, traveled widely around the country, and read a great deal of Spanish literature. Spain was fascinating because it was a Catholic country, but many of the intellectuals were free thinkers. They didn't like the Jesuits who controlled education. Giner de los Ríos had started an educational movement in Spain, based on ideas he had taken from Germany, France, and England, as an alternative. He founded a students' residence—*Residencia de los Estudiantes*—which was rather like the *Cité Universitaire* in Paris. All the writers and intellectuals were drawn to it. They came and gave lectures and held discussions, and I used to go to them. I learned more from Spain than any other country, and I met most of the important contemporary writers. What I was really rather sorry about was that I had had no adventures. I knew Spain very well; my book *Marching Spain* was a return to it. But there were no adventures. I always wondered how it was that Robert Stevenson always seemed to have adventures; why don't I have adventures? The only adventure in that book was running into the brigands, which was quite entertaining. The rest was simply an account of the journey.

INTERVIEWER

Did you meet those writers who became known as the "Generation of '98," such as Unamuno y Jugo, Ortega y Gasset. . . .

PRITCHETT

Yes, all of them. I went to their lectures and met them privately too. Ortega was particularly kind to me. I read Unamuno's *Del Sentimiento Trágico de la Vida*, which made a great impression on me. It helped me to understand what I had not yet understood about the Catholic faith. And although I was not tempted to become a Catholic myself, those two years in Spain were very fruitful.

INTERVIEWER

Then you came back to London. Did you find it easy to get a job?

PRITCHETT

By then I was a published writer and journalist. I wrote for *The New Statesman*. Its literary editor was Raymond Mortimer. I reviewed and wrote for him through the war.

INTERVIEWER

Many of your essays were on classic writers, such as Cervantes, Tolstoy, and Balzac. Was that your idea or his?

PRITCHETT

There was a shortage of paper during the war and there were fewer new books. So Raymond Mortimer thought that it would be a good idea to write also about writers of the past. It was an opportunity to write a piece about something I particularly admired.

INTERVIEWER

In your case you made your apprenticeship through journalism. There are different views on this sort of training. Michael Frayn says that every writer of fiction ought to work as a reporter for a while because it keeps one in touch with reality. On the other hand, Evelyn Waugh believed that journalism was detrimental to writers and that they ought to get out of it as soon as they can. Even more damning of the profession was Chekhov, who wrote that although he was forced to work as a journalist, he hoped he would not die as one. What is your view?

PRITCHETT

I had no other way of starting. I think the experience is indispensable. I know writers who have never touched journalism, but they have private means. A creative writer is better formed by himself than by institutions. But it is a risk; one has to be certain and prove oneself. So, I don't regret having been a journalist. I think it was a good apprenticeship.

INTERVIEWER

Do you think living and writing conflict?

PRITCHETT

I have always thought that life and literature are intermingled and that this intermingling has been my quest.

INTERVIEWER

Let us talk about that quest. You have defined yourself as "a man of letters." As Anthony Burgess remarked in his review of your essay collection of the same name, this expression has a pleasantly old-fashioned ring, denoting a broader, grander sweep than we are used to. Indeed, you have covered almost every literary genre in your oeuvre except poetry and drama. You said that you originally wanted to be a poet. Did you ever try?

PRITCHETT

Oh yes, but it was no good. I scribbled reams of love poems for a girlfriend when I was seventeen. But I realized I couldn't do it, and I gave it up.

INTERVIEWER

What about drama? Your dialogues are so accurate and concise that I wonder if you have ever considered transferring them to the stage.

PRITCHETT

No, I have never attempted to write for the stage. That requires a special skill that I don't have.

INTERVIEWER

Over the years, have you developed any rules of thumb for writing dialogue?

PRITCHETT

It's hard to answer that. It comes naturally to me to write dialogue. I'm not a plot writer. I find it very difficult to invent a plot of any intricacy. Much more exciting to me is the intricacy, the plot form, of dialogue. The speaker is making up his drama as he goes along, and he doesn't know how good he is or how bad he is. It's natural, so therefore dialogue gets me out of any chip I have about not being able to think of a good plot. Dialogue is one of the things which I seem to be able to do, hit upon doing, and like. Dialogue is my form of poetry. I can't write poetry to save my life. Dialogue is the nearest I can come to the poetic.

INTERVIEWER

And the surrealistic streak in your writing?

PRITCHETT

Well, there is that. One constantly hears people's minds going off at an astonishing angle. When I reread some of the strangest remarks in my stories, I think, "I must have heard that somewhere, I certainly didn't invent it. Someone said that to me in a train or I heard it on a bus." For example, the dialogue of the people I worked with in the leather trade was absolutely astonishing to listen to. It was a remarkable narrative, a sort of lopsided narrative, but nevertheless with its brilliant moments, which they muddled in marvelous ways.

INTERVIEWER

Your most popular and acclaimed works have been your

short stories and travel books. What attracted you to the short
story as opposed to the novel?

PRITCHETT

The short story appealed to me straight away because of its
shortness, and I preferred it to the novel. It represents a certain
vision of reality which consists of isolating the incident. The
great thing about the short story is the detail, not the plot.
The plot is useful, but only for supplying the sort of detail
which is not descriptive but which pushes the action forward.
Many critics have noticed this about my stories.

INTERVIEWER

How did you come to write your first novel?

PRITCHETT

In 1927 I went back to Spain, walked across the country and
wrote a book about it. The publishers of that book, *Marching
Spain*, accepted it on condition that I write a novel for them.
I didn't think of myself as a novelist and said I couldn't do it.
Instead, I gave them a collection of short stories, which again
they only accepted with the pledge of a novel. *Marching Spain*
sold six-hundred copies, but the short stories sold more than
any of the novels I wrote subsequently. The collection was
called *The Spanish Virgin*.

INTERVIEWER

So, in a way you were bullied into writing a novel?

PRITCHETT

Yes, *Clare Drummer*. And it wasn't good, rather turgid. It
was about a love affair in Ireland, and it had a number of Irish
eccentrics in it. The critics demolished it, though one or two
were kind enough to say that it was promising.

INTERVIEWER

But you went on writing novels—five in all. Which made
a mark, either critically or popularly?

PRITCHETT

I wrote a novel based on my experiences in the leather trade. This novel, *Nothing Like Leather* (1935), sold about eleven thousand copies. *Dead Man Leading* (1937) is an account of an exploration in Brazil and a trip up the Amazon. I had never been anywhere near the Amazon, but I fancied myself an explorer and read it up at the British Museum Library. To my amazement, it was highly praised. Unfortunately, it coincided with Munich and failed commercially. But I did write one more novel, *Mr. Beluncle* (1951), which was published after the war. This highly-fictionalized autobiography did well.

INTERVIEWER

In *Mr. Beluncle* you wrote about your father. Did he ever read it?

PRITCHETT

I think he started it, but it bored him stiff. He said, "I can't make anything out of this." He didn't like reading.

INTERVIEWER

But he knew it was about him.

PRITCHETT

Yes, he did, because somebody told him it was.

INTERVIEWER

You said once that the short story tells exhaustively about one thing, while the novel offers up a whole universe. Did you always want to be principally a short story writer?

PRITCHETT

I think I really wanted to be a short story writer because I thought I was a man of short breath. I haven't got the breath to write novels.

INTERVIEWER

You've actually written a number of very long stories, almost novellas.

PRITCHETT

Long stories I think are admirable. I like those. That is quite
another matter because you have your central theme, which
is sustained and helps you along. But a novel is like an enormous tree with so many branches going off from it in all directions. At least the nineteenth-century novel is like that, and
that's what I was brought up on. That's no good to me, but
the short story and the long short story are. I've written quite
a lot of them.

INTERVIEWER

You're known for boiling one hundred twenty pages down
to twenty.

PRITCHETT

It has happened. I've written some stories that absolutely
said, "No, no, this has got to be cut down."

INTERVIEWER

Is it usually a question of getting rid of entire scenes, or of
thinning it out?

PRITCHETT

I think it's been a question of speeding up. You may fall in
love too much with certain conceits, and elaborations. The
thing is to keep it running well, keep it lightly clad.

INTERVIEWER

Keep it athletic.

PRITCHETT

Yes, exactly. "Athletic" is the word; I think that's a good
word to describe my attitude to stories.

INTERVIEWER

It's actually your own word.

PRITCHETT

Is it? There you are—didn't know I was so clever.

INTERVIEWER

You've said that it was a big discovery to find you were a humanist, and it is a writer's duty to justify the characters to themselves. Is the aim of a balanced story that every character be given a chance to speak on his own behalf? Or do you mean that they should all be treated fairly?

PRITCHETT

I think they should all be treated fairly. In the story I wrote about the secondhand trade, "The Camberwell Beauty," there's a very wide range of characters. The minor ones are observed, I think, as closely as they need to be, never more. Also, one must never regard a character as totally disposable. He may somehow have to reappear at some moment. In fact, it makes the others truer to life if he suddenly crops up later on. But you've then got to make him feel that he's got a right to do that — that he's on some other business. He's carrying on his life, as well as the larger characters carrying on theirs. I think in that story the minor characters work very well. They keep coming back, but in another way.

INTERVIEWER

So characters in stories may judge each other, but the writer should never give the impression of judging them.

PRITCHETT

That's right. Let them do it to each other.

INTERVIEWER

That's a very anti-nineteenth-century idea.

PRITCHETT

Yes, very. I hesitate on sweeping judgements, and, after all, it's the variety in human nature that's interesting. A human being is rather like a tune; he has various notes in his emotions, in his thoughts, in his life. Some are his best, some are very fine, some are ripe, but not all.

INTERVIEWER

Let's talk about distinctions between first and third person. You've said that you first cast your famous story, "Sense of Humor," in the third person, and then you decided it should be in first person. Did you ever find a way to decide early during a story's progress about the voice?

PRITCHETT

I'd written the first part in the third person, and then suddenly I realized that I'm so much better at dialogue than I am at writing this awful, elaborate analysis. If only I could jump away, this man could tell his own story. People are much brighter than you think they are. I shan't be interfering with him. I shan't give him my thoughts. They will be his as a person. One knows that from listening to people. You take characters from life. In general, I've found this almost indispensable. If I took you for a story, I would have to find some other person, a second, or a third to fill out the character. Then the fixity of the original "you" vanishes. A real character emerges from three.

INTERVIEWER

Did you know Joyce Cary? He was a master of the first person.

PRITCHETT

He was. I didn't know him very well, but I did know him. A most extraordinary man, a very strange man. He used to live in Oxford, and I went to see him there. He seemed far too accomplished; he seemed to have everything. He'd been a very distinguished civil servant in Africa. He'd been a great book collector and was a rather able painter—not a genius, but he painted better than most of us. His background was very amusing. He had a rather wild Anglo-Irish background, which was immediately recognizable to anyone who knew Ireland at that time. He was very serious. Oxford made him seem a bit solemn, but he wasn't really solemn. He was very restless. For example, when we were talking at Oxford, suddenly there was a noise at the front door. He clapped his hands and said, "That's my cutlet! That's my dinner! Dear old so-and-so's dropped me in my cutlet!" Someone had dropped some meat in through the letter drop. He rushed to the door, picked it up, opened the door and said, "Oh, she's gone." I heard him shout down the street, "Thank you! Thank you! Thank you!" He was very excitable.

INTERVIEWER

Let's talk about your essays, another genre in which you are an acknowledged master. When did you start writing reviews?

PRITCHETT

The kind of advance you got for a novel or a travel book was something like twenty-five pounds—not enough to live on. So, I started reviewing to have a regular source of income.

INTERVIEWER

You once said that one or two good stories are worth all the criticism in the world. Is that because stories are more imaginative? More creative?

PRITCHETT

If a story is really good it simply lives on, regardless of what other people think of it. Criticism, however, comes and goes. It changes with the fashion of the time. A story is always a story.

INTERVIEWER

Is there a different approach to writing criticism?

PRITCHETT

I think the critic must first of all clear his own mind. Someone who has worked on a book, perhaps for years, and succeeded in getting it published, must have some quality. What is it? The critic has to sort him out and look for his merits. I always look for the real voice of a writer because most good writers have a distinctive voice. If he doesn't have a voice, however important the subject may be, the book is not interesting.

INTERVIEWER

Do you think there is a conflict between criticism and imaginative writing?

PRITCHETT

Not really, though they are different, of course. When you write a story you try to become the characters you are writing about. In criticism you try to enter a world that someone else has created, and that is also an imaginative, creative act.

INTERVIEWER

Which critics do you particularly admire?

PRITCHETT

When I was a young man I thought Lytton Strachey was splendid, and I admired Virginia Woolf too. Later I got bored with her, but now I think she is very good and alive. I liked Edmund Wilson as a critic because he had an impressive, gathering mind.

INTERVIEWER

You have written biographies of Balzac, Turgenev and Chekhov. They differ from the usual, factual biographies. They are more the work of a storyteller, a personal reflection on the life and work of a fellow writer. Why did you choose those writers as your subjects?

PRITCHETT

Partly because I was asked by the publishers to do them, and partly as personal tributes. When I was young I hero-worshiped Balzac. He was the first French writer I read, and I lived near his home in Paris. I went around with a copy of his *La Peau de Chagrin* in my pocket, and later, whenever I was traveling, I took one of his books with me to read. A lot of his small businessmen and shopkeepers reminded me of members of my family, especially my father. Even Balzac himself was like my father, only more grand. As for the other two, I have had a life-long interest in the nineteenth-century Russian writers.

What was their special attraction?

What I particularly like about them is their naturalness and clarity. They are pre-industrial people outside the European structure; their novels flow from the emotions of the people, their characters, and what they feel—not grandiose emotions—the sort of things we all feel which come to the surface in the daily course of life. Clarity is very important to me. When I began to write I went in for dramatic, extravagant images and descriptions. But now I think clarity is everything—I seek to keep the cutting edge clean. Some Spanish writers have clarity, so has Stendhal. Tolstoy and Turgenev are marvelous in that respect. Their language is plain and taut. Dostoyevsky is different. He sees clearly through the mass of conflicting emotions and thoughts of his characters.

Your own style has been praised for its clarity and naturalness. Molly Keane described it as, "Not a word too many, not a word too few." Did you consciously cultivate this style, or did it evolve naturally?

I just wanted to write in my own manner, rather than adopt someone else's, however much I admired him or her.

Is writing easy for you? You give the impression that it is, that you're a natural.

PRITCHETT

No, it is not easy at all. It is hard getting it out. I do like the process of writing, but it is not easy.

INTERVIEWER

Do you have a clear sense of the merits and shortcomings of your work?

PRITCHETT

When I look back I know very well, yes. When I look back I think: Oh, this is not good, but this is very good, or *this* is much better than anyone ever told me. I do rewrite quite a lot.

INTERVIEWER

When you're writing a story, what's the process it goes through?

PRITCHETT

I write longhand, always. My typing is absolutely hopeless. I make several false starts, or perhaps it starts right, but it doesn't go on right. Then suddenly I'm able to go on once more. It's erratic. Once I get going, then I do write really quite fast. Invention invents itself. You have to get yourself into it. One is very dull when one starts. You have to give yourself several good kicks in the behind.

INTERVIEWER

Your work goes through several drafts, which your wife types?

PRITCHETT

Yes, my work would stop if she didn't type these things for me. Then I go through and alter a good deal, so she has to do it again.

INTERVIEWER

Do you still work every day?

PRITCHETT

Every day of the week. It's simply because journalism does that to you. You always have to work on Sundays, so therefore that makes up the week. It makes you quite different from anyone else. You don't get a mid-week day off by law. And I find writing takes a long time. I write most days. I didn't write yesterday. I think I tried to write the day before. I don't think it is a good idea to write if one doesn't have anything to say. I don't start writing a story until I have a governing idea or feeling.

INTERVIEWER

How does the idea of a story come to you?

PRITCHETT

It is usually given to me by meeting people. The first story of mine which was very much praised was "Sense of Humor." It came about while I was in Eniskille, a small place in Ireland. I used to go to a bar where I met a commercial traveler who talked non-stop, and the interesting thing about him was that he had a car, but it was not an ordinary car, it was a hearse. It emerged that his girlfriend was the daughter of an undertaker, so he drove around in this hearse. But I don't necessarily write the stories of the people I meet; it's rather that something about them gives me an idea.

INTERVIEWER

Do you ever get hollow periods, when you don't have ideas for stories? Do you worry about them?

PRITCHETT

No, I don't worry, because I usually have something else to do—a review or something. I have a huge package of "failures"—stories that haven't worked. I keep them, thinking: you never know. For example, I wrote a story which happened on Lake Como. I was mad about the lake and started writing about it and its beauty, but of course that doesn't make a story. So I put it away.

INTERVIEWER

Once you have started a story, do you know where it is going and how it will end?

PRITCHETT

Not always. It begins to make itself, as long as you keep close to your characters and think about them. I once wrote a story about a man who was blind. I thought I must find out what it is like to be blind. I closed my eyes, analyzed what blindness is, and so on. . . . It was called "Blind Love."

INTERVIEWER

Are you working on stories now?

PRITCHETT

I have got a story which I'm trying to get going. I'm getting long-winded. I'm trying at the moment to think of something very short. I wrote one which hasn't been published: "A Family Man." About a girl, an artist, who is very honest. Suddenly someone knocks on her door on a stormy night. A lady has come and accuses her of sleeping with her husband—which she has done, in fact. The girl is absolutely taken aback. She becomes exalted and makes up a marvelous denial and is so carried away by her own denial that she convinces the lady. She even invents her father. The lady says, "Well, who lives in that room?" and the girl says, "My father, please don't disturb him." "Wouldn't he like a cup of tea?" "Just a moment, I'll go and see." And he is not there! There's nobody there. "He must have gone for his little walk." "Ah, you've got to keep your eye on them," says the lady. Suddenly they're allies.

INTERVIEWER

Do you have any advice that you'd give to a young writer?

PRITCHETT

Just to write. Write, write, write. I think a good idea is to write a little — about two lines, not more, or three lines, about any person they wish. Don't write too much, if you write too much about it then you're afraid you'll kill it.

INTERVIEWER

You said somewhere that one difficulty for a young writer is knowing what you have to write about. And when it works you have the sense of something from the past being struck on the flint of the present. Do you still feel this way?

PRITCHETT

Sometimes. The odd thing is I wrote a very good story about two or three years ago. And it came about only because I remembered some schoolboy sitting in a railway station down in the country with the boys all going home from school. And he was very fat and greedy and ate chocolate. All the boys tried to cadge chocolate off him. Sooner or later there was a scene. They started fighting, someone threw his cap onto a railway line. I thought: "My God, this is a very good incident, I must use it. But I must put this into a totally different story."

INTERVIEWER

How long ago was it that you saw this boy?

PRITCHETT

Oh, forty years, fifty years.

INTERVIEWER

There's an idea that we go round and round in our lives; that there's a youth of youth, a middle age of youth, and an old age of youth, followed by a youth of middle age, and so on. What are you in now?

PRITCHETT

I think I'm half in the madhouse, you know. I feel like I'm getting rather dull now.

INTERVIEWER

The edges are going?

PRITCHETT

Well, I'm very old. After all, I'm ninety. I'm rather annoyed at the thought of being ninety. I put my faith in Bertrand Russell, whom I remember meeting when he was about ninety. And I thought that that's all right, if I can be like that I won't mind!

—Shusha Guppy
Anthony Weller

Les Murray

Presence

Translations from the Natural World

Eagle Pair

We shell down on the sleeping-branch. All night
the limitless Up digests its meats of light.

The circle-winged Egg then emerging from long pink and
    brown
re-inverts life, and meats move or are still on the Down.

Irritably we unshell, into feathers; we lean open and rise
and magnify this meat, then that, with the eyes of our
    eyes.

Meat is light, it is power and Up, as we free it from load
and our mainstay, the cunningest hunter, is the human
    road

but all the Down is heavy and tangled. Only meat is good
    there
and the rebound heat ribbing up vertical rivers of air.

Layers of Pregnancy

Under eagle worlds   each fixed in place
it is to kangaroo   all fragrant space
to feed between long feet   to hop
from short to ungrazed sweet   to stop
there whittling it   down between eyed knees
cocked to propel   away through shadow trees
as Rain the father   scenting ahead through time
for himself   who is all
he can scent, does   and expels a blood-clot to climb
wet womb   to womb of fur
and implants another   in the ruby wall.

I glory centennially slowly in being Guugumbakh the
strangular fig bird-born to overgrow
the depths of this wasp-leafed stinging-tree
through muscling in molten stillness down
its spongy barrel crosslacing in overflow
even of myself as in time my luscious fat
leaves top out to adore the sun forest high
and my shade-coldest needs touch a level that
discovered as long yearned for transmutes
my wood into the crystal mode of roots
and I complete myself and mighty on
buttresses far up in combat embraces no
rotted traces to the fruiting rain surface O I one.

Insect Mating Flight

Iridescent in accord, clear wings
row, and the pressure of air-ocean
breathing and upholding him, Ee sings:
with our chew eyewords' whim
moth reed haze racing vane,
butts hum and buoy or, fairer moan,
ex pencil eye fits elf, is gain.
Microbes leap ova neither lung
disdances leery quid threw awed.
Clewings eerie dissent inner cord.

Two Dogs

Enchantment creek underbank pollen, are the stiff scents
  he makes,
hot grass rolling and rabbit-dig but only saliva chickweed.
Road pizza clay bird, hers answer him, rot-spiced good. Blady
  grass,
she adds, ant log in hot sunshine. Snake two sunups back.
  Orifice?
Orifice, he wriggles. Night fox? Night fox, with left pad
  wound.
Cement bag, hints his shoulder. Catmeat, boasts his tail, twice
  enjoyed.
Folded sapless inside me, she clenches. He retracts initial
  blood.
Frosty darks coming, he nuzzles. High wind rock human-free
  howl,
her different law. Soon. Away, away, eucalypts speeding—
Bark! I water for it. Her eyes go binocular, as in pawed
hop frog snack play. Come ploughed, she jumps, ground.
  Bark tractor,
white bitterhead grub and pull scarecrow. Me! assents his
  urine.

Cockspur Bush

I am lived. I am died.
I was two-leafed three times, and grazed,
but then I was stemmed and multiplied,
sharp-thorned and caned, nested and raised,
earth-salt by sun-sugar. I am innerly sung
by thrushes who need fear no eyed skin thing.
Finched, ant-run, flowered, I am given the years
in now fewer berries, now more of sling
out over directions of luscious dung.
Of water the crankshaft, of gases the gears
my shape is cattle-pruned to a crown spread sprung
above the starve-gut instinct to make prairies
of everywhere. My thorns are stuck with caries
of mice and rank lizards by the butcher bird.
Inches in, baby seed-screamers get supplied.
I am lived and died in, vine-woven, multiplied.

Lyre Bird

Liar made of leaf-litter, quivering ribby in shim,
hen-sized under froufrou, chinks in a quiff display him
or her, dancing in mating time, or out. And in any order.
Tailed mimic aeon-sent to intrigue the next recorder,
I mew catbird, I saw crosscut, I howl she-dingo, I kink
forest hush distinct with bellbirds, warble magpie garble, link
cattlebell with kettle-boil; I rank ducks' cranky presidium
or simulate a triller like a rill mirrored lyrical to a rim.
I ring dim. I alter nothing. Real to real only I sing,
Gahn the crane to Gun the chainsaw, urban thing to being,
Screaming Woman owl and human talk: eedieAi and uddyun
    nunoan.
The miming is all of I. Silent, they are a function
of wet forest, cometary lyrebirds. Their flight lifts them barely
    a semitone.

Shoal

Eye-and-eye eye an eye
each. What blinks is I,
unison of the whole shoal. Thinks:
a dark idea circling by—
again the eyes' I winks.
Eye-and-eye near no eye
is no I, though gill-pulse drinks
and nervy fins spacewalk. Jinx
jets the jettisoned back into all.
tasting, each being a tongue,
vague umbrations of chemical:
this way thrilling, that way Wrong,
the pure always inimical,
compound being even the sheer thing
I suspend I in, and thrust
against, for speed and feeding,
all earblades for the eel's wave-gust
over crayfishes' unpressured beading,
for bird-dive boom, redfin's gaped gong—

Prehistory of Air

Fish, in their every body
hold a sac of dry
freeing them from gravity
where fish go when they die.
It is the only dryness,

Fish, in their every body
hold a sac of dry
freeing them from gravity
where fish go when they die.
It is the only dryness,
the first air, weird and thin—

but then my beak strikes from there
and the world turns outside-in.
I'm fishes' horror, being
crushed into dimensions,
yet from their swimming bladder
hatched dry land, sky
and the heron of prehensions.

The Gods

There is no Reynard fox. Just foxes.
I'm the fox who scents this pole.
As a kit on gravel, I brow-arched Play? to a human.
It grabbed to kill, and gave me a soul.

We're trotting down one hen-stalk gully.
Soul can sit up inside, and be.
I halt, to keep us alive. Soul basks in
scents of shadow, sound of honey.

Call me the lover in the dew
of one in his merriment of blur.
Fragile as the first points of a scent
on the mind's skin settle his weights of fur.

A light not of the sky attends
his progress down the unleaped dim —
There's a young false-hoofed dog human coming
and the circling gunshot scent of him

eddies like sickness. I freeze, since their
ears point them, quicker than a wagtail's beak.
I must be Not for a while, *repressing*
all but the low drum of the meek.

Dreams like a whistle crack the spring,
a scentless shape I have not been
threads the tall legs of deities
like Hand, and Colour, and Machine.

Cattle Ancestor

Darrambawli and all his wives, they came feeding from the
  south east
back in that first time. Darrambawli is a big red fellow,
terrible fierce. He scrapes up dust, singing, whirling his bull-
  roarers
in the air: he swings them and they sing out Crack! Crack!
All the time he's mounting his women, all the time more
  kulka,
more, more, smelling their *kulka* and looking down his nose.
Kangaroo and emu mobs run from him, as he tears up their
  shelters,
throwing the people in the air, stamping out their fires.
Darrambawli gathers up his brothers, all making that sad cry
  mar mar:
he initiates his brothers, the Bulluktruk. They walk head down
  in a line
and make the big blue ranges. You hear their clinking noise
  in there.
Darrambawli has wives everywhere, he has to gallop back and
  forth,
mad for their kulka. You see him on the coast, and on the
  plains.
They're eating up the country, so the animals come to spear
  them:
You have to die now, you're starving us. But then Waark the
  crow
tells Darrambawli Your wives, they're spearing them. He is
  screaming,
frothing at the mouth, that's why his chest is all white
  nowadays.
Jerking two knives, he screams *I make new waterholes! I bring
  the best song!*
He makes war on all that mob, raging, dotting the whole
  country.
He frightens the water-snakes; they run away, they can't sit
  down.
The animals forget how to speak. There is only one song
for a while. Darrambawli must sing it on his own.

Mollusc

By its nobship sailing upside down,
by its inner sexes, by the crystalline
pimplings of its skirts, by the sucked-on
lifelong kiss of its toppling motion,
by the viscose optics now extruded
now wizened instantaneously, by the
ridges grating up a food-path, by
the pop shell in its nick of dry,
by excretion, the earthworm coils, the glibbing,
by the gilt slipway, and by pointing
perhaps as far back into time as
ahead, a shore being folded interior,
by boiling on salt, by coming uncut over
a razor's edge, by hiding the Oligocene
underleaf may this and every snail sense
itself ornament the weave of presence.

Cattle Egret

Our sleep-slow compeers, red and dun,
wade in their grazing, and whirring lives
shoal up, splintering, in skitters and dives.
Our quick beaks pincer them, one and one,
those crisps of winnow, fats of air,
the pick of chirrup—we haggle them down
full of plea, fizz, cark and stridulation,
our white plumes riffled by scads going spare
Shadowy round us are lives that eat things dead
but life feeds our life: fight is flavour,
stinging a spice. Bodies still electric play for
my crop's gravel jitterbug. I cross with sprung tread
where dogs tugged a baa-ing calf's gut out, fold on fold.
Somewhere may be creatures that grow old.

The Snake's Heat Organ

Earth after sun is slow burn
as eye scales darken.
    Water's no-burn.
Smaller sunlives all dim slowly
to predawn invisibility
but self-digesters constantly glow-burn.
Their blood-coals fleet
    glimmering as I spin
lightly over textures.
    Passenger of my passage
I reach round upright leaf-burners, I
reach and follow under rock balances,
I gather at the drinking margin.
Across the nothing there
    an ardency
is lapping blank, which segments serially up
beneath the coruscating braincakes
    into the body,
three skin-sheddings' length of no-burn negatively
coiled in a guttering chamber:
    a fox,
it is pedalling off now,
a scintillating melon,
    gamboge in its hull
    round a dark seed centre
and hungry as the sun.

Great Bole

Needling to soil point
lengthens me solar,
my ease perpendicular
from earth's mid ion.

Health is hold fast,
infill and stretch.
Ill is salts lacking,
brittle, insect-itch.

Many leaves numb
in tosses of sear,
bark split, fluids caramelled,
humus less dear,
barrel borer-bled.

Through me planet-strain
exercised by orbits.
Then were great holding,
earth-give and rain,
air-brunt, stonewood working.

Elements water brought
and solar, so sharing out
it's forever past one
enveloped me spiralling.

In no one cell
for I am centreless
pinked a molecule
newly, and routines

so gathered on
that I juice away all
mandibles. Florescence
suns me, bees and would-bes.
I layer. I blaze presence.

Echidna

Crumpled in a coign I was galactic with my hatchling
till he prickled.
He entered the earth pouch then
and learned ant-ribbon,
the gloss we put like lightning on the brimming ones.
Life is fat is sleep. I feast life on and sleep it,
deep loveself in calm.
I awaken to spikes of food-sheathing, of mulling fertile egg,
of sun, of formic gravels,
of worms, dab hunting, of fanning under quill-ruff when
budged:
all are rinds, to sleep.
Tongue-scabbard, corner-footed, I am trundling doze
and wherever I put it
is exactly right. Sleep goes there.

Yard Horse

Ripple, pond, liftoff fly. Unlid the outswallowing snorter
to switch at fly. Ripples over a day's gigantic peace.
No oestrus scent, no haem, no pung of other stallion,
no frightening unsmell of sexless horses,
the unbearable pee-submissive ones who are not in instinct.
Far off blistering grass-sugars. Smoke infinitesimal in air
and, pond gone, his dense standing now would alert all mares
for herded flight. Fire crowds up-mountain swift as horses,
teeters widening down. Pond to granite to derelict
timber go the coat-textures. Large head over wire
contains faint absent tastes, sodichlor, chaff, calc.
The magnified grass is shabby in head-bowed focus, the earth
it grows in only tepidly exists; blots of shade are abyssal.
In his mind, fragments of rehearsal: lowered snaking neck
for directing the mares; bounced trot-gait of menace
oncoming, with whipping headshake; poses, then digestion.
Moment to moment, he is a climate of mirrorings
and his body is the word for every meaning he conveys.

The Communist Manifesto
by Karl Marx and
Friedrich Engels: a story

Daniel Stern

*Until now the philosophers have
only tried to understand the world . . .
the point, however, is to change it.*

— *Karl Marx*

*The point is not to change the world.
All the worst people change the world.
The point is to understand it.*

— *Maurice Marx*

Bixby, Mettro, Manishin and Marx.
  Ah, Bixby, Mettro, Manishin and Marx. Sitting here in my
high-ceilinged under-priced West End Avenue Co-op, waiting

for my wife to come by and leave the keys for the last time, I am giving a party in my head. A party for Bixby, Mettro, Manishin and Marx: for all the soldiers of my formative years, the shock troops of my imagination — the drill sergeants of my character and achievements; the Unknown Soldiers of my finest failures. One glass is all I need for this party. It is full of ice and yellowish vodka, colored and flavored by a spear of buffalo grass. I raise it to my guests, one by one, each of whom had a key point about the living of life to impart; points I seem somehow to have missed.

Bixby, sword-skinny, wild-blonde hair, long, long fingers gesticulating, apparently independent of each other and the hands to which they were attached; Bixby wearing the remnants of an Air Force uniform he'd never been issued, and whose age remained a mystery — he could have been anything from twenty-two to forty. Vitamins, he said, vitamins were the secret, he took thirty-eight different pills a day. Thin as a skeleton, but a healthy, energetic skeleton. Depression-prone, Bixby shone with a mad optimism; optimism about playing the piano; those lighter-than air fingers were self-taught and full of dazzling technique — optimism about writing the Second Great American Marxist Science Fiction Novel (He had already written the first, but its whereabouts were buried in the puzzles of piles of old *Cosmos Magazines* in which it had been serialized) even optimism about Dianetics. Bixby was one of the first "clears" in a still-muddy America, long before Dianetics had become the menacing Church of Scientology; optimism extending even to the coming triumph of Marxist socialism and the possibilities of a revival of interest in the works of Scriabin.

All things were harmonized in Bixby. When you were in his presence there seemed to be no contradiction between the tight constructions of Marxist thought, the wild fantastic leaps of Dianetics, or the heated sevenths and ninths of Scriabin.

Mettro and Manishin, too, turned out to have their own weird take on Marxist thought. No, not thought. Everything, then, was how to *live* life — what to *do*! Not merely what to think. Thought as a possible way of being was an old story in

Europe. But it wasn't due in America until years later. For the moment the streets were packed with Marxist madmen and madwomen — knowing and unknowing; all set on changing the world one way or another. Everybody was hellbent on the unity of theory and practice! (Otherwise known as "If you think it but can't *do* it something is wrong.") We'd just won a war. It gave us the idea that we could make things work.

I was one year out of the Army, a passionate student of drawing at the Art Students League, of creative writing at The New School for Social Research. The more credits I enrolled for, the more money I got on the G.I. Bill — plus more text books to sell on the open market. How serious was I about drawing and writing? Well, you decide! And bear in mind the fact that I also managed to squeeze in an enrollment at the Arthur Murray Dance School in Washington Heights. The first ballroom dance studio to be accredited by the naive, guilt-ridden, postwar U.S. Government.

Bixby was from Indiana. Mettro was from too many places to count but California was the basic starting point. He was studying public relations at The New School in the evening, the cool spring nineteen forty-seven evenings. That was something new you could do then, *study* to be in public relations. During the day Mettro fixed cars. He was frail, dark, and Jewish, but being from California he naturally knew all you could know about cars. When he was ten Mettro had taken apart a Pontiac and put it back together, landing on network radio in the process. He also loved music, his specialty being early twentieth century. Which was how I got to meet Bixby. Mettro was watching me dance one evening at the Arthur Murray School. He sat smoking his Gauloises and observing my attempts to get as close as I could to the young southern lady who was teaching me to move, keeping exactly a forearm's length between our bodies. At the piano the still unknown Bixby played waltzes, rhumbas, even congas, as richly textured as if he were being paid by the note. On the floor I counted 1-2-3-4 and tried to engage Miss Surrey's eyes with mine. After having failed at this for twenty minutes I took a break and bummed a Gauloise from Mettro.

"Bad luck," I said.

"Did you hear the pianist?"

"I'm talking about Miss Surrey."

"Never mind; listen to that pianist. He's playing Scriabin. I can't believe it. "The Poem of Ecstasy" in waltz time, "The Poem of Ecstasy" in rhumba time, "The Poem of Ecstasy" in conga time." He was right. The next time I was on the floor I forgot about my frustration and listened in amazement. It was a virtuoso dazzlement of notes and rhythms all, indeed, based on that luxuriant hothouse piece by the mad Russian.

Miss Surrey, for all her distant southern charm, could not compete. Mettro and I waited till the end of the session. By the time a porter danced across the empty floor with a broom, Bixby, in his melange of uniform parts from various services topped off with a snappy Air Force officer's cap, was ours. Scriabin brought us together like old friends. Only Miss Surrey could keep us apart. He had a date with the dancing belle. By the time it was clear that he had been stood up it was almost midnight.

"Screwed again," Bixby sighed. "As it were."

"Get your music," Mettro said. "We'll have a drink."

"I don't use music."

"Never?"

"I can't read it."

"*Incroyable*," Mettro said. He had been in France when the war ended and had a few souvenirs to show. "On that, I'll buy the drinks." And off we went to midtown Manhattan where drinks could be had to celebrate new admirations, new friendships.

Actually, I must pause to tell you that we did not end up at a bar, we bought, much more characteristic of those days, hamburgers and coffee, right there in ugly old Washington Heights. This is not an idle digression. The point is—I almost changed Hamburger Harry's, in which the sawdust was so wet you had to walk very carefully, into a chic midtown bar, martinis, scotch, and all. The truth is—and the whole thing about not missing the point is truth, isn't it? The truth is this pseudo-Marxist trick of presenting earlier experiences in the style of

later ones is absolutely terrible. Whether it's Trotsky the hero
of the revolution becoming Trotsky the counter-revolutionary
monster, or a hamburger joint becoming a chic cocktail lounge,
it screws up the possibility of ever learning anything. Which
is one of the reasons I am sitting here, surrounded by suitcases,
entertaining ghosts.

"All those notes," I marveled to Bixby.
Bixby popped vitamin pills and drank vegetable juice.
"The more notes I play, the more they pay me. They want
quantity, I give quantity. For myself, I get it back by using
Scriabin."
Scriabin, he told us, was a great unsung genius of modern
times and his day would come. As for Miss Surrey, he was not
too concerned about her disappearance. It seemed that Bixby
was impotent, a dark result of some shadowy experience in the
war in which he had never taken part, whose uniform he had
bought in Army surplus stores. Instant converts to Bixby-
Scriabin, we did not question. This did not mean that we believed him. With his wild blue eyes, his dramatically high
cheekbones—a legacy from a Welsh grandfather and an American Indian grandmother—he compelled suspension of dis-
belief. We suspended, willingly.

Two days later, after my creative writing class, there was Bixby
waiting for me.
"I heard the story you read," he said. "You're going to be
good."
"I don't know," I said.
"I know. Listen, lend me eighteen bucks, will you. I've got
to see somebody," he said mysteriously. The oddness of the
number disarmed me. I complied.
"Thanks," he said. "I'll give it back to you tomorrow at my
office." Office? There was, then, a daytime Bixby?
The office turned out to be *Cosmos Science Fiction Magazine.* Now as solid as the Smithsonian Institution, *Cosmos* was
then struggling to be heard, as was science fiction, itself. Bixby
was passionate about this, as about so many things. Sur-

rounded by empty typewriter chairs and desks—it was the end
of the work day—he expatiated on his science fiction-Marxist
vision. Karl Marx and Fredrich Engels had sounded the first
note in *The Communist Manifesto*. The note of the unreality
of modern experience. If I was going to be a writer—and I was,
Bixby had decided—I had better listen to that note.

"Unreality," I said. "Marx and Engels?" It was as close as I
could come to a challenge. I was on uncertain ground. Because
of a certain secret involving my family, I had never read much
by the big Marxist thinkers, including Numero Uno, the big
K.M. himself. It was an inhibition I think you'll understand
later on; around page 270, I think.

But now, the word "unreality" seemed to light a fire under
Bixby. He leaped up and ran up and down the room past a
row of jumbled books. Finally he extricated a ragged soft-
covered book—as much pamphlet as book—and opened it.

"Listen to this," he said. He read:

*Constant revolutionizing of production, uninterrupted dis-
turbance of all social relations, everlasting uncertainty and
agitation, distinguish the bourgeois epoch from all earlier
times.*

He waved the book at me like a flag. "Do you know what
this means for a writer?"

"It sounds—"

Schmuck! If I was going to be a Bixby-born writer I should
learn to recognize a rhetorical question when I heard one.
Bixby poured on.

"Get this: *All fixed, fast-frozen relationships, with their
train of venerable ideas and opinions, are swept away, all new-
formed ones become obsolete before they can ossify.*

"And here's the kicker. *All that is solid melts into air, all that
is holy is profaned, and men at last are forced to face with so-
ber senses the real conditions of their lives and their relations
with their fellow men.*

"Look how exciting Marx makes the bourgeois period. *Unreality*, my ass. All that is solid melts into air, all that is holy
is profaned . . . "

"Then you think I should read Marx—"

"God, no." He tossed the little book at me. I shoved it into my pocket like an obedient student. "You'll probably get stuck on the labor theory of value and Hegelian dialectics. Worst thing in the world for you at this stage. I want you to hear their mysterious song. Understand?"

I did not, of course, in any conventional way. But I was learning from Bixby the way youth learns best — by the communicated passion and person of the teacher. "There was a touch in your story, yesterday. The part where the man dies in the synagogue, killed by prayers. That fantasy moment is your key."

Such enthusiasm was impossible to fight. I must not, however, Bixby warned me, go commercial. Most of Sci-Fi was junk. BEMs and SO (Bug-Eyed Monsters and Space Opera). I must read Arthur C. Clarke, a young writer named Ray Bradbury, the books of Charles Fort. The glorious conversation climaxed with an offer to submit my story to *Cosmos* for publication. Then Bixby asked if he could return twelve of the eighteen dollars he'd borrowed the day before and owe me six. The modern artist, he added, as he handed me the ten dollar bill and two singles, is the first ever to have to create from his own insides. The center does not hold, no foundation all the way down the line. What the artist needed to survive in addition to silence, exile, and cunning was a direct line to his time. That line was to be fantasy and science fiction. And the best kept secret of our day was that Karl Marx was one of the great modernists along with Joyce, Proust and Valery. I had read neither Yeats nor Saroyan, neither Joyce nor Marx, so I got none of his references. I simply nodded and went home to type up my story for editorial submission and to think about silence, exile, cunning, and art, none of which I had thought much about before. It seemed to me though, as if I had been secretly thinking these thoughts for years. It may have been truth or it may have been the music of Bixby's passion. To dwell on that at the moment seemed to me, to be missing the point.

Lying in bed that night I opened the beat-up *Manifesto* at random. I read: *Modern bourgeois society, a society that has conjured up such mighty means of production and exchange is like the sorcerer who can no longer control the powers of the underworld that he has called up by his spells.*

I felt my skin ripple with eerie anxiety. Perhaps because Bixby had told me, specifically, not to read what I had just read. Or perhaps it was the Frankensteinian imagery. The whole question of 'productivity' was a family mystery. In the Vienna from which my parents had come, anyone with enough nerve, luck and some relatives to supply capital, could do well in a small business: jewelry, factoring (the lending of money to textile manufacturers to get through a season)—anything. When they got to America this family was crazy enough to ignore the post-war phenomenon of the college education. With the exception of my older brother who went to medical school, everyone else seemed to be floating around in a vague soup of small business hopes. Petit-bourgeois indeed.

It's difficult to express the particular sort of cultural/money mixture that makes up a certain kind of second-generation family life. Perhaps it was only my special family-plant which flourished on Mosholu Parkway in the Bronx. Daily life seemed to be all about values: education, decency, old-fashioned, traditional liberal Jewish politics . . . But the latent content, the substructure was an immense, all-pervading anxiety, a rage, about and for money.

Don't get the wrong idea—there wasn't any money around—at least not at first. But in the unreal life of the Anxiety of Affluence, a ten dollar bill will stand in perfectly well for ten thousand dollar bills. My grandmother taught herself to read English by reading the Scott Moncrieff translation of Proust. Eccentric but admirable in a seventy-year-old Austrian refugee. Yet, when my father wished to restart his career as a businessman all over again, in America—retail jewelry—she loaned him the starting money at the prevailing interest rate, prime plus two points. More like Balzac than Proust you might say. But sensibility was sensibility and money was money: as simple as that.

Not so simple to me. When it filtered down to me, the whole question of money had an eerie aura about it. *Money* . . . The word spoken or implied had deep reservoirs of unspoken power—and along with it—danger. This may have been connected with an extraordinary incident involving my father's younger brother, Irving.

My family had specialized in an exquisite confusion of values. Study the violin, read books, learn, and above all make a good living, marry, and raise a family. Art, culture, money, and family were what life was all about. All unspoken but clear. Clear as mud—so I dismissed them all by age fourteen. The exception was my Uncle Irving, the outlaw Voltaire, the Thomas Mann of Attorney Street to whom employment did not come naturally, the black sheep of the family, who had devised a sort of personal extra-legal, aesthetic and economic philosophy.

"Look, kid," he said, "nobody owns nothing. Everybody is born—they grow up, they walk down the streets of the world and they see buildings, stores, cars, barrels, trucks, signs—sometimes farms or mountainsides and, since you're human, it all seems to belong to you. Even if it did—which it probably doesn't—you're going to die sooner or later—probably sooner—and then it's not going to belong to you *again*! So the trick is: *act as if it does! Use the illusion!* People only have to believe you for a little while, if your luck holds out. This, my boy, is as true for the average American Jew as it was for J.P. Morgan or Jenny Grossinger. At the start, anyway."

So much for theory. But my Uncle Irving believed in the unity of theory and practice as much as any orthodox Marxist. (You understand, I knew none of these slick left-wing terms at the time. I learned them later when Manishin made it a condition of our continuing courtship for me to attend the Jefferson School [formerly the Workers' School] on East Sixteenth Street.) What Uncle Irving did next was exemplary. He was the manager of a cigar store—retail sales being the only refuge of the willfully uneducated. He bet the store on the World Series—and lost. This would not have been as bad as it turned out, except for the fact that he did not *own* the cigar store, he'd only *acted* as if he'd owned it. Consistent, my Uncle Irving, as perhaps no philosopher has been before or since.

And, some people, professional gamblers, had believed him

for the little while he'd asked. But not long enough. The men he'd bet with did not have a philosophic turn of mind. They called on my father to find out where his brother was hiding.

"Forget it," my father said, "he hasn't got a dime."

"We know," one of them with a sense of humor said, "The dime he doesn't have is ours."

"Look," another one said, "He bet with us and won for months. The first time he loses he cops a big one—and he welches."

"He got overconfident," my father said. "He's an immigrant like me, an idealist. Couldn't believe the Brooklyn Dodgers could lose."

"He told us he owned the store. Some idealist?"

"He'd like to own it," my father explained patiently. "That's what idealism is, as opposed to materialism, where you *really* own it. He'd run it better, too, believe me."

"Look, we don't want to kill anybody. Maybe just work him over a little. A lesson to others. That's a promise."

I recall my father's fine moment of dignity. He stood slowly, at the rickety kitchen table and placed his hands before him, flat down, like a lawyer.

"I have a photographic memory," he said carefully. "One hand on him and you're all in jail."

When Irving returned from exile in New Jersey, months later, I told him some of the highlights of the conversation. He seized, at first, on what I thought was an odd, minor point.

"Your dad was right," he said. "That *should* have been my store. A great location and Greenblatt does nothing with it. No in-store promotion, no outdoor advertising. Just waits for people to come by for a cigar, a pack of cigarettes, a Zippo lighter. I tell you, if I'd won, I would have bought the place from Greenblatt and turned it into a winner."

"But it wasn't yours," I said, stupid with literal morality. "How could you bet it as if you owned it?"

Instead of getting angry, Irving reached over and hugged me. He was skinny and bony, a little like Bixby. All the people who have exhorted me about life, over the years, have been like skeletons, for some reason.

"It's a comfort, kid. A great comfort. I mean you appropriate something for yourself, from all the things in the world around you — you pick something and you say — mine! Even if it doesn't finally work out — it makes you feel less helpless. Babies don't know any better and they do it, right? Mine, mine . . . And maybe nobody should. But it's a torment — a world full of money and music and women and vicuna jackets and foreign cars. Your average person has to do *something* to feel better. Do you understand that?"

I hadn't. But I tried to now, faced with the new electricity of Bixby's injunction to use my family's cash-craziness. *All that is solid melts into air.* . . . I began to sketch out a story, something growing out of Irving and his special approach to private property. As for myself, I had neither money, nor cashmere blankets nor cars — my only music came from Bixby and his Scriabin-piano and my woman was a somewhat unsatisfactory young Army officer I'd picked up in Central Park during a rainstorm.

In those days my connections with women seemed to have a built-in time limit. Some would burst brightly in less than a month, for non-reasons: temperament, sudden travel arrangements, entropy. Others would gradually develop cracks and flaws based on "real" differences and dissolve in nine months or less. Those seemed to be the magic numbers: one month or nine. It rarely troubled me. Love was not covered by the G.I. Bill.

That night I lay in bed next to the current connection, Marie Sullivan, a recently discharged WAC who spoke in her sleep all night; spoke in some indecipherable tongue. While she spoke I turned over what Bixby had said. I remembered my Uncle Irving and his bony hungry smile. The next day after typing up my story and mailing it to *Cosmos*, I sat down to write a new story for that week's class. Strange images were sucked from my typewriter's keys onto the paper. My imagination seemed to come from someone else. Odder than Scriabin in waltz-time, a story shaped itself in less than a day. Based on Irving the outcast, it exalted him as the metaphysical outsider, ennobled his passion for gambling and sang a sweet mystical song of criminality. When I read it to the class I was astonished when, at the end, there was a pause, then a smack of applause cracked the air. That finished me off. Or, rather, started me off. For the next six months I swam in a sea of productivity, with Bixby at my side. *Cosmos* rejected the first story but by the time I received the form letter it touched me not at all. I was already deep into Joyce, Flaubert, H.G. Wells, Wilkie Collins, Henry James, and Mme. Blavatsky. The mixture of great moderns and trash mysticism was just right for my unravished mind and new talents.

In the meantime Bixby kept touching me for modest, odd-numbered sums of money, none of which ever quite got paid back. Tight as I was for cash, as we all were in those days, it seemed a small price to pay for Bixby's infusion of energy and point into my life. I began sending stories out to the little magazines. Needing more sleep for this energetic new life, I moved out of Marie Sullivan's apartment; her sleep-talking tolled my sleep too much. Besides, by this time Bixby had her into Dianetics and there were meetings in the apartment at all hours when I wanted to work. Bixby was living there too, having as it turned out no fixed home of his own.

"Bixby is for fun, for listening to at the piano. But you have to admit he's weird." Mettro had doubts. I admitted nothing. Fond of Mettro as I was, I had doubts about *him*. His public relations education had already yielded some freelance jobs. Khaki pants had given way to slacks and sport coats. There was a lot less talk about Paris. The Gauloises had given way to Pall Malls. Mettro had always been my connection to reality. After all, anybody who could take apart a car and put it back together again had to be in touch with things as they are. If there was a point to Mettro it was a kind of easy-going practicality to daily life. But Mettro's point had collided with Bixby's, somewhere in my floating soul of the time. For the moment Bixby's point was sharper, though Mettro's impinged more each day. For one thing, I was being thrown out of the Art Students' League for demonstrable lack of talent, as well as absenteeism which reached a new high, post-Bixby. For another, I had only one more year left on the G.I. Bill. Mettro's reality would soon be breathing hard on the neck of Bixby's imagination. So much for Bixby and Mettro. It is time for Manishin.

Here is Manishin greeting us at the door at eight-fifteen P.M. on Wednesday, April 23, nineteen forty-eight. She is quite small, looks up at me and Mettro, the whole top part of her drenched in long, red hair. Beneath all the hair you could see a kind of Mexican patterned shawl and a determined smile.

"Hey, I'm Manishin," she said. "The game hasn't started yet?"

Ah, Manishin, Barbara Manishin, hippie and feminist before your time, Beat Generation twenty years too early, smoker of marijuana when it was still called "tea" and "mary jane," raiser of two daughters according to the principles of George Bernard Shaw, the game had indeed just started; the longest game either of us would ever play. While Mettro helped Bixby and a few others set up the chips in neat piles on the table, I suddenly had an inkling as to where those peculiar sums of money Bixby had been borrowing for months had gone. Manishin and I spoke. It was one of those first conversations that happen, I think, only in New York. Intimacies and epiphanies tumbled over each other in the first rush of realizing we found each other interesting, or at least attractive. Questions brought answers not evasions; statements brought surprises.

"Why do you call yourself Manishin—your last name."

"Hey," she said. Manishin seemed to enjoy getting your attention with that silly word. "Hey, it's my father's name. Women are given women's names to keep them in their place. I haven't decided my place yet, so I'm Manishin not Barbara. What do you do?"

"I'm a writer."

I'd never said that before. It startled the hell out of me. So much so, in fact, that I poured out Bixby's dream of revitalizing the modern tradition by the Marxist magic of fantasy and science fiction.

"Yes," Manishin said. "I know all about it."

"You do?"

"Sure. Bixby sings beautiful songs. I like him."

"Do you—are you—have you?" I stumbled.

"Not anymore. We tried it. Then I got married to a nice man—turned out to be a forger. I have two daughters and I'm going to NYU Law School. Want a toke? It's good tea. How about you and women. What goes?" Her abruptness compelled some kind of honesty. I told her all the fragments of my fragmentary life with women for the last two years. I told her the peculiar development of each affair—the gradual involvement, the movement towards intimacy, the dropping of the guard, the slow moving in of shirts, underwear, records, books; then traced the beginning of each provocation in a variety of shapes and sizes.

Lilla, the red-headed Quaker girl who spent Saturdays and Sundays copying the Caravaggios at the Metropolitan Museum and all week long was an executive secretary on Wall Street. I borrowed three-hundred dollars from her, seriously questioned Quakerism as religious thought, and never returned the money—until after she'd sent me packing.

I told her of Jamie, the lovely pre-Raphaelite actress who wanted to marry me and have children at once . . . and how I teased her with promises of reform, of getting out of bed early in the morning . . . of getting a job, renting an apartment, opening an account with the New York Telephone Company; promises all welshed on as Jamie's delicate features, her soft gray eyes and light-line mouth grew weary and finally bitter. Then, one day, she vanished with a road company of Saint Joan and left me alone once again.

All these fragments poured out to Manishin. She nodded her small, oval, red-haired noggin wisely and smiled that knowing smile women have when they see a point you have not seen yet seen.

The cards might have been Tarot cards for all the sense I could make out of them that night. I was entirely enchanted by the red-haired elf who counted out her chips and, businesslike, plunged into poker, dealing, raising, bluffing. For many months I had allowed women as little time and attention as possible. I had preferred their conversation to be on the order of Marie Sullivan's—my sleep talking former soldier.

Now, instead of counting my cards I was counting the minutes, the hours, until I could walk Manishin home.

All of the players appeared to be science fiction writers, editors, and patients or practitioners of Dianetics as well as Marxists of one persuasion or another—often not clear which—a poker game as much a scrimmage of beliefs as it was of chance and bluff. It was one of those evenings that burned itself up in the energies and conflicts of the players. Prickly, edgy, competitive—like the science students I'd known in high school—they badgered and bit at each other's styles and souls until an eruption was inevitable.

The fight, itself, when it came, started because someone accused the host of cutting the pot for more money than was needed to pay for the sandwiches and coffee. From there it moved to angry ideological small-talk. The small talk became shouts and the shouts became fists with astonishing speed.

"Twenty bucks for seven sandwiches?"

"It's my apartment. I maintain it. That takes money and work. So I get an extra cut. It's the labor theory of value."

"It's sophistry, otherwise known as bullshit. If you're basing the extra cut on land ownership—you're talking Henry George and the single tax theory. This is the kind of doubletalk they dished out at the Moscow trials."

"The Moscow trials were necessary to cleanse the revolution."

"Cleanse? They were filthy set-ups. How can you defend them?"

"Those guys—Bukharin and Zinoviev had to be guilty. Otherwise, why didn't they defend themselves?"

"Don't ask me. Read *Darkness At Noon*."

"The pot's light. Somebody didn't ante."

"Not me. And how can you defend Stalin—betrayer of Communism?"

"Who's to say what Communism really is?"

"It's been said. 'Soviet power plus rural electrification equals communism.'"

"I can't believe you said that."

"I didn't. Lenin did."

"I raise."

"You can't! There's a limit. Three raises."

"A bourgeois convention. See my raise or get out!"

"Get out? I'll throw *you* out first!"

Chips started to fly, chairs were turned over. It was the Marxist New York version of a western. Before anybody could shoot out the lights, Bixby appeared at my elbow, eyes wide with revelation.

"You see," he said. "This is what I warned you about." He ducked to avoid a stream of chips followed by a shower of pastrami.

"Listen," he said, "you don't belong with these people." He seemed to have forgotten that I was there at his invitation. "This is what their so-called revolutionary imaginations come down to—this earthbound Socialism. Go home and write. Create a socialism of the imagination. MAKE IT NEW!" With that he threw himself into the fight with a fine Welsh-Indian rage and Manishin, Mettro, and I fled.

My God! No one had ever said, "Make it new" to me before that moment. And, since Ezra Pound had not been invited to my Bar Mitzvah, there was no way for me to know that Bixby was, to put it kindly, "adapting." It didn't matter. Bixby was bringing me the news of the twentieth century—and if it was coming late in the game, it was certainly at the beginning of *my* game.

We left Mettro at the Sheridan Square subway station and walked west to Hudson Street where Manishin lived. We exchanged lives, as young people do on such impromptu occasions. I remember nothing of all she told me and we stayed up talking until the morning tugs hooted into the Hudson dawn—except for one tale. She told me of her grandmother in Odessa—a ferocious revolutionary in her heart—Manishin's model. She'd joined every subterranean organization for change she could find—while bearing eight children; seven boys and one golden girl. One Friday afternoon she'd rushed home from a secret political meeting, in a desperate hurry to prepare the Sabbath meal in time for sundown. It was May and her four-year-old golden girl was playing with her playmates; there was a Maypole and she had been Queen of the May. Then, flushed with excitement, she ran home. Her mother was sitting in the kitchen peeling potatoes. The little girl ran up to her, her face covered with a fine dew of perspiration; she was happily out of breath. Then, a smile of delight on her face, she laid her small head on her mother's lap—and died.

Manishin told it to me in wonder. One moment alive, Queen-of-the-May young; the next moment gone, her head on her mother's unsuspecting lap. She even shaped the tale for me as she told it: the awful intrusion of irrational death into rational political life.

"Engels breaks your heart writing about the exploitation of working-class children in the industrial nations," she said. "They die awful, early deaths, too. But this was full of extra mystery." In a thousand years, Manishin mused, sadly, after we've won all the battles, after each person is giving according to his abilities and each is receiving according to his needs—a child could still come back to her mother's lap to rest from play—and die.

"Hey," she said, trying to break the mood, "that's no excuse for child labor. It's just some extra mystery."

I walked home that morning, balancing this delicate tale on the one hand and Bixby's mad admonition on the other. Politics and fantasy. I wrote the story in two days and I knew as I wrote it that it would change my life one way or another. I knew Bixby would be delighted with it. But when I searched him out to show it to him—he was gone. My former night-talker Marie told me he'd left for the coast.

"He owes me three-hundred and sixty dollars," she said. "Your friend."

"Don't blame him on me," I said. "Besides, he owes me a hundred and eighty."

"Why does he always ask for these odd numbers?"

"Damned if I know."

"Listen," Marie said. "It's lonely here now. Do you want to stay over?"

"I can't," I said, though I could have, and instead went over to Mettro's place. I had a hunch I might find Bixby there. Somehow in those young days everyone's place seemed to be for friends, acquaintances, encounters, even friends of friends, to hole up in. The grown-up bourgeois notion of your "home" as exclusive rather than inclusive came much later. Even so Bixby was running out of places to shack up. Mettro might be the last. I'd guessed right. Bixby was there, (Mettro wasn't) — and he was packing.

"What's up?" I asked.

"I'm getting out of here."

"To where?"

"The coast."

I sat down, as confused as the sprawl of luggage on the bed.

"Why west?"

"Because the East is played out." As always Bixby spoke in prophetic tones.

"But how about the life you've gotten me into?"

Bixby stopped packing the pounds of khaki underwear; (He had actually been folding khaki handkerchiefs.). "Time, please," he muttered, "It's time . . ." wasting his quotation on me, who had never played darts in an English pub and had not read *The Wasteland*. Both of which, of course, Bixby had triumphantly done. And for the next ten minutes I tried to decipher the lyrics of Bixby's departure-song.

It was time apparently for me to give up the fantasy motif and recognize the secret of my family's dirty little secret: what Marx called "the callous cash nexus." The story about my Uncle Irving and the betting of the cigar store he did not own had made an impression — even though *Cosmos* had turned it down. It was time for me to recognize the criminality of the petty-bourgeoisie which was my family's legacy.

"Your big temptation is going to be the cash nexus. Fight it! You could be the first real Marxist modernist. But it means you may have to learn to eat rocks. The bourgeois culture is not going to reward you with money for trying to replace it with something better. Don't listen to Mettro."

"He hasn't said a word."

"Wait! He's developing a revisionist theory of the *Manifesto.*"

"I thought he was getting into public relations."

"Both! They will intersect, soon. The trick is for you not to be standing exactly where they meet. It's all going to be about money. Hold fast!"

"Are you giving up the struggle?"

He stopped packing and sat down next to me.

"I need sunshine, the doctor says. I have diabetes." The connection between a sugar and insulin imbalance and the California sun escaped me. I didn't press it.

"Do you remember what I told you about —"

"Yes?"

"About how I couldn't — you know — have sex?"

"I heard, I forgot from who. But Manishin said that you and she —"

"Manishin," Bixby said, "was a misunderstanding. We both tried hard to penetrate and we were both afraid to yield so it all got mixed up and we didn't know who should do what to whom or how . . ."

"Sounds a mess."

"What a mess. But that was before she married her *gonif* and started a new life." I was feeling something unpleasant in my stomach, my place where jealousy has always lodged. It was a strong, painful sensation. But not strong enough to erase my identity as the eternally agreeable, ambitious acolyte, "Okay," I said. "But you haven't read this new story."

Bixby paused to pop a handful of vitamins past the important presence of his Adam's apple.

"Listen," he said. "Can you lend me ninety dollars?" I did some fast figuring. That would leave me about thirty dollars till the end of the month. I was helpless before Bixby. But I also couldn't resist asking him the basis for the odd needs that always seemed to require sums divisible by eighteen.

"Didn't I tell you?" he said as he folded the check into his shirt pocket, "that my Grandmother was Jewish and eighteen is the numerical equivalent for life: *Chai?* A sacred number."

"Welsh, you said your grandmother was Welsh."
I was growing panicky dealing with a vanishing Bixby. He seemed to be growing less substantial every minute, both in the present and in his past history. He had never carved out much air and space for the eyes to hold onto. Which may have been why it was so important to me that his history should hold up under scrutiny. Bixby, a skinny dancer-on-air, player of Scriabin siren-songs on his piano and on my needy imagination.

"Oh," he smiled a thin khaki-smile. "That was my other grandmother."

"She was Indian, you said."
He snapped the suitcase shut and sat down, suddenly.

"My father's father married a lot of women. I didn't know them all. But one of them was Jewish. Anyway, I'm good and scared.

Fear and Bixby: an impossible combination! He was the Fred Astaire, the Simon Templar of combined commitment and insouciance. It turned out that what he was terrified of was flying. So much for the Air Force officer's cap he'd rakishly sported since we'd met. These contradictions, these strands of not-quite-truths or imagined truths gleaming in the midst of Bixby's quotidian Marxist ordinary truth did not throw me. Was he a part-Jew who had slept with my night-talking WAC, Marie as well as my past, present and future Manishin, or was he an impotent Welsh-Indian, self-taught pianist with a knack for science fiction, a passion for a mysterious brand of his own literary Marxist modernism, and a flying phobia? Did anyone in their youth have a more comic-book Master?

Bixby, creator of an impossible socialism, is going to California to dream.

I left him sitting amid luggage and anxieties with a copy of my story in his hand. From a street phone I called Manishin and arranged to be invited over for a drink—or as it turned out—to begin the second installment of what was to be an endless courtship.

I picked up a bottle of Polish vodka with a spear of buffalo grass in it—my only addiction. It was one hundred proof. I wasn't sure if the extra proof was for me or for Manishin.

"The last time I was here the poker got pretty intense."

"Hey, that wasn't poker. That was ideology."

"Tough game. It's harder to tell who wins and who loses."

"Easier to cheat at, too. Thanks for this vodka. It tastes weird but nice."

"It's the grass, I think. And maybe some chemicals."

She was dressed in various shades of red and her red hair, I now saw, came down to her waist. There were flowering plants and Ivy everywhere. I'd never seen so many plants outside of a greenhouse where I once had a summer job.

I came right out with what was on my mind. Either because I was falling in love or because I was young.

"I just saw Bixby. You and he were a big thing, right?"

"Wrong."

"Aha."

"Bixby is fantasy, I'm science fiction. You can't have a big thing with a fantasy."

"Not to mention his famous organ problem."

"Yes—I would say not to mention that."

"Discretion? Delicacy?"

"Maybe it's fantasy . . ."

"He's vanishing. I just saw him."

"I know. A restless soul."

"Listen, we stayed up all night, you and me—after that crazy poker game."

"You and I."

"The two of us."

She swigged some of the greenish vodka and said: "I'm going to Columbia Law School. I'm preparing myself to be very precise. I'm going to be a judge, someday. A judge has to be very precise.

"When was the last time you stayed up all night with somebody?"

"Hey—" she said. "Hey. You're stuck in a groove! Jealousy

is just a claiming of private property. Even an ordinary, every-day Capitalist knows you have to acquire the property first. You going to be jealous of Bixby and every other man I ever went with—at this stage? Why don't you just kiss me, first. Let's do things in order!"

Great idea! It was one of those first kisses that comes loaded with promise. I mean it felt like a thousandth kiss. When we started gasping for oxygen, Manishin reached up and pulled her red shift over her head.

And that's not what astonished me. Not just her apparent willingness. What got to me was: she was *naked*. She'd been sitting there, a Columbia Law School student, independent mother of two little girls, wearing no underwear, in nineteen forty-nine. In the days and months to come, Manishin was to make a hundred, a thousand political statements about men, women, private property, freedom, and the origins of the family and the state. But none of it equaled the pure political intensity of pulling that red, cotton sheath over her head, to reveal that slender, boyish body, cup-like breasts with tiny, dark red aureoles prickly with the flow of air or desire. And after our first kiss!

"I want to marry you," I murmured.

"Why? Because we stayed up all night, talking?"

"Because we're perfect together."

"As simple as that?" She had not stopped kissing me since I'd asked her to marry me. I was standing there fully dressed, she was naked. It was weird. But not as weird as what happened next. She grabbed my hand and pulled me into the adjoining room. Books cluttered the floor, the walls, a desk in the corner facing the summer buzz of Second Avenue.

Manishin ran along the wall running her hand across the spines of books until she found the one she wanted. More naked waiting—shuffling and thumbing of pages and then: aha! She read, in her loud, clear Manishin-voice:

"Although romantic idealists generally insist on self-surrender as an indispensable element in true womanly love . . ."

"Hey," I said borrowing her favorite expletive, "what is that book? I never said anything about surrender . . ."

Like all smart teachers, dressed or undressed, she knew
enough to ignore student interruptions.

"*. . . its repulsive effect is well-known and feared in practice
by both sexes . . .*"

"What . . . ?"

"*Love loses its charm when it is not free; and whether the
compulsion is that of custom and law, or of infatuation, the
effect is the same . . .* Here—" she gestured the book at me
like a conductor's baton. "He says, *It becomes valueless and
even abhorrent, like the caresses of a maniac . . .*"

In a matter of moments I'd gone from being a welcomed
present or future lover to a caressing maniac. Who was this
son-of-a-bitch she was reading to me? I tried to grab the book
to see, but she danced away. Some of her long, bright red hair
trailed over the page and she flipped it off, impatiently, over
her shoulder.

"Here it is," she said. "Here: *The intense repugnance inspired by the compulsory character of the legalized conjugal
relation that leads, first to the idealization of marriage whilst
it remains indispensable as a means of perpetuating society;
then to its modification by divorce . . .*"

I got hold of the book. "Whilst?" was all I could think of
to complain about. "What writer uses a word like 'whilst?' "
She had the book back in a second. It was clear who was in
charge.

You'd think I would have taken offense at the mention of
divorce only a few undressed minutes after our first kiss and
my proposal of marriage. But, no, all I could think of was the
damned foreign-sounding foolishness of 'whilst.'

"It's British for 'while,' " she said. "This is George Bernard
Shaw. My hero. Look how he finishes off the idea of marriage
with a metaphor: *Marriage is thus, by force of circumstances,
compelled to buy extension of life by extension of divorce,
much as if a fugitive should try to delay a pursuing wolf by
throwing portions of his own heart to it.*"

"Isn't that beautiful—a kind of Marxian poetry."

She tossed the book at me. It smelled of her perfume, now;

something very light and flowery; very Manishin. The book was *The Quintessence of Ibsenism*. I wonder if I was to have it to keep and put beside Bixby's copy of *The Communist Manifesto*.

"He makes the same point in Major Barbara," Manishin said. "I'll take you to see the movie. Rex Harrison is wonderful."

"If you want me to stop asking you to marry me, you'd better lend me the book. And don't tell me how wonderful other men are."

"Take it," she said putting her arms around me. "I don't believe in private property anyway."

We collapsed into an even longer kiss than the first.

"You know, we're in the bedroom," she said. She kicked the couch next to us. "This opens up."
Suddenly nervous, I said, "Where are the kids?"

"Trotskyite sleepaway camp. Two weeks."
I began to fumble with furniture and while I was pulling I said, "What pushed you to where you are? How'd you get to all this politics about men and marriage?"

"I was so miserable being married. When you're that miserable you weep and weep—and when your eyes calm down and clear up, you read. A friend gave me a pamphlet called "Lenin on the Woman Question." By the time I was divorced, I'd worn out three hardcover copies."

"Listen," I said. "Forget Lenin, forget Bernard Shaw, Manishin. Marry me."

"I'd rather die," Manishin said, kissing me passionately and struggling with the knot in my tie at the same time.

It seemed she instinctively knew the point of my amorous *vita interrupta* with all the women in my post-war life. A point which, if it existed, I had missed thus far. But, like all good analysts, like all good prophets, she taught only by indirection, by example. Her method in my case, consisted of loving me very calmly, studying carefully for her law boards, making no demands, lending me no money, and refusing to respond to any provocations. Nothing I did could make her either leave

me or marry me. It was maddening! She was entirely—in the
early fifties, imagine—her own woman. And she insisted that
I be my own man. It was no use my telling her that parallel
lines meet only in infinity. That was an old wives' tale. Parallel
lives, she said, were the only ones that could meet in the present. So, I made my own way in the present the best way I
could.

I wrote stories, I planned novels, I read the peculiar mixture
of great modernists and questionable freaks that constitute
the influences prescribed by the vanished Bixby. (I'd learned
from the G.I. Bill grapevine that Bixby had actually fled to the
Coast chased by an angry husband who refused to believe his
tales of impotence.) In any case, his exhortations of me had
'taken' like an injection of some magical elixir. The story of the
Queen of the May was accepted by *The New Yorker*. I stopped
drawing; I stopped dancing. To hell with the G.I. Bill. I was
a writer! Obeying the prophet of Scriabin, I did not squabble
over pennies: I wrote. I saw few pennies. *The New Yorker* publication was the first and last sale. The rest of the stories I wrote
were given away, mostly to magazines bearing the names of
states or localities; *The Colorado Quarterly* cherished my
work; *The Southern Review* allowed me below the Mason-
Dixon literary line; *The Antioch Review* paid me in copies of
the magazine. Nevertheless, I was talked about sometimes in
oddly Bixby-ish terms; one article mentioned me as a link between the early English line of fantasy and the modernist
movement. Heady stuff like that. Interestingly, Marx was never
mentioned.

Until I showed up on Mettro's doorstep, one early spring
evening (Is it my imagination or was my youth entirely composed of spring and summer evenings?) to touch the most successful member of our little band for a loan. It was the second
anniversary of my first meeting with Manishin and a celebration was indicated—but the means were not.
I explained this to Mettro who was most understanding.

"It was only a question of time," he said, ladling out the cost of dinner for two at a Village restaurant and maybe a cab home, afterwards, mostly in singles—a heavy wad.

"What do you mean?"

"I mean you've been a prisoner of Bixby's romanticism for long enough." He had forked over the money and was now shining his shoes; Mettro, the only shiner of shoes or, indeed, wearer of shined shoes, I can remember from that un-shiny time.

"A voluntary prisoner," I said, defending Bixby by defending myself. "And pretty productive."

"Marx said—" (the first time I'd heard the name fall from Mettro's lips) "that Bixby's beloved Bourgeoisie had a special genius for wringing the profit out of thinkers and artists. Well, where's your profit?" Before I could perform one of my specialties, which was the answering of rhetorical questions, he held up his hand. "No mystery," he said. "You've just been ignoring the one form created by and for the bourgeoisie: *the novel.*"

"I've been writing short stories."

"Right. For elegant little non-paying magazines. Besides, your kind of literary modern short story is an expressive device, the novel in the marketplace is a fungible artifact. That means it can be an effective medium of exchange. . . . The cash nexus—don't be a schmuck—it goes for art the same as for industrial enterprises."

"Will I find that in *The Communist Manifesto?*"

"Look at that shine," Mettro said. "It's like a mirror. You can see your face in it."

I took this to mean 'no.' Bixby's warning that Mettro was preparing a cash-rich revisionist theory had been right on the button.

Which would have cooled me off on Mettro except that he had apparently read my story about Irving the Outcast; not only had read it but thought it would make a novel that would sell. The trick about any era, Mettro said, the bourgeois one included, was to survive it.

Crammed with pasta, overflowing with wine, love and lust for Manishin, after our Mettro-financed anniversary celebration, I returned to my typewriter and began my novel, *The Doctor Faustus of Rivington Street*. It took me seven months to turn a tense, ironic short story into a sprawling Lower East Side novel with demonic overtones. Mettro introduced me to Martha Maxwell, a sharp-tongued, sharp-suited young woman who was an editor at Random House. I thought she might be a lesbian. But I was on guard against received ideas—and she might simply have been the first young businesswoman I ever saw who wore a different suit each time we met.

"I love the manuscript," she said. "It needs work—but I think it is just the answer to the pseudo-moralities which are flooding the marketplace, after the recent unpleasantness (that's the war—a joke—Ha, I said.) Everybody has a moral or political philosophy to sell, except your character Oscar (read Irving. I'd naturally changed the name to protect the guilty.) He's the only man in contemporary literature who has a kind of ontological approach to Making It. Betting that cigar store is like Gide's Gratuitous Act in *The Counterfeiters*. Have you read *The Counterfeiters*?"

"No," I said. "Will my book sell?"

"If I have anything to say about it, it will," said Martha the Mouth as Mettro called her. I assumed he was referring to her verbal energies. Astonishingly, Random House put their money where Martha's mouth was. They accepted the novel and paid me two thousand dollars as an advance. I was in the world, at last.

But disaster and disappointment led the way to publication. Halfway through, Martha Maxwell quit to to go to McGraw-Hill and nobody at the publishers seemed to know who or what I was, after that. The reviews were amazing. They understood me perfectly. I was invited to live and write at a writers' colony on the west coast. Only the sales failed to arrive. Three thousand copies. I was left, owing the publisher about a thousand dollars. Thus, I was slightly lower on the cash nexus scale than I'd been before.

Mettro's revisionist theory had failed me—or I had failed it; it was not clear which.

While this was going on I pursued Manishin in and out of bed, into dreams of permanence and on into frustration. She loved me but was having none of it. Marriage, she chanted, was the end of friendship. Permanence was a confession of the failure of individual moments. It was useless for me to complain that witty, depressing epigrams were no substitute for happiness. If she wanted to put an end to one or another of my campaigns Manishin had only to point out that rebuilding the modern tradition in literature boiled no pots, fed no children. (Though she was by this time clerking for a judge in Brooklyn and could look forward to a good salary as a lawyer.)

"If men shouldn't support women anymore, neither should women make children out of men by supporting them." She had more theories than I had strength.

"Furthermore," she added, "I have two kids in private school."

"And if I *could* support them . . . ?"

"It wouldn't make marriage less of a master/slave relationship. We're alert to each other, physically and emotionally. It's terrific! We have everything husbands and wives have except the detachment that comes from constant exposure, and my taking care of your laundry."

"Is that Shaw again," I sniffed a point I was only partially getting.

"Partly," Manishin said.

"I can't stand this," I said. "The other man in my life is in his eighties and has a small, gray, pointed beard."

I gave up for the moment and followed Bixby to the coast. I carried with me my Bixby-born seriousness of purpose, my noisy silence, my portable exile, and my financial cunning to a writer's colony in the Pacific Palisades Mountains; scattered cottages, rolling lawns, a swimming pool, and hot noons as still as graveyards.

It was a paradise of sorts; one of those places run by a foundation and established by somebody who, in his lifetime, worshipped art and the artist. Such philanthropists are superb artists at Missing the Point. By setting up sylvan retreats where writers will be entirely undisturbed, they exquisitely miss the point that writers wish for nothing so much as to be disturbed. Of course they also want the food and shelter such places contribute. But they would much rather have it sent to them in the form of cash—at their home address. However, since the terms of the will were otherwise, I went west. I had no idea where Bixby was. Mettro had joined the West Coast exodus a year before. Southern California, he'd told me as farewell, is the fatherland of public relations. The slacks and sport coats that had replaced Army surplus khaki pants had given way to three button gray suits. The forties were over. The fifties had arrived.

I was restless in Paradise. I could not concentrate on my third novel. Five thousand dollars in debt, two rejected novels, and a tiny, red-headed beauty who would sleep with me but would not marry me. I did not yet know that I might be missing the point; or, in fact, what the point might be to each of the recent movements I had made, either complete or abortive. Surrounded by the bald and foolish palm trees of Southern California, I pondered the sheer American-ness of what I'd been doing—to listen to outside voices. Thus, I had listened to Bixby's voice and taken up the flowering pen of Joyce and James and vows of modernist poverty; had listened to Manishin, had stayed (reluctantly) free and single.

Mettro arrived one day for a visit driving a stripped-down lean animal of a Maserati with an Alfa Romeo engine he had installed himself, piece by piece. We sat by the pool and shared my box lunch. I wore a bathing suit, Mettro wore a three button gray silk suit. I sweated. He did not. The crickets stitched the only sounds; the noon heat congealed around us like invisible cream. Mettro said, "This place is marvelous. So isolated. I makes me nervous. But I'm not an artist."

I said, "It makes me nervous, too. Yet there are people who go from one of these places to another all year, every year."

"How are you and Manishin doing?"

"Fine, except she won't marry me."

"Is it money?"

"It's confused. Independence, friendship-preservation. She reads a lot of Shaw. I don't know."

"It's always money. I read that novel about your Uncle Albert. . . ."

"Irving . . ."

"The Spinoza of Houston Street . . ."

"The Doctor Faustus of Rivington Street. Close enough."

"It was good. It had balls. Bixby lent me his copy."

"Bixby? You see him?"

"Bixby," Mettro said, "is a will-o'-the-wisp. He has abandoned Scriabin and Marxism. It's Romanticism, now—the English Romantics—Vaughan Williams, William Walton . . . He is also apparently involved in a non-stop, high-stakes poker game he cannot afford. He owes me eighteen hundred dollars. Ah, Bixby . . ."

"Listen, I owe you thanks for the novel about my uncle. You gave me that pep talk about switching from stories to novels. The cash nexus, the novel as fungible artifact . . ."

"What a memory," Mettro said. "You'd be great in P.R."

"Are you having fun?"

"It's a snap. I've got a job for you."

"Who said I wanted a job?"

"It's written all over you. You want to marry Manishin; a job can maybe make that happen. Listen I was there when Bixby brought you into *The Communist Manifesto*—the new relations between people. *All that is solid melts into air. . . .* Don't forget I met Bixby before you. Did he ever tell you that Marx said the bourgeois genius was to make any human way of behaving morally okay—'valuable' he called it, philosophically, as long as it becomes economically possible."

I laughed, nostalgically happy to be hearing the old rhetoric from when we were young, after the war.

"No," I said. "There were some conversations he'd had with the old boy which Bixby kept to himself. But I remember *you* preaching me the financial gospel of the novel versus the short story. Look around you," I said, a wave of my arm indicating the free grass, the free cottages and, less visibly but all around us, nevertheless, the free time to sweat out my slow-in-coming third novel. "Pretty valuable. Free, in fact."

"Nothing's free," Mettro said. "Listen to this." He closed his eyes and muttered, "I hope I can still remember. It's been awhile. *The bourgeoisie has resolved all honor and dignity into —* Shit! I've lost it."

"Hold it," I said, willing and eager to continue the game. "I've got my copy of the *Manifesto* here." I returned from my cottage and tossed it at him. It was, of course, *not* my copy, but Bixby's tattered relic which had helped to change my life, for wrong or right. It felt good to be the tosser of the book for once. He leafed the pages with dazzling speed and continued —"*. . . resolved all honor and dignity into exchange-value.*" More wild leafing. "*The Bourgeoisie has transformed the Doctor, the lawyer, the Priest, the poet, the man of science into its paid wage-laborers.*"

"This means," I said, "that I should get a job?"

"Well—"

"You know," I said, "You and Bixby both, for years, every time you talk about Marx or quote Marx it's really about how extraordinary the Bourgeoisie is. What kind of Marxist *is* this? If I should be transformed into a paid wage-laborer, in whose God-damned name is it? The old or the new?"

"No, no, no . . ." Mettro got excited. "Marx sees modern bourgeois culture as part of modern industry. You realize how long ago he saw that? My God! He was the fucking first! I'm talking about eighteen sixty-eight."

"But he seems to — so approving . . ."

"No, it's just that he knows that whether you create pictures, books or industrial products — it's all the marketplace. *In the meantime! Until Socialism, Communism or any version of the real ultimate thing!*" We're in the U.S. That's the meantime".

"Ah," I said, "the great 'meantime.' " I threw my arms out into the yellow sunshine. "Mettro," I said. "That's why I'm here. California is just another word for 'meantime.' " I closed my eyes against the pastel haze. "Manishin and I came to a big, endless 'meantime.' And this offer came along."

Mettro leaned back and propped the beat-up paperback

against his narrow chest, insulated by its grey vest. "What's Manishin's 'meantime?' "

"She doesn't want to support me and make me a child."

"In short—she wants you to enter the marketplace."

"A paid wage laborer . . . or else stop pushing to get married? Maybe something like that. Actually she's amazingly pure—she's happy to keep things the way they are. Is that suit make of silk?"

"Right."

"It's nice."

"Are you forgetting what I told you about the short story and the novel?"

"Are you kidding? It's what got me this deal. The novel is the hard currency. I owe you."

Mettro sat up and tossed *The Communist Manifesto* back at me. I dropped it and it fell into a clump of dry leaves.

"Listen," he said. "I have a theory about you: you are a potential public relations magnate." (For a moment I thought he'd said Magnet and thought he was joking or sun-struck.) "Don't laugh," he went on. "You attract people; they see you as some kind of symbol, or some kind of Human Resource Opportunity." Mettro was talking in Capital Letters now and growing impassioned.

"Like Bixby," he said, "and that teacher at school you told me about. And your gambler uncle. People want to get involved in you." I thought—like Bixby he's exhorting me. Mettro was right; something in me made people exhort me, made them want to take me in hand, to convince me of one or another course of action for my life. Mettro himself was doing it while describing it.

"And that's why you could be a public relations whiz. So it's not writing fiction, but it's fiction of another kind. Manipulating metaphors, painting images. You'd be a great success. People will believe you because they'll want to be involved with what you're becoming."

"That's not for me."

"It doesn't matter. You're for it! The job is in New York— the East Coast branch of Rogers & Cowan. You'll love it."

"But I just *got* here!"

"No rush. You can start in two weeks," Mettro said blithely. "I should have brought my bathing suit. I don't have any appointments until five o'clock." He smiled a California smile, white-toothed, delighting in innocent evil. "I told you it was an easy dollar. Meantime."

"I'll lend you a bathing suit." I said. "Enjoy yourself. But the answer is, 'No!' "

Before I fell asleep that night I decided. There are exhortations and there are exhortations. Bixby the believer, Bixby the keeper of the Marxist/Modernist flame, the seller of fantasy in an unimaginative world: He had earned the right to change my life. His message made sense. And it had led me into a career which kept me broke but also kept me in touch with something of value in myself. Mettro's proposition was another matter. As if he'd heard me and wished to convince me otherwise, Mettro called the next day and invited me to go with him to a party. "I hear Bixby may show," he said.

Bixby showed. He looked not a day older. Tanned, tubercular-thin, and gay, he shone like a bright jagged piece of bottle glass in that crowd of smooth-edged agents, producers, screen writers and public relations magnets. He played the piano, unheard but rapt; played only music I'd never heard before. Not a note of Scriabin. What had happened to the great Scriabin revolution? I'd been afraid that when he saw me there would be some embarrassment over the money he owed me. But debts apparently shared a special amnesia with Scriabin. And, it turned out, with his former religion of modernism and fantasy.

I made a stab at getting his attention, one attempt to revive his old love for the young disciple I'd once been.

"Did you know that Molotov's real name was Scriabin? It turns out he was actually a relative of the composer." I meant, of course, to point out how mysteriously History and Music had come together in the Bixby I remembered. The point hung, fresh, in the air until Bixby staled it with a remark.

"Are you still doing that kind of thing?" he said. "That's all dead and buried. Stalin buried *The Communist Manifesto* and the funeral is being held all over Eastern Europe. It's *sauve qui peut*, now."

The Bixby I'd known spoke no French. But if *he* could believe it was every man for himself, how well had I known him, my comic-book Master?

"The name of the game is Romanticism," Bixby said, looking about him, distracted.

"All that is solid melts into air . . ." I hazarded. "The bourgeois period . . ."

"No, No, for God's sake. It was always only what you could imagine. That's why I'm trying to get some assignments writing music for movies . . . for TV. Romantic music — that never dies. The best kept secret in modern times is this equation: *Marxism is modernism and modernism is romanticism.*" He spoke, still, in italics and left me to digest this aperçu while he played William Walton's violin concerto on the stereo for a producer who undoubtedly did not know that Bixby could not read or write music. It didn't matter because in a few moments Bixby was the center of the party, elegantly miming a waltz passage as a waltzing violinist, sans violin, but with a skeletal dancing grace. He drew applause, laughter, and the arm of a pretty model five inches taller. Later, when he had left with her, I heard someone behind me sketch out Bixby's present life in a few choice California sentences.

"It better be *her* place," the voice of Los Angeles said. "Because he's living with Paul Randolph. There's only one bed. When Paul has the rent money, Paul gets the bed and Bixby gets the floor; when Bixby has it, Bixby gets the bed. Bixby has yet to pay a month's rent." Outside in the Beverly Hills night, facing the long curved floodlit driveway, I had a replayed vision of Bixby — not my remembered or fantasized Bixby, but the flesh-Bixby, pushed by the pump of blood flushing the bony red face — the physical presence of the man as he'd waltzed with his invisible violin to the Walton Concerto. (Had he not played Scriabin in waltz-time at the Arthur Murray Dance School in those G.I. Bill days of long ago?) The words were all different now, but Bixby was unchanged. I'd been taken in by words! Bixby had preached a particular kind of communist sainthood, the Gospel According to Saint Marx, and then coolly danced on, apparently taking his anarchic life day by day. Leaving me (or so it felt at that end-of-the-evening moment) to dance the Bixby waltz — and end up in disappointment and poverty.

Behind me, through the French doors, I caught a glimpse of Mettro looking for me. He was my ride home but I did not want to see him. Better even the unthinkable thought of a bus in southern California. The next morning I called Mettro and reversed my decision. I was sick of the way my private relations had worked out. I was ready to try Mettro's public relations. Of course the day I arrived in New York, Manishin warned me she was not to be bought — or even rented — by my change in employment status. Lying entangled in that long red hair I said. "Let's get married."

"Let's be friends," she said.

"Let's do both."

"I'm not sure that can be done."

"Are you in love?"

"Yes."

"Am I in love?"

"Yes."

"Then we're in love . . ."

"You're just conjugating. Look, I've *been* married. If you want, forget Shaw, forget all the social stuff. Something mysterious, something peculiarly chemical happens when people get married. They stop being themselves . . . they start to represent things; it's all a nutty masquerade. A balance of power without countries. Give me a toke will you."

"You smoke too much of that stuff." I took a deep draw myself and waited for illumination. Nothing! I handed it back and asked Manishin, "Has it ever occurred to you that there's something odd about our friends — the ones who have been swallowed up by California?"

"Odd?"

"They're hooked on Marxism."

"A lot of that going around."

"But it's a strange kind — all about the past and the present. I thought it was supposed to be about the future. What I get from our friends is the bourgeois this, the bourgeois that. Never a word about the working class or suffering proletarians. And they never talk about Russia, which is supposed to be the future. Mettro says it's because we're living in the 'meantime'."

"Between what and what?"

"It's like they're giving lessons in How to Survive until the Revolution Comes. But not a word about how great it will be afterwards. Strange."

Manishin yawned. "Nothing personal," she said.

"It's two Ayem. I'm on California time but you're not."

"Mmmmm."

"Put it out and let's go to sleep."

"Hey, don't husband me."

"I've got an idea. You keep your name, how's that?"

"Thanks," she said dryly. "It was always mine. And we can both lose everything else."

"Can any two people be with each other as much or as closely any other way?" Another yawn. "Shaw says marriage is the most licentious of institutions. It combines the maximum of temptation with the maximum of opportunity."

"How was his marriage?"

"Unconsummated, they say."

"Ah, Manishin, you lawyer. Stop tempting me part-time. Marry me!"

That summer, in the year nineteen fifty-five I joined Rogers & Cowan as a junior account executive at seven thousand dollars a year. In nineteen fifty-six Manishin and I were married. Mettro flew East to be the triumphant best man. By nineteen sixty-three I was making seventy thousand dollars a year. The go-go sixties were on the way. Manishin's two daughters were happy with me; their father, after serving a brief term in jail for forging checks, vanished into the Midwest, from which hiding place Manishin never attempted to extradite him.

But how to tell about those years. The Romantic poets were wrong — youth is not like a dream. Youth is sharp, clear, sur-

real, flooded by the sunny light of memory and hope. It's
when your life seems to *begin*, when you seem to set your feet
on a continuing path that the years go by as in a dream. That's
how it was with our life together. Friends were made, groups
came together, broke apart; children had accidents; once I
contracted a strange fever and almost died, but recovered, still
undiagnosed but alive. Manishin gained fifteen pounds, lost
them again and turned down an appointment as State Supreme Court Judge; a long ribbon of trivia, dramatic and ba-
nal by turns.

But what was the point of those years? Just look at two high
points. Two years after Mettro introduced me to the golden
days and nights of public relations-he went private. Suddenly
he was just—gone. Not a word to any one. Certainly no one
at the office could find out where he was. It took months for
information to drift in. He was in France, it turned out, living
with a Japanese dancer. The gray suits had, apparently, been
turned in for Basque sport shirts, a beret and a carved walking
stick. One of Manishin's colleagues had seen him so attired at a
cafe in a small village in Provence. That was the early information. The later information was even more interesting. It
seemed that Mettro's venture into freedom from commerce had
been financed by his being on the take. Several of Rogers &
Cowan's best clients affirmed this. Ah, Mettro, Pied Piper of
the rat race, who led me in only to flee, himself. No one was
very surprised. Except me. I was, as usual in these matters,
astonished.

The name of the village was Menerbes; so small, I was
warned, it didn't have a drug store. I changed planes in Paris
and flew to Nice where I rented the tiniest of cars, a Fiat, and
drove north towards Avignon. At a town called Cavaillon I
stopped for lunch. I asked the waiter about Menerbes.

"Any Americans in Menerbes? *Est'ce qu'il y a des Ameri-
cains à Menerbes?*" I said carefully.

"Why do you stop in Menerbes?" the waiter said. "They'll
only serve you melons from Cavaillon."

"Life is not all melons," I said.

Apparently he disagreed because the conversation ended there. I drove on, pondering what Manishin had said when I told her I was going to find Mettro.

"We can't afford the plane ticket," she'd told me, "But I'm glad you're going."

"Why?"

"Because just once you're going to confront one of those voices you've listened to. You're going to ask it—"

" . . . about the Unity of Theory and Practice," I butted in.

"What's that?"

"It's a notion in philosophy. I forget where it started—but it ends up in Marx. And Mettro—with all his talk about the cash nexus—never once mentioned stealing or crime. He talked about the making of money as if it were the healthiest, most natural activity in the world. Not a hint of any fascination with the criminal, with the underground imagination. My Uncle Irving had a number going in that direction. But that was different. That was *my* inheritance, which I decided, a long time ago, to ignore except by writing about it."

"Do we *know* that Mettro stole the money for his great getaway? I'd hate for you to be embarrassed after flying thousands of miles."

"It was nothing so gross as simple stealing. Quite elegant, this woman at the L.A. office said. She called it 'skimming.' Apparently if you skim long enough, you end up with a great big pot of money—and because you didn't take it all at once it's hard to trace."

I couldn't articulate for Manishin, or yet for myself, the sense that I might have run into a Bixby/Mettro Marxism that was weird but, somehow, very American. A Marxism designed to make the middle class feel okay; to make the privileged comfortable in their skins, in their selfishness. A Marxism in which the working class is, as usual, invisible.

When Manishin stretched on tiptoe to kiss me goodbye at the gate, I said: "Maybe I just want to know why I'm always so surprised at the way things turn out."

"You mean people."

"Yeah. Weren't you blown away with surprise when I told

you about Mettro?" Manishin shook her head — a flaming little 'no.'

"Are you sure you have to go all this way to find out?"

"If I was sure," I said, "I wouldn't have to go and I wouldn't have to stay."

I wasn't surprised at her lack of surprise and I kissed Manishin again and got on the plane for France and the missing Mettro.

In a run-down cafe at the top of the village perched on a steep hill I found my man. There were almost as many dogs as there were patrons. Mettro was wearing a purple and orange sport shirt and a navy blue beret. I decided on a light approach; no heavy-handed morality. The trick was to find out what had really happened and why. Mettro was going through a pile of photographs with great care. When I sat down across the table from him he looked up and smiled; another one who had an inoculation against surprise that seemed to have skipped me, alone.

"Well," he said. "I was wondering if you'd be in touch one way or another." He handed me a batch of the photographs. "I've been discovering some new talents. Like photography. What do you think?"

They were carefully posed shots of a pretty young Japanese woman. Her face was flat, like the surface of a Matisse painting, the eyes staring mischievously at the camera, sometimes directly, sometimes over her shoulder, a parody of high fashion magazine photographs.

"Terrific," I said. "Who's the model?"

"Ishekanawa. Here she comes."

And she appeared moving delicately from the dark interior of the cafe to the sunny table where we sat. She was startlingly tall for a Japanese woman and she wore a simple loose robe.

"Ishekenawa," Mettro gestured towards me, and then burst into a babble (to me) of Japanese in the midst of which I heard my first and last names; obviously an introduction.

"She doesn't speak any English," Mettro said. "Have some red wine. Local stuff. That's what we drink here in the afternoons in Menerbes."

"Just coffee. I don't want to fall over."

The coffee was foul, the cafe shoddy; Mettro had not escaped to a jewel thief's exotic Riviera; but Ishekenawa was exquisitely made with small shapely breasts and long, long legs and the warm Provençal sun, a steady scent of lavender in the air and the sloping hills down to the valley were thrilling. So Mettro had bought a mixed bag of Paradise with his subtle 'skimming.' I was shaky with jet-lag and it was not the time to evaluate anything. It was the time to ask what I'd come to ask. (I'm not sure I could have done it if Ishekenawa spoke English.)

"Is it true?"

He didn't play games, for which I gave him instant credit. No. "Is *what* true?" and the usual sparring.

"Of course," Mettro said.

"Of course? You mean as in—naturally, or—to be expected?"

"I mean of course, as in the idea of taking the money occurred to me a few times and I blocked it out as wrong or dangerous or both. Then one day I was daydreaming after a client lunch—General Electric, big stuff, they wanted us to help them diversify, maybe get into show business, and I was trying to get revved up to work on the account even though I was full of Chateaubriand and brandy—I was actually more fed up with the work than I admitted to myself—and I suddenly remembered a passage from, oh, I forget, it's either *Das Kapital* or *The Communist Manifesto* or *Theses on Feurbach*—something explaining why Capitalism would have to fall—this memory, by the way, was like a dream—anyway the idea was that because the giant corporations would finally have to merge and become international monopolies and cartels, like G.E. for example—(those are the new words, after it happened, that's not what Marx called them . . .")

"Are you sure you're telling me what happened or the rationale for what you did . . . ?"

"It's the same thing," Mettro said. Ishekenawa watched both of us, intently. "So," Mettro continued, "Squeezed by the laws affecting international expansion and the demands of bigger and bigger trade unions, the corporations would be ripe for overthrow by the workers. But then," Mettro took off his beret and wiped his forehead of the midday Provençal sweat, "then there was a mention of something I'd never thought of. Marx says, *Of course the possibilities of bribery and other illegal means of prolonging the life of the free marketplace are endless.* That was a big moment."

"A big moment for *you?*"

"A flash of light in the darkness of southern California. I mean the same as you and all of us normal middle-class characters trying to get ahead and make sense of life at the same time, I always assumed that things like Bribery or Theft, criminal activities with capital letters in the front of the words, were done by Others."

"I used to steal books," I said.

"And I stole money from my father's pants," Mettro said. "Youthful highjinks. A kind of complaint through action."

I was getting a clear picture, for the first time, why Mettro was good at public relations. He had a phrase for everything. All you needed was the right phrase. The trick was: never be at a loss. Which meant: never be at a loss for words.

"But if bribery could actually hold off Socialism, extend the criminal life of Capitalism — then why not seize the day. *Carpe diem.* The really bad stuff — bribing people, real stealing was a little like murdering somebody. Or, at least, it was clearly criminal. It had nothing to do with the middle-class — with people like us. But suddenly, I saw it differently. I saw myself bribing one of the people at G.E. to work out some 'skimming' of fees to the agency. And here's the key — *suddenly I saw it as simply taking on a partner and starting a new business venture.*"

"Listen," I said. "I changed my mind. I'll have some of that wine."

"*S'il vous plaît,*" Mettro called out and got me a glass of the local red.

I drank up and leaned towards him trying to ignore Ishekenawa's steady, quiet presence and gaze. This was the moment I'd come for. (Actually that moment was to arrive a little after midnight, but I couldn't know that, yet.)

"Listen," I said, intensely, "You know, now, that was all just game-playing, just word-magic, right? You know exactly what you did and that all this partner-bullshit was just so you could get yourself to be a crook. It has nothing to do with any of the stuff you fed me about the cash nexus and fungible artifacts and, how does it go, the bourgeoisie has resolved all honor and dignity into exchange value . . . something like that . . ."

Mettro grinned happily at me: a teacher proud of his student. "No," he said, "Not something like that. That's *exactly* how it goes."

"You know, I feel involved in this stuff—what you've done."

"I know. You're wrong, but I understand."

"I mean it's like you and I were partners before and now you've taken in new partners with a very different idea. A scary idea."

"That's why you came all this way, right? To understand. I assume you're not going to turn me in. You could have done that in New York."

"You assume, as usual, correctly."

"Where are you staying?"

"I didn't make reservations. I was told this town didn't even have a drug store, but I figured there'd be some kind of hotel or pension."

"Never mind. You'll stay with us."

He blew off some more Japanese steam at Ishekenawa. She nodded and kept her gaze on me.

"Absolutely not! No way!" I said.

Mettro's house was a simple one on the top of a steep street. Three stories but small—stone and wood, reddish. The real news was out in back. Three cars: a red Jaguar convertible, a BMW and a Maserati. The Maserati's hood was up; it was more of a Mettro work-in-progress than a finished car. I think I was looking at seventy-five thousand dollars worth of automotive equipment.

"A ride," Mettro said.

I shook my head. A ride would implicate me even more. I had

come to ask questions, to judge, to understand. I was not going to become the newest partner.

We whirled up and down those narrow streets, the three of us crammed into the silly seat; I was laughing against my will; Mettro twirling the wheel, Ishekenawa not laughing but smiling a broad distant smile. Later, over dinner at a small outdoor restaurant, just six tables in a sort of garden, a place of dreamy charm called Chez Marie, Mettro ordered more of the local wine and I drank too much of it.

"Do you know," I said to Mettro in mournful reproach, "because of you I'm a published novelist? Was."

"I know," Mettro said.

"Do you know," I continued, "that because of you I'm married to Manishin?"

"I know."

"But do you know that I don't know what I know?"

"I know. I've given up knowing what I know. The trick is—" I stood up as swiftly as I could given the wine and jet-fatigue. But the point is: I stood up *before he could tell me, yet again, what the trick was.* I'd given up listening to Mettro.

Outside, a dry, lavender breeze, struck me in the face and across the knees. Mettro and Ishekenawa got me into the car, then into the house, then, with a little more of a struggle, upstairs and into a bed.

I woke into the unaccustomed stitch of night-insect sounds and lavender smells with a desperate urge to pee. When I left the bathroom, I found Ishekenawa standing outside. Stupid with sleep and the early start of a hangover, but ever the *bourgeois gentilhomme*, I gestured towards the bathroom door and said, "do you have to—" She took my arm and guided me back towards my bedroom.

"Are you feeling better?" she asked. "I couldn't sleep."

"I thought you couldn't speak English."

She stretched out next to me and reached up the longest arm I'd ever seen and snapped off the bedside lamp. The moon kept pouring in through the open shutters, so much moonlight that the lamp being off made no difference. Ishekenawa kissed me.

"What is this?" I said. And then, suspicious again, "Did *he* send you in?"

"He's asleep."

Her skin smelled like lavender soap and she answered questions like Mettro, without answering anything. He could have sent her in *and* been asleep, by now. Who knows what he might have in mind? Perhaps buying me off; Ishekenawa, another one of his famous fungible artifacts; adding pimping to skimming now that he had joined my Uncle Irving on the other side of the law. *Carpe diem*, my ass, I thought as I started to explore Ishekenawa. If I wasn't involved before, I am now.

It wasn't until the morning, when I woke, alone and starving, that it occurred to me that she might have simply been attracted to me and been moved, on her own, to betray Mettro. I rejected the explanation and flew back to New York, from Nice, that afternoon, with Bixby and Mettro both behind me, at last. But what was ahead? At the duty-free shop in Paris, while waiting for the plane to New York to arrive at the gate, I bought bottles and bottles of perfume for Manishin. Chanel Number Five, Shalimar, White Shoulders—by the ounce, no micro-ounces and no eau de toilette, the real stuff. I knew I was overdoing it, inviting not responsive passion or gratitude but more likely a knowing irony from my knowing, ironic little redhead. I couldn't help myself.

Bixby had folded on me.

Mettro had run out.

Manishin was my last chance.

Which brings us to the other high point: the day Manishin decided to leave me. The reasons were both elusive and somehow beside the point. The sandpaper of ordinary married life had rubbed off the sensitive skin of money, sex, power, helplessness. All the things everybody ends up fighting about—no matter how special they think they are.

Here is Manishin after I have given her several pieces of luggage she had forgotten in the bedroom closet. She is sipping her drink and, with my encouragement, is expatiating on one small but central point I'd missed: why she had to leave.

"Don't go," I said.

"I warned you."

"That was years ago."

"Makes no difference. True is true."

"But I love you, you love me, I loved you, you loved me."

"You're still conjugating. Changing tenses doesn't change anything. I told you—we were better off as friends. Everybody is. I warned you people stop being themselves when they get married. You can't be friends if you're not yourself." As always Manishin was in the advance guard. Half the people we knew were choosing to live together, or apart, as 'friends' instead of getting married. *Time* magazine did cover stories; *The New Yorker* did a profile. Years later, marriage would again regain its status as the privileged class in the class structure of relationships. But for now, as usual, Manishin was ahead of her time. Old George Bernard Shaw would have been proud of her.

"Okay," I said desperate, adaptive, "Let's be friends. We'll live together."

Manishin flashed a smile. "You're missing the point, again. You always have."

"What do you mean?"

She sighed. It was to be an unusual moment. Sighs were not in the Manishin repertoire. "The point you missed," she said very slowly, "is simply that love, ambition, literary and financial, modernism, Marxism—all that stuff, they're just a chorus of voices singing at you all your life, since you were a kid. There was always somebody to tell you what you should do or think or feel. And you got caught up in the web of words. It's words that made you miss the point. You listened—Oh, God, you're a great listener. But what you never did was . . . look . . . to see what the people you believed actually did. Bixby turned you onto *la vie bohème*—then quietly went Hollywood-anarchist-romantic. Mettro sucked you into the rat race and then hit out for the expatriate life in France on funny money. But there must have been something to tip you off that they weren't what they seemed. You're a real artist—an artist at Missing the Point! And even with us, just now, you—"

"Missed—"

"Right!"

I took a deep breath and then took a chance. Not a big one since I'd already lost. I played the Ishekenawa card. Not a big risk, also, since I'd confessed very soon after returning from Provence.

"Was it—Ishekenawa?"

"No."

"I told you it never happened before and never happened again. It was like being run over. An accident!"

"Who ran over who?"

"It *was* Ishekenawa!"

"It was you. I just can't go on being married to Candide." She jumped up and paced around me. "THIS IS MY LIFE, DAMMIT, NOT THE BLUEBIRD OF HAPPINESS." As usual, I missed the references. I had read neither Voltaire nor Maeterlinck. "Even" she continued, whirling around me like a prosecuting Imp in an imaginary court, "Even if you and I agreed on whether or not you participated in an act of white slavery . . . "

"*White* Slavery?"

"You said you knew what Mettro was up to."

"I said I *thought* he *might* have been up to something. . . ." She sat down, suddenly exhausted of all that frenetic energy. "Anyway—she wasn't the point. If you would promise to stop listening, stop thinking, stop developing world views, stop latching onto ideas about life and how it should be lived . . ."

"I will . . . *I will!*"

"No," Manishin said. "You'll promise. And worse, you might even do it. Then I'd hate you. Because the real horror is—that that Candide stuff I hate about you, is also what pulled me to you. It's hopeless."

Now it was my turn to be drained of energy; of hope, actually.

"You mean you think I'll always—"

"Miss—"

"The . . ."

"Point." Manishin popped the word at me, like a period in a life sentence. "The only way for us to be friends, now, is to break up. We've done the other thing. So, here I go." She hefted her luggage and kissed me on the mouth, cool and dry. She is gone now; I am on my own.

Again, or at last.

Bixby, Mettro, Manishin—you've met them. But what of Marx?

Myself: Maurice Marx, my grandmother a second cousin to Tussy Marx, the old boy's daughter, the apple of his eye. Thus, I am a direct descendant of Karl. And if you've wondered why I had never read any of the stuff Bixby, Mettro or Manishin were laying on me, just think about my father growing up in a Viennese bourgeois home with a mother full of family pride about her connection to the scourge of Middle-Class Europe. The black-bearded specter who was haunting Europe was my second cousin once removed. Thus, our entire side of the family removed themselves from any connection to the life of thought. Thought carried a bomb in its hand and a knife in its teeth, promising new worlds and destroying old ones. My father, the son of a Mediaeval scholar became the first Marx on his side of the family to skip college and go right into business. The rest of us, too, avoided education as the first step towards damnation.

And I, a refugee child, as nervous about my name as I might have been had it been the middle of World War One, when people with German names were being ostracized or turned in to the F.B.I., only I knew that I was not an innocent Marx—but a real one. A relative of HIMSELF. The Ur-Marx. Now, having thought much about this, and having, finally, read all I could of and about him, I think I rather take after him.

I admire the old man immensely. Only those who plunge headlong towards a point end up missing it so completely. Marx, by jumping ferociously at an economic, materialist view of the universe, missed the point of the psychological—that monkey wrench in the machinery of theory. And I, heir to old Karl, continued in the family tradition.

I was ready for any explanation—any guide to the jungle of reality. As long as it had nothing to do with the subtle confusions of personality, the ambiguity of motives, the fact that my Uncle Irving might have been, not an existential hero of the delicately criminal gesture, but simply a psychopath nut who was out to lose, to get caught and to finally simply enjoy the pleasure of weaving a web of philosophical explanation around a compulsion; that Bixby might have been only a garbage can of failed received ideas; the very rancidness of whose mixture—Dianetics, Marx turned upside down to become Joyce and H.G. Wells—was what attracted me to him—just a *luftmensch* hustling exhortations in return for loans divisible by eighteen—his only hold on life . . . that Mettro might have been, not a poet of self-interest, a singer in the entracte between the past opera of selfish capitalism and the future opera of altruistic socialism—his precious "meantime"—in whose lyrics I'd heard another of my songs of salvation . . . but simply a California con man en route to his ultimate destiny, like many a con man, surviving on the lam through silence, exile and cunning.

Thinking about this now, surrounded by the luggage-debris of a marriage, I wonder if the essential trouble comes, perhaps, from the fact that we do not live alone; that we live in the world. There are other voices out there from the start. How to know when to listen and when to be oblivious? How to know which point is *the* point? It's difficult. The inner voice is soft, tentative. It often seems to be without any point at all. The temptation to listen to others is very great. As soon as they speak—*all that is solid melts into air* . . .

That is the general condition. But there is also the specific. My father, brother, and I came to this country as refugees from Austria in nineteen-forty. My brother, deaf from a childhood accident, my father a dispossessed businessman, merely deaf to other people's ideas; willful and stubborn. It fell to me to pick up all the hints, nuances, directions that could help us find our way in a strange place. Foreigners must listen to what the natives tell them. In such ways are lifetime habits formed. My brother is now a surgeon in Tulsa, Oklahoma, with his hearing restored by several operations. My father lives, retired, in Florida, where he has grown more malleable with age. He is now, however, quite deaf. And I—I have just listened to Manishin say goodbye.

Even at this point, a grown man, I am ready to listen to others. Finally, too, it is a matter of faith. There is no other way to take or refuse the world, except on faith. It's too hard to prove anything. I won't even bother to play around with the now commonplace notion that the Marxist idea is and was a question of belief, replacement for old, dead religions, etcetera, etcetera. That's just another opinion and I'm through with the scrimmage of opinion.

I'm interested in knowing or *not* knowing. Was Bixby's grandmother really Welsh and his grandfather really Indian? Which one was Jewish? Is Scriabin really a great and neglected composer or the second rate mystic maker of program music he's often thought to be? Did Manishin really want her independence or did she want me to overwhelm her with reasons to get married? How deaf is my father? Sometimes he seems to hear quite well, other times such as when I try to explain to him about Manishin and our breaking up—total, reproachful silence.

I am pouring myself another vodka from the bottle with the tall spear of buffalo grass floating mysteriously in its depths. I stare at it closely. It looks like any other tall blade of grass. How does it impart that odd, yellowish color to the vodka— and that special slightly briny flavor to the usually colorless, tasteless liquid? I'm sure a scientist could tell me. But, in spite of what Manishin says, looking may be as complicated a route to knowledge as listening.

Still, I can't complain. My mistakes have all given me something. My work in public relations is as easy and lucrative as the otherwise dishonest Mettro promised. The clients often ask to have 'the writer' assigned to their accounts, knowing that I once published short stories and novels, too difficult to read, but elegant to refer to. It gives a different kind of satisfaction than Bixby and I had in mind for my career. But a satisfaction, nevertheless. Other satisfactions impend, too. A young woman at the office, hair not so red as Manishin's, mind not so sharp, but still . . .

I will finish the bottle and go to sleep. I will sleep a slightly murky sleep; sleep the color of yellowish buffalo-grass vodka; sleep secured by the sense of resting in a universe of 'missed points,' religion, art, war (and its G.I. Bills and its Bixbys), commerce, economics (and its Mettros) philosophy, love (and its Manishins). I was afraid to sleep alone this first night. But now I know I am not alone. If it is, finally, in the nature of all points that they be missed, then everyone in the world may sleep well in that sweet security.

The party in my head is over. Good night Bixby, good night Mettro, good night Manishin, good night.

NOTES ON CONTRIBUTORS

FICTION

Jeffrey Eugenides has published one story previously, which appeared in the *Gettysburg Review*. He lives in Brooklyn.

Reynolds Price is the author of many books, including a collection of poetry, *The Use of Fire*, and a volume of three novellas, *The Foreseeable Future*. His most recent novel, *The Tongues of Angels*, was published last spring.

Daniel Stern is the author of nine novels, a play and several essays. His collection of short stories, *Twice Told Tales*, for which he received the 1990 Rosenthal Award from the American Academy and Institute of Arts and Letters, was recently published by Paris Review Editions. He was the recipient of *The Paris Review*'s John Train Humor Prize in 1989.

Ruth Tarson is a former actress and comedienne. She has published a story in *Groundswell*. She learned of her *Paris Review* acceptance this fall one hour before receiving anesthesia for open heart surgery. She called her cardiologist with the news and was wheeled into the operating room laughing. Tarson is recovering speedily.

POETRY

Margaret Atwood is the subject of an interview in this issue.

Blaise Cendrars (1887–1961) is the Swiss-born French author of many poems, novels, and works of nonfiction. **Ron Padgett**, his translator, is the editor and translator of an anthology, *The Complete Poems of Blaise Cendrars*, which will be published in the fall of 1991 by the University of California Press. The poem in this issue is a selection from that volume.

Jorie Graham has published four volumes of poetry: *Erosion, Hybrids of*

Plants and of Ghosts, *The End of Beauty* and *Regions of Unlikeness*. She works and lives in Iowa.

Carolyn Kizer won the 1985 Pulitzer Prize for her poetry collection *Yin*, and in 1987 won the Theodore Roethke Prize for her collection *The Nearness of You*. She is a recipient of the Frost Medal for Lifetime Achievement in Poetry from the Poetry Society of America.

Christopher Logue is the author of several volumes of poetry and a pornographic novel. His book-length poem, *War Music*, a modern account of Books 16–19 of Homer's *Iliad*, was published by Farrar, Straus & Giroux. His *Kings*, from which the poem appearing in this issue was excerpted, is an account of Books 1 and 2 of the *Iliad*. It will be published in 1991.

Les Murray's many books of poetry have been published in Australia and the United States. Two books of his verse, *Rabbiter's Bounty* and *Dog Fox Field*, are forthcoming from Farrar, Straus & Giroux. He lives in Bunyah, New South Wales, where he was born in 1938.

Donald Revell is the author of three volumes of poetry: *The Abandoned Cities*, *The Gaza of Winter* and *New Dark Ages*. He teaches English and creative writing at the University of Denver.

John Tranter's most recent collection of poetry is *Under Berlin*. He was recently awarded a three-year Creative Artist Fellowship by the prime minister of Australia.

INTERVIEWS

Shusha Guppy is the London Editor of *The Paris Review* and contributes regularly to *The Daily Telegraph* and British *Vogue*, among other periodicals. Her memoir *The Blindfold Horse* was published by Beacon Press. A collection of her interviews with British women of letters, *Looking Back*, is forthcoming from Paris Review Editions.

Mary Morris is the author of two collections of short stories, two novels and a travel memoir. A second travel memoir, *Wall to Wall: From Beijing to Berlin by Rail*, will be published in June, 1991. She lives in New York.

Anthony Weller has published poetry, short stories and travel writing, and has just completed his first novel, *Garden of the Peacocks*. He divides his time among coastal Massachusetts, Cyprus and Europe.

ART

Mike Kelley was born in Dearborn, Michigan, in 1954, and lives in Los Angeles. Recent exhibitions of his paintings, sculpture, and drawings have been held at Metro Pictures, New York; Galerie Jablonka, Cologne; and Rosamund Felsen Gallery, Los Angeles.

Jim Shaw was born in Midland, Michigan, in 1952, and lives in Los Angeles.

His work has recently been exhibited at the University Art Museum, Berkeley; and Linda Cathcart Gallery, Santa Monica.

Jacqueline Humphries was born in New Orleans in 1960, and lives in New York. She has recently exhibited paintings and drawings at John Good Gallery in New York.

ERRATA

The Paris Review regrets that it neglected to run an acknowledgment of copyright for a work of fiction in its last issue. It follows:

From "A Man Asleep" by George Perec. Translated by Andrew Leak. Copyright 1967 by Editions Noel. Translation© 1990 by William Collins Sons & Co., Ltd. American edition published by David R. Godine, Publisher, Inc. Reprinted with permission of the publisher.

David R. Godine published the Perec novel in November.

THE PARIS REVIEW IS PLEASED TO ANNOUNCE ITS 1990 PRIZEWINNERS:

THE BERNARD F. CONNERS PRIZE HAS BEEN AWARDED TO CHRISTOPHER LOGUE FOR HIS POEM "KINGS" APPEARING IN THIS ISSUE.

THE AGA KHAN PRIZE HAS BEEN AWARDED TO LARRY WOIWODE FOR HIS STORY "SUMMER STORMS" APPEARING IN ISSUE 114.

THE JOHN TRAIN HUMOR PRIZE HAS BEEN AWARDED JOINTLY TO ROBIE MACAULEY FOR "SILENCE, EXILE, CUNNING" AND TO PADGETT POWELL FOR "MR. IRONY" AND "MR. IRONY RENOUNCES IRONY".

NAMPALLY ROAD

"Like Meena Alexander's poetry, her first novel is a deeply moving blend of lyric beauty and uncompromising toughness. Nampally Road plunges into the tumult, squalor, and corruption of post-colonial India, yet stands back from it at the same time; . . . a grim, beautiful book."
—Walter Kendrick

MEENA ALEXANDER
Mercury House
Words Given Wings

The Long Lost Journey
A novel by Jennifer Potter

"Maverick, memorable characters . . . evokes a time, a place, and a torturous romance"
—Publishers Weekly

"My journey has begun. I've stood on the sands of Arabia, smelt the heavy salt winds blowing in from the southwest . . ."

Mercury House
Words Given Wings

New Releases from The Paris Review.

Twice Told Tales
Stories by Daniel Stern
$18.95 cloth

"Daniel Stern's ingenuity—his originality—is his transformation of the great Modernist Seminal Works into the heroes of his stories.

Brooksmith, for instance, is the glorious protagonist of Stern's 'Brooksmith by Henry James'. If you are reminded of Borges you will not be wrong, but put the thought aside; Stern's half-dozen antic and sorrowful tales more powerfully, and more bouncingly, suggest Ring Lardner, or else the lively diversions of Alice's tea table.

A child named Tulip is reared in the hatcheck room of a New York restaurant. A lover blindfolds himself in order *not* to find his way back to his love. A man writes a novel against his will. And, throughout, Freud, Hemingway, Trilling, Forster preside; famous names swarm; the hearts of artists and would-be artists blaze; the winter sun slants; New York lives; comedy whispers and sometimes roars; wit triumphs."

—Cynthia Ozick

Imaginary Paintings
Poetry by Charles Baxter
$7.95 paper

Charles Baxter's *Imaginary Paintings* is the first book of poems by an emerging master of the short story. Baxter transforms the details of Midwestern landscape, intimate domestic tableaux, and the experience of art into a vision that is powerful and symphonic, deeply in the American grain.

"I read Charles Baxter's *Imaginary Paintings* with intense pleasure. This is poetry of the first order, characterized by an anguished, almost inconsolable lyricism, utterly immersed in the life that is, a life that tends to be ignored in our art, whatever the form."

—Jim Harrison

See Order Form elsewhere in this issue.

The Writer's Chapbook

A Compendium of Fact, Opinion, Wit, and Advice from the 20th Century's Preeminent Writers

Edited by George Plimpton
$19.95 cloth

"The most candid, stimulating, and instructive handbook for would-be serious writers the world has so far seen." — Kurt Vonnegut

A fascinating and delightful survey of writers on writing in this collection of excerpts from *The Paris Review* interviews. Here are Hemingway, Faulkner, Eliot, Doctorow, Roth, among many others, discussing the nitty-gritty of the craft of writing in pithy and sometimes aphoristic statements. The highly personal observations about subjects ranging from the development of plot, writer's block, narrative voice, and the influence of alcohol and other drugs on writing, provide a rare glimpse of what being a writer is really like.

"A superb, utterly fascinating book. If *Writers at Work* was the wine, this is the brandy. Very good brandy indeed. Indispensable for anyone with even the slightest curiosity about the mysterious work of writing."
— Frank Conroy
Director, Iowa Writers' Workshop

The Paris Review Anthology

Edited by George Plimpton
$25.00 cloth

. . . Beckett . . . Calvino . . . Gunn . . . Wright . . . Milosz . . . Simpson . . . Gordimer . . . Dubus . . . Bly . . . Ashbery . . . Bass . . . Brodkey . . . Minot . . . Brodsky . . . Dickey . . . Hughes . . . Merwin . . . McInerney . . . Salter . . . Simic . . . Boyle . . . Ginsberg . . . Southern . . .

"Venerable at 35 and justly venerated for its unequalled mix of fiction, poetry, interview and essay, *The Paris Review* remains the single most important little magazine this country has produced. A glimpse through the table of contents of this new compendium will demonstrate why: the editors have launched a thousand careers and consistently published the best work of some of the best writers of our time." —T. Coraghessan Boyle

Recent Books from Paris Review Editions

Bennett's Angel
a novel by Barton A. Midwood
$18.95

"The discerning reader and lover of literature
should follow Bart Midwood in his literary career. He is a master of dialogue. His humor
is genuine. . . . Bart Midwood is a writer
capable of bringing us many surprises."
— Isaac Bashevis Singer

Memories of Amnesia
a novel by Lawrence Shainberg **$16.95**

"A fascinating and intriguing novel, *Alice Through the Looking Glass* rewrit-
ten in the language of modern neurosurgery." — J.G. Ballard

Shine Hawk
a novel by Charlie Smith **$18.95**

"Charlie Smith seems to have sprung fully armed from the head of Zeus, with
zest and plenitude all in his pocket. He reads like a dream."
— Edward Hoagland

Love and Will
twenty stories by Stephen Dixon **$18.95**

"A master of the short story . . . shows his talents at their peak. Here craft
and technique are truly realized, and so is the message they convey. Mr.
Dixon is a highly distinctive writer, one whose work has grown richer and
deeper over time." — The New York Times

Atoms, Soul Music and other poems
by Baron Wormser **$7.95, paper**

"*Atoms* is the finest political poem I've read in a long time—'political' in the
broadest sense. It is intelligent; it is thorough, it is extraordinarily inventive
and compelling. Everyone should read it." — Hayden Carruth

Morning Run
poetry by Jonathan Galassi **$7.95, paper**

"Thoughtfully constructed and limpidly phrased. Jonathan Galassi's poems
will stay in the mind for many seasons to come." — James Merrill

See Order Form elsewhere in this issue.

Selected Back Issues of The Paris Review

 The Paris Review *Fifth Anniversary Issue* (1957).
Legendary interview with Ernest Hemingway, first published story by
Philip Roth, portfolio of drawings by Giacometti, poetry by W.S. Merwin
and Robert Bly, and more.
Original Edition, $25.00

Issue Twenty (1958)
Original publication of Philip Roth's First novella, *Goodbye, Columbus.*
Plus an interview with James Jones, drawings by Marc Chagall, poetry
by Louis Simpson, Robert Bly, Charles Wright, William Stafford, and
others.
Original Edition, $20.00

Issue Sixty-Four (1975)
Interviews with Kingsley Amis and P.G. Wodehouse, fiction by Thomas
Disch, portfolio by Vali Myers with commentary by ed. George Plimpton,
and more.
$10.00

Twenty-Fifth Anniversary Issue (1981)
Fiction by Raymond Carver, William Faulkner, William Gass, Terry South-
ern, essay by Ernest Hemingway, poetry by John Ashbery, Amiri Baraka,
Thom Gunn, John Hollander, Kenneth Koch, Joyce Carol Oates, William
Stafford, Charles Wright, and many more, plus *The Paris Review Sketch-
book*—a rich history of *The Paris Review.*
Double Issue, $12.00

Issue Eighty-Two (1981)
Interviews with Carlos Fuentes, Gabriel García Márquez, fiction by Julio
Cortázar, Jamaica Kincaid, Jay Williams, translations from the poetry of
Baudelaire by Richard Howard, Rilke by Stephen Mitchell.
$7.00

Issue Eighty-Six (1982)
First published fiction by Jay McInerny, plus fiction by Norman Mailer, in-
terviews with Erskine Caldwell and P.L. Travers, portfolios by Sandro
Chia, Francesco Clemente, cover by Sandro Chia.
$10.00

One Hundredth Issue (1986)
John Hersey, John Irving interviews, Mary McCarthy, Ezra Pound, James
Laughlin, Gertrude Stein features, Nadine Gordimer, Alice Munro fiction,
John Ash, Harold Brodkey, Raymond Carver, Allen Ginsberg, James
Merrill, Czeslaw Milosz, Robert Pinsky, Charles Simic, Charles Wright
poetry.
Double Issue, $10.00

Keith Haring poster now available.

THE PARIS REVIEW PRINT AND POSTER SERIES

Anuszkiewicz · Christo · Chryssa · Clemente · Crash d'Arcangelo · Paul Davis · Dine · Jimmy Ernst Janet Fish · Glaser · Frankenthaler · Freilicher · Haring Arnold Hoffman · Hockney · deKooning · Indiana Kanowitz · Krushenick · Katz · Kelly · Kushner · Lewitt Lindner · Lichtenstein · MacConnel · Marca-Relli Marisol · Motherwell · Salle · Nevelson · Rauschenberg Steve Poleskie · Oldenburg · Rosenquist · Ortman Shahn · Stamos · Sultan · Trova · Steinberg · Summers Ungerer · Vicente · Warhol · Wilson · Wesley · Winters Youngerman

For catalogue or information write: Joan Krawczyk, The Paris Review, 541 E. 72nd St., New York, NY 10021.

"Simply quite wonderful"*

TOO LOUD A SOLITUDE

BY THE AUTHOR OF
*I SERVED THE KING
OF ENGLAND*

BOHUMIL HRABAL

"From Czech writer Hrabal, another melancholy but movingly buoyant tale about life under communism, this time in a charming, intelligent... allegory about a man and books... a cry from the heart as culturally timely now as ever."
*—Kirkus Reviews**

"Absorbing... a showcase for Hrabal's dazzling writing talent." *—Publishers Weekly*

HARCOURT • BRACE • JOVANOVICH

Available at bookstores everywhere

HBJ

ELAINE

LOVES

THE PARIS REVIEW

ELAINE'S

1703 SECOND AVE
NEW YORK CITY

reservations: 534-8103/8114

An invitation to subscribe to the "premier" intellectual journal published in The United States.

The New York Review is offering a special, introductory subscription which brings you a full year of issues (21 in all) for only $19.95–a $19.05 saving on the regular subscription rate. *The Review* is known internationally for its brilliant reviews and essays by Gore Vidal, John Updike, Timothy Garton Ash, Elizabeth Hardwick, Milan Kundera, Susan Sontag, Joseph Brodsky, V.S. Naipaul, Nadine Gordimer, Václav Havel, John Kenneth Galbraith, Alfred Brendel, and countless other writers and scholars who are themselves a major force in contemporary literature and thought.

This special invitation is entirely risk-free — a full refund of the subscription cost is guaranteed at any time during the year — and you keep all issues received with our compliments. So do subscribe now and find out why *Esquire* calls *The Review* "the premier literary-intellectual journal in the English language."

- -

The New York Review of Books

Subscriber Service Dept, P.O. Box 2094, Knoxville, IA 50197-2094

Please enter my subscription to *The New York Review of Books* for a full year, 21 issues, at the special introductory rate of $19.95 –almost 50% off the regular subscription price and a saving of over $30 off the newsstand price.

Name _____

Address _____

City _____ State _____ Zip _____

❏ $19.95 enclosed. Or charge my ❏ American Express ❏ MasterCard ❏ Visa

Signature _____

Acct. No. _____

Exp. Date _____

❏ Send Bill. Your paid or charge order adds an *extra issue* to your subscription without charge. Full refund guarantee.

Offer good for new subscribers only. Please allow 6-8 weeks for receipt of your first copy. Add $12 for Canada and UK, and $15 for all other countries. Add $50 for airmail (suggested to Far East only).

PO5

Skowhegan
School of Painting & Sculpture

June 15 – August 17, 1991

An independent work program for sixty-five advanced painters and sculptors with eleven resident and visiting artists working in a rural Maine community.

Application deadline: February 15

For information write: 329 East 68th Street / New York, N.Y. 10021 • Telephone: 212 861-9270

Generous financial aid available according to need including minority and other assistance.

Resident Artists	**Visiting Artists**	**Paul Mellon Distinguished Lecturer**
Gregory Amenoff	Sue Coe	Yvonne Rainer
Peter Gourfain	Ann Hamilton	
Per Kirkeby	David Hare	
Thomas Lanigan Schmidt	Will Insley	
Joan Semmel	Brice Marden	

Ploughshares
Read It and Reap

"*One of the best literary magazines in the country . . . a national treasure.*"
—Frank Conroy

Since 1971, *Ploughshares* has been committed to providing its readers with dynamic literary perspectives. To this end, the paperback magazine has had a different writer edit each issue, becoming, in effect, a unique anthology series. Some of these guest editors have included Raymond Carver, Tim O'Brien, Jayne Anne Phillips, Seamus Heaney, Tess Gallagher, and Derek Walcott. Personal visions, diversified aesthetics, with the common agenda of cultivating the best in contemporary fiction and poetry.

Published three times a year: usually a fiction issue in the fall, a poetry issue in the winter, and a mixed issue in the spring.

Subscriptions are $15/yr for individuals and $18/yr for institutions. Please add $4/yr for international orders. Sample back issue: $5.

Ploughshares • Emerson College
100 Beacon Street • Boston, MA 02116

The Paris Review
Booksellers Advisory Board

THE PARIS REVIEW BOOKSELLERS ADVISORY BOARD is a group of owners and managers of independent bookstores from around the world who have agreed to share with us their knowledge and expertise.

STUART BRENT, *Stuart Brent Books, Chicago, IL*
ANDREAS BROWN, *Gotham Bookmart, New York, NY*
TIMOTHY CARRIER, *Odegard Books, St. Paul, MN*
ROBERT CONTANT, *St. Mark's Bookstore, New York, NY*
JOSEPH GABLE, *Borders Bookshop, Ann Arbor, MI*
MARGIE GHIZ, *Midnight Special, Santa Monica, CA*
JAMES HARRIS, *Prairie Lights Bookstore, Iowa, IA*
ODILE HELLIER, *Village Voice, Paris, France*
RICHARD HOWORTH, *Square Books, Oxford, MS*
KRIS KLEINDIENST, *Left Bank Books, St. Louis, MO*
FRANK KRAMER, *Harvard Bookstore, Cambridge, MA*
TERRI MERZ AND ROBIN DIENER, *Chapters, Washington, DC*
PETER PHILBROOK, *Books & Company, New York, NY*
MICHAEL POWELL, *Powell's Bookstore, Portland, OR*
DONALD PRETARI, *Black Oak Books, Berkeley, CA*
ENCARNITA QUINLAN, *Endicott Booksellers, New York, NY*
JACQUES RIEUX, *Stone Lion Bookstore, Fort Collins, CO*
LEWIS ROSENBAUM, *Guild Books, Chicago, IL*
ANDREW ROSS, *Cody's, Berkeley, CA*
HENRY SCHWAB, *Bookhaven, New Haven, CT*
RICK SIMONSON, *Eliot Bay, Seattle, WA*
LOUISA SOLANO, *Grolier Bookshop, Cambridge, MA*
DAVID UNOWSKY, *Hungry Mind Bookstore, St. Paul, MN*